What is Artificial Intelligence?

**A Conversation between an AI Engineer
and a Humanities Researcher**

What is Artificial Intelligence?

A Conversation between an AI Engineer and a Humanities Researcher

Suman Gupta
The Open University, UK

Peter H. Tu
General Electric Research, USA

World Scientific

NEW JERSEY · LONDON · SINGAPORE · BEIJING · SHANGHAI · HONG KONG · TAIPEI · CHENNAI · TOKYO

Published by

World Scientific Publishing Europe Ltd.

57 Shelton Street, Covent Garden, London WC2H 9HE

Head office: 5 Toh Tuck Link, Singapore 596224

USA office: 27 Warren Street, Suite 401-402, Hackensack, NJ 07601

Library of Congress Cataloging-in-Publication Data
Names: Gupta, Suman, author. | Tu, Peter H., author.
Title: What is artificial intelligence? : a conversation between an ai engineer and
    a humanities researcher / Suman Gupta, The Open University, UK,
    Peter H. Tu, General Electric Research, USA.
Description: Hackensack, NJ : World Scientific Publishing Europe Ltd., [2020] |
    Includes bibliographical references.
Identifiers: LCCN 2020010080 | ISBN 9781786348630 (hardcover) | ISBN 9781786348647 (ebook) |
    ISBN 9781786348654 (ebook other)
Subjects: LCSH: Artificial intelligence. | Artificial intelligence--Philosophy. |
    Artificial intelligence--Government policy.
Classification: LCC Q335 .G87 2020 | DDC 006.3--dc23
LC record available at https://lccn.loc.gov/2020010080

British Library Cataloguing-in-Publication Data
A catalogue record for this book is available from the British Library.

First published 2020 (hardcover)
Reprinted 2026 (in paperback edition)
ISBN 9781800619135 (pbk)

For any available supplementary material, please visit
https://www.worldscientific.com/worldscibooks/10.1142/Q0255#t=suppl

Desk Editors: Ramya Gangadharan/Michael Beale/Shi Ying Koe

Typeset by Stallion Press
Email: enquiries@stallionpress.com

Preface

Peter H. Tu

Born and raised among the Great Lakes of North America, I would describe myself as a simple country engineer. After days spent solving equations, assembling derivations and formulating proofs, we engineers are often given to moments of fellowship and camaraderie. This usually involves high-spirited discussion and dare I say good-natured debate. For the humble engineer, a drop-the-mic moment is something along the lines of, 'Therefore the left side of the equation equals the right side. QED!' Since the values of entities such as $\cos \pi^3$ are independent of the engineer's opinion let alone her identity, there is little room for offence to be given or taken. However, I fear that the beliefs of non-engineers are held closer to the heart. In such cases, opinion and identity are hopelessly intertwined. At a cocktail party for the good and the great, the engineer cannot help but feel like a bull in a china shop. When the non-engineer inevitably poses the question 'By the way, do you actually think you are funny?' one knows that it is time to slip away. My high school English teacher once remarked: 'Peter, although you may find it hard to believe, some of the smartest people in the world are actually in the humanities!' One can only imagine what offence I must have given to earn such a rebuke. The good reader can certainly empathise with my trepidation as I made my way to Oxford University, where behind every dreamy spire there lurks a sensitive poet or an angst-ridden political scientist.

The college system of Oxford is designed to encourage interdisciplinary socialisation. For my first year of graduate school, I was assigned a room at Exeter House, a decommissioned nunnery that now serves as graduate student accommodation. It turned out that my soon-to-be-friend Suman had the room next to mine. Suman has a number of admirable qualities. He maintains an impressive collection of international teas, is an accomplished cook, is a Rhodes Scholar, is a student of the humanities and is uncharacteristically indifferent to most forms of offence. I also bring a few things to the table. I am always open for a cup of tea. At the risk of sounding immodest, I am more qualified than most to both admire and consume a fine meal. In addition, I have a rather remarkable set of personal possessions including an adventure hat, a camera with remote control and a modest collection of whimsical taxidermic art. It turns out that we both seem to enjoy holding forth on just about any topic regardless of personal conviction, level of expertise or subject matter knowledge. Like Bogart and Louie — it was the start of a beautiful friendship.

One dark and stormy evening, our conversations meandered into ominous territory — our research interests. The danger of asking graduate students about their thesis topic is that they might just tell you. This is then followed by two to three hours of excruciating nuance and detail. Eventually, I came to understand that Suman's research had something to do with how critics interpreted James Joyce's novel *Ulysses*. I questioned the importance of critical opinion. Why not just focus on what Joyce himself intended to say with his writings? To my surprise, Suman declared that the intentions of the author are irrelevant. All that matters are society's interpretations. This point of view is completely alien to the engineering ethos, which is focused on inferring the state of an objective reality given a set of observations. I contend that this contradiction has been the backdrop of our conversations to date and is at the heart of why we have decided to write this book.

Unlike most scientific investigations, the field of AI is riddled with philosophical questions which to date have been meticulously avoided by AI engineers focused on narrow feats of strength. While dabbling in such murky waters certainly have made for many a pleasant after-dinner conversation, such dialogues usually ended with myself saying something along the lines of, 'Suman, you don't have the math needed to understand what I am saying', followed by the quick retort, 'And you, Peter, are not sufficiently well read to understand what I am saying'. A never-ending stalemate of sorts.

A few years back, I had reason to make a brief and unexpected trip to London. Upon arrival, I gave Suman a quick call to see if he was free for lunch. Given that I was at the GE Hammersmith offices, Suman suggested a rendezvous at a new pie shop near Putney station. Out of politeness, Suman started our lunch by inquiring about my work. I mentioned that the field seems to have transitioned from theoretical proof to 'the proof is in the pudding'. To make my point I described how a chair detector is now instantiated by first constructing a rich feature description followed by the search for some sort of discriminant. Suman brought up Ludwig Wittgenstein's idea that the meaning of an object such as a chair is established less by description and more by multiple agents partaking in a kind of referential game. Once again, we see the dueling themes of inference based on observation and agreement established by society. It turns out that recent formulations known as Emergent Languages fuse rich descriptive embeddings with Wittgensteinian referential games. At the risk of being accused of maintaining some form of latent religiosity, I cannot help but feel that our pie lunch at Putney was in its way positively portentous.

Preface

Suman Gupta

This preface is the only opportunity I have ever had in exchanges with Peter of getting the last word in, and not just in what follows. All that drop-the-mic training has given Peter an unerring instinct for grabbing the moment before the full stop. His instinct has been honed through a career that is more cosmopolitan than country and has a negligible connection with anything simple.

Those pies were edible, the Thames sluggish, we had time on our hands. From the beginning of the meal I could see that Peter was manoeuvring to make sure that he gets the last piece of the pie. It has ever been so and I know how to deal with it. A few steps before the last piece one has to announce, 'Peter, that last piece is mine.' We then go through a verbal negotiation and careful calculation of the fairest way to achieve this goal. Practice in this process has the great advantage of disregarding the claims of anyone else who might happen to be dining with us.

As Peter has truthfully reported it, our conversation was following a not dissimilar path. The only difference was that we weren't sure what the last piece of this conversational pie was. Since it was a leisurely afternoon, we were reluctant to simply put a full stop where it suited (one of) us. 'Let's put our argument out there and let others decide,' we thought. 'But what about that other unresolved argument?' one of us said. 'Okay, let's put a few of our arguments out there and let others decide,' we agreed. Before afternoon waned, the idea of a book emerged. 'If we write up arguments by turn,' we conceded, 'things might even become clearer between us before others adjudicate.' Writing them up would at the least circumvent doubt-ridden moments like this:

'As I said a few minutes back …'

'But you said nothing like that!'

'Yes, I did.'

'No, you didn't. What you said was …'

'Okay, let's say I said that but then it doesn't make sense that you said …'

'No, I didn't say that at all!'

'Yes, you did.'

'No, I didn't.'

Writing must have been invented, we concurred, to avoid prevarication like that.

So we got down to it and also pitched the idea of the book to WSPC Commissioning Editor Jane. Jane was encouraging and even signed it up. Peter and I had fun writing it. Peter had all the last words, but that doesn't necessarily mean he had the upper hand. I don't think we really homed in on the last piece of any of the pies. Then, all eager to know how readers will lay these arguments to rest, we sent the fruits to Jane. Jane was … well, not discouraging, but Jane managed to convey a furrowed brow over email. She was not sure we had hit the right note, that we would engage readers. Before they adjudicate on unresolved arguments, they have to read said arguments, she said. Not sure it would grab them enough to begin with, she said. 'But, come on, surely these are the pulse-of-our-time issues?' I said. 'I have generally managed to say things without reeling out some math,' Peter observed righteously. 'There are even a few witty moments,' I pointed out meekly. To which, Jane: 'At least write a Preface, explain to readers why you have written this book and why they should read it. Keep it chirpy.' What she meant was: 'Guys, be courteous and invite — nay, entice — your readers to share the pie on the table with you.'

You are warmly invited to the conversation that follows and exhorted to continue with it. By way of encouragement, please note the following:

- (Let's say this before any gentle reviewer) It's an eccentric book, as likely to amuse as inform and most likely to bewilder;
- The issues it deals with are not amusing at all but deadly serious, and you owe it to present and future generations to have your say on them — this book is merely to cajole you into doing so;
- We can't even resolve things between ourselves so are unlikely to inform you of much, but you are undoubtedly better informed already and should set us right before this book does any harm;
- The only way to deal with these bewildering times is to raise questions — this book certainly poses more questions than answers about our world and it's up to you to set the world to rights.

About the Authors

Suman Gupta earned his MPhil degree in English from the University of Delhi, India, and DPhil in English Literature from the University of Oxford, UK. Prior to joining the Open University in 2000, Gupta lectured at Nottingham University and the University of Surrey Roehampton (now Roehampton University). He has led a series of international collaborative projects since 2002, including: *Globalization, Identity Politics and Social Conflict*, 2002–2006; *The Nigerian Film Industry* and *Independent Publishing in English in India*, 2006–2008; a cluster of projects on *English Studies in Non-Anglophone Contexts*, 2007–2014; *Framing Financial Crisis and Protest, Northwest and Southeast Europe*, 2014–2016; and *Entrepreneurial Literary Theory*, 2016–2017. He has held visiting positions in Delhi University, India; Peking University, China; University of Texas Austin, USA; Federal University of Campinas, Brazil; CRASSH, Cambridge University, and Wolfson College, Oxford University, UK. He is Honorary Senior Research Fellow at Roehampton University. Gupta has authored 16 and edited 10 books, and published around 70 scholarly papers and chapters, in the areas of literary studies, cultural theory and politics. Books include: *Corporate Capitalism and Political Philosophy* (Pluto, 2002), *The Theory and Reality of Democracy* (Continuum, 2006),

Globalization and Literature (Polity, 2009), *Imagining Iraq* (Macmillan, 2011), *Philology and Global English Studies* (Macmillan, 2015), *Usurping Suicide* (Zed, 2017, co-authored with M. Katsarska, T. Spyros and M. Hajimichael), *Digital India and the Poor* (Routledge, 2020).

Peter H. Tu earned his BS degree in Systems Design Engineering from the University of Waterloo, Canada, and DPhil in Engineering Science from the University of Oxford, UK. In 1990, Dr Tu joined Sony Research in Tokyo, Japan, where he developed a number of computer vision algorithms for man–machine interfaces. While at Oxford University, his research was devoted to the development of computer vision methods for the automatic analysis of seismic imagery. In 1997, he became a senior research scientist working at General Electric's Global Research Center. In partnership with Lockheed Martin, he has developed a set of latent fingerprint matching algorithms for the FBI Automatic Fingerprint Identification System (AFIS). He has also developed optical methods for the precise measurement of 3D parts in a manufacturing setting. Dr Tu was the principal investigator for the FBI ReFace project, tasked with developing an automatic system for face reconstruction from skeletal remains. Starting in 2006, he was the principal investigator for a series of National Institute of Justice programs. This work was focused on behaviour recognition and face recognition from surveillance video. In 2008, Dr Tu led the GE video analytics team that participated in the DHS STIDP demonstration program — the goal of STIDP was to establish an effective defence against suicide-bomber attack. Algorithms associated with these efforts have been incorporated into GE's Intelligent City offerings, where large networks of street lights are equipped with computational and video analytic capabilities. He is the principal investigator for the DARPA-sponsored effort associated with group-level behaviour recognition at a distance. He is also a principal investigator for the DARPA GAILA and CREATE programs, which are focused on language acquisition via visual grounding and multi-agent cooperation. Currently, Dr Tu is GE's Chief

Scientist for Artificial Intelligence. He has helped to develop a large number of analytic capabilities, including: person detection from fixed and moving platforms, crowd segmentation, multi-view tracking, person reacquisition, face modelling, face-expression analysis, face recognition at a distance, face verification from photo IDs and articulated motion analysis. Dr Tu has over 50 peer-reviewed publications and has filed more than 50 U.S. patents.

Acknowledgements

We are grateful to our respective employers, The Open University, UK, and General Electric Research, USA, for allowing us space and time to engage in this conversation.

Thanks are due to Terrence McDonough, Mike J. Hartman, Fred Wheeler, John Kaufhold, Tao Gao, James Kubricht, Mark Grabb, Colin Parris, Alberto Santamaria Pang, Weina Ge, Milena Katsarska, John Seed, Ayan-Yue Gupta, Anne Tu and Cheng Xiao. They have variously offered valuable comments on arguments made here, allowed us to refer to their insights and experiences, been forthcoming when we have tested ideas in conversation with them and helped to bring this book together.

If errors are found in this book, we would typically be unwilling to accept responsibility for them. First we would try to ascertain whether we have unwittingly replicated someone else's error; if it originated within these pages, we would each then look to blame the other; eventually we may come to some consensus about shared responsibility.

Contents

Part 1

Questioning AI

To Begin …

These pages feature a conversation on Artificial Intelligence (AI). The conversation is between Peter, an AI engineer, and Suman, a Humanities researcher.

The agreements with which this conversation was undertaken were these.

Suman will argue that AI does not exist at present and is unlikely to in the future. Peter will maintain that it does to some degree and is very likely to become fully fledged before long.

That is to say, Suman will mostly be raising questions and doubts about the existence of AI. Peter will usually be offering explanations of and solutions for the existence of AI.

This conversation will not take recourse to articles of faith and convictions based on feelings. Nor will it accept unquestionable assertions of self-evident truth. Reasoned argument is all here.

That's it.

It is not clear at the beginning whether Suman and Peter are talking about the same topic when they say 'AI'. Both think they know what AI means. It is Peter's job to figure out what AI could functionally consist of.

It is Suman's business to make sense of what people from different walks of life mean when they say 'AI'. These are different standpoints.

Conversations can only begin from the different standpoints of the conversationalists, on the assumption that they share an understanding of their topic. The process of the conversation will establish whether they actually do. At the least, the conversation should clarify their different ways of understanding the topic. Through that process, the topic itself may become clearer.

So, Suman and Peter must begin this conversation with the assumption that they are talking about the same topic, AI. As their conversation proceeds, it will become evident where their ideas of AI connect and slip, to what extent they agree or disagree on the meaning and prospects of AI. In the process, it should gradually become clearer what AI means and is. At the bottom of this conversation is that question: what is AI?

1

Setting Terms

Suman

- The distinction between artificial and natural systems are outlined
- The dictionary definition of *intelligence* as the capacity to understand is noted
- It is anticipated that the definition of *intelligence* would be at the heart of this conversation

---

By way of terminology: capacities which are considered as revealing of 'intelligence' here are attributed to 'systems'. A 'system', in this sense, may refer to an entity (individual) or collective of entities (social) that behaves according to a functional programme or network (operating a set of instructions).

A system could be 'artificial' or 'natural':

1. A system is 'artificial' if it is constructed, at least in its original form, on the basis of an available/recorded pre-existing blueprint. A system is 'natural' if no such pre-existing blueprint is available/recorded, even when some such blueprint may be inferred or suspected after the fact.
2. A system is 'artificial' if it has the signatures of artifice on it, i.e. the recognisable trace of the tools and designs with which it is produced (in the way a wooden table will have a planned table shape and traces of sawing and chiselling).

We think of the natural system as *born* and the artificial system as *made*. There could be various system states between artificial and natural.

Once a system exists as such, whether born or made, it is apt to *change* (grow, evolve, adapt, transmute, decay, die, etc.). How a system undertakes change is considered as revealing of its 'intelligence' or lack thereof. Loosely speaking, planned voluntary change in response to a circumstance is considered intelligent while spontaneous involuntary change in response to a stimulus is not considered intelligent. But that's a very loose way of speaking.

I expect this conversation would largely be about clarifying what the overloaded term 'intelligence' means. The term 'intelligence' in different registers evokes as many definitions as mystifications, and they have all been implicated in talk about AI. So, that is best approached gradually.

Our usual reference for an intelligent natural system is the human (person) or collection of humans (society). Our usual way of thinking about an intelligent artificial system (AI system) is to think of it as emulating and building upon human persons/society. These are the *usual* ways, which does not mean that they are the *only* ways in which systems may be considered intelligent. Non-humanlike natural intelligence may be found. However, that remains to be considered. Let's start with human intelligence as the base model.

The relevant Oxford English Dictionary definition of 'intelligence' is 'faculty of understanding; capacity to understand'. That's okay to begin with, but very much less than enough for our purpose.

2

More Terms

Peter

- The concepts of *classification* and *detection* are presented
- How the meaning of a concept may emerge based on analogies with other concepts is discussed
- Sayre's views on *recognition* are introduced

In the spirit of defining terms, I would like to refer to Kenneth Sayre's *Recognition* (1965). In this work, Sayre focuses on defining several key terms which include classification, detection, perception and, finally, recognition. I will attempt to summarise these thoughts as follows:

- **Classification:** Determining whether a given sample is a member of a specific class or category. For example, a ring with a certain diameter could be a good classifier for large eggs. If an egg cannot be passed through the ring without breaking the shell, then the egg can be classified as a large egg. While somewhat underwhelming as our first example of AI, there are many examples of how this type of approach is used to great advantage by intelligent agents. With a little bit more formalism, we can talk about observable variables X and unobservable or latent variables Y. The ability to estimate the value of Y given a sample X is known as inference. In the cases where Y can be thought of as the class label, inference of Y given X can then be viewed as an act of classification. For example, given an image patch centred on a camel seen in profile, the set of pixel intensity values can be viewed as the observed variables X. The designation 'camels in profile' would be the class label Y. In another example, the words in a book can be thought of as the observations X, and the value of Y can range over various book categories such as non-fiction, science fiction or poetry. The mechanism by which one can infer the value of Y given X is known as a model. One approach to producing a model is to make use of training data which is composed of a comprehensive set of samples X and their associated class labels Y which have been established through some sort of ground truth process. The means by which the parameters of a model are established is often referred to as machine learning.

- **Detection:** Given a stream of samples one must determine which, if any, of the samples belong to a given class. For example, given a large image we may wish to detect the presence of a rabbit which, if it is in the image, only takes up a small percentage of the pixels. One approach to this problem is the concept of a sliding window classifier. In this paradigm, a set of rectangles of different sizes are systematically translated across the image. At each location, a rabbit classifier is applied to the rectangle. If the classifier produces a positive result, then a rabbit has been detected. Questions of computational efficiency start to arise when one attempts to simultaneously detect large numbers of classes over a wide range of imaging conditions.

- **Perception:** According to Sayre, perception goes beyond detection and classification and towards the concept of meaning and this has to do with semantics. The grounding problem, which is an attempt to establish the semantic meaning of class or category, has been the topic of study for many years. Terrence Deacon's book *The Symbolic Species* (1997) makes the argument that the meaning of a semantic or symbolic class such as camels in profile, rabbits and romance novels may emerge based on a dense web of connections to other semantic classes which are themselves also densely connected. In their book *Surfaces and Essences* (2013), Douglas Hofstadter and Emmanuel Sander make the argument that such connections are essentially analogies, which they view as the currency of thought. With this view in mind, the act of perceiving an object is to see the object through the lens of everything else that one knows.

- **Recognition:** Sayre argues that recognition goes beyond perception, in that it is a type of 'attainment' where the mind enters into a state of awareness where observations can be incorporated into a kind of narrative. In this case, a narrative can be contrasted with a simple series of events or chronology, in that it lends itself to a sense of understanding. For example: given a set of radar returns, motion at the Polish border is detected. After a deeper analysis of the radar signatures, the sources of motion are classified as a large set of troop transports. Based on an analogy between the motion patterns of the troop transports and the pincers of a crab, these events were perceived as aggressive. At this point, the general recognises that Poland is once again preparing for war. A final thought on recognition as it relates to AI comes from Douglas Hofstadter: 'Given unforeseen circumstances, an intelligent agent will get the gist of things and then take the right action'. I think that this capability is what we are shooting for.

3

Questioning Terms, and a Provisional Concept of Intelligence

Suman

- Sayre's four terms are interrogated, especially *recognition*
- A concept of *numinous terms* is proposed and *recognition* is placed as such a term
- A return to Turing's question is mooted, though not to his test
- A model for understanding *intelligence* as distinguished from *automation* is suggested, focused on tasks and purposes

Terms

Useful to have definitions of more terms, Peter. I will not dig back into your sources, simply take the definitions as you state them. I find your definitions of 'classification' and 'detection' to be clear, that of 'perception' to be fuzzy but possibly serviceable, and I don't think your definition of 'recognition' is doing very much. However, the onus of understanding 'intelligence' seems to be on 'recognition', for which the other terms are preconditions.

Let me put it this way. Say I am making an artificial system called … MacHine. I can feed instructions into MacHine so that it can process those and act to fulfil any task that I set it (i.e. it is constructed and programmed

9

accordingly). From your definitions, I can tell by observing MacHine when it is 'classifying', 'detecting' and even perhaps 'perceiving'. If I give MacHine a basket of many different kinds of things, and task it with picking out peanuts and putting them into one bowl and putting hammers into another bowl, and it does, I know MacHine can 'classify'. If I task MacHine with finding the cockroach in the basket and it does, it is 'detecting'.

If I task MacHine with coming up with a set of general rules for distinguishing one (or one kind of) thing in the basket from everything else in it, and it prints out a set of rules for that task and hands it to me, I know it is 'perceiving'. There are a couple of quibbles here. First, in principle this task is easier to fulfil if the things in the basket are more or less fixed; trickier if we keep changing them and adding to them. The latter is more the case if the analogies with (presumably natural) 'semantics' and 'thought' made in your definition are to hold. But, let's say MacHine can do this to a *necessary* extent to fulfil its task at a given moment in time, and learn from that for another task in the next moment in time. Second, the key here is not whether MacHine can do this, but how do we know whether MacHine is doing it — that is, the key is the language of the printout with the general rules that MacHine gave me. The parameters of this language are where a connection to natural 'semantics' and 'thought' lies, and, as it happens, using this language (giving the rules in a 'narrative') is not necessarily a sign of intelligence — though in defining 'recognition' you suggest later that it is.

From your definition of 'recognition', I can't tell how I will know whether MacHine is demonstrating an ability to 'recognise'. The problem is with the vagueness of your definition, not with my ability to observe or with MacHine's to act in a tasked way. There are three problems with your definition:

1. The terms you use for the definition of 'recognition' (including 'recognition' and 'intelligence' themselves) are what I think of as *numinous terms*. That is, their meanings are understood by reference to each other and all are attributed a preconceived and mystical significance. Let me put it this way. The words you use here — the ability to 'recognise', 'know', 'think', 'be aware', 'be intelligent' (and 'understand', 'be sentient') — are all more or less synonymous with

each other. They are swappable with a qualifier or two thrown in. To define one by using the others begs a definition for each of the others and leads to circular definitions or tautological definitions. For example, to be 'intelligent' is to 'understand'; to 'understand' is to be 'intelligent'; to 'know' is to 'be aware'; to be 'aware' is to be able to 'recognise' which shows that one 'knows'.

2. The only non-numinous part of your definition is the ability to 'incorporate in a kind of narrative'. As it happens, 'putting into narrative' is not necessarily equivalent to being describable by any of those numinous terms. A 'narrative' depends upon the base linguistic structure of narrativising. For instance, I can put together a simple 'language game' (in Wittgenstein's (1953) sense), i.e. appoint a set of words and appoint some syntactical rules to govern their usage as a simple language. Then I could put some random phrases which are within the possibility of the simple language, and a certain number of narratives will become possible. If I programme MacHine to work with my simple language, it may compute all narratives that are possible for a number of phrases relevant to a task. That won't show it is recognising, knowing, thinking, aware, understanding … intelligent. That just shows MacHine has acted on its programming for a given task.

3. Your quotation from Hofstadter at the end is a cop-out insofar as it says 'take the right action'. I don't see anything in your definition which enables me to know that MacHine has taken the right action unless that is in accomplishing the task I set it. If it took the right action by any other terms, I won't think it is right. If it takes the right action according to my tasking it, that just shows I am intelligent, not MacHine.

Basically, I can discern what you think are the preconditions of 'intelligence' (or the numinous term 'recognition' if you prefer it) — but I don't understand what you mean by 'intelligence' ('recognition').

A Distinction

Let me come at the issue above from a different direction. There's an old and fundamental question that's implicit above, the Alan Turing (1950) question: how would I, as an intelligent system, know when another system is demonstrating intelligence? Raising the Turing question does not bring back his test model, which we have moved on from; the question that the test was meant to answer is more important than Turing's solution. The point is to try and define 'intelligence' without depending on equivalent numinous terms.

For this, it is necessary to make a distinction between 'automated behaviour' and 'intelligent behaviour'. In this regard, I make a proposal briefly below and will elaborate/adjust if it can be taken further. In the brief statement here, I do not reference the various familiar conceptual sources it is drawn from.

[By the way, it is now fashionable in scientific as in media, policy, commercial and other circuits to dub (even moderately) complex automated systems as intelligent systems (AI). This is based either on genuine misunderstanding or a deliberate desire to mislead. I think it's deliberately misleading because doing so serves some political and business interests — but that's a separate argument, can be taken up later.]

To give this proposal a general statement, before fleshing out in common-sense words: Let's consider a system S which is constituted/programmed to negotiate a series of tasks $T1$, $T2$, $T3$, ... , Tn such that on reaching Tn, a final purpose (FP) is served. S is designed to find the most rational or efficient way to deal with its interim tasks $T1$, $T2$, etc. so as to get to Tn whereby the FP is served. Moreover, the FP is such that the relevance of the tasks and their sequential direction can only be understood if FP is set before the tasks are determined. Otherwise, FP cannot necessarily be inferred from the tasks themselves, and what the significance of Tn is and why S should move from $T1$ to $T2$ and onwards towards Tn cannot be stated with any rational certainty. Then:

1. S is an automated system if it works towards an extrinsically given Tn irrespective of the goal to achieve an FP. This is obviously so if S is constituted/programmed to reach Tn via a given set of interim tasks $T1$, $T2$, etc. as efficiently as possible. This is also so if S is constituted/programmed to vary, modify or change the interim tasks and their pathways so as to fulfil Tn more efficiently than otherwise (i.e. is a learning system). That is to say, even when S can change the pathway

of interim tasks (e.g. skip $T1$ and go straight to $T2$) or modify the interim tasks (as $T1_a$, $T2_a$, and so on) or introduce new tasks ($T\alpha$, $T\beta$, etc.) so as to reach the given Tn with maximum efficiency, it is still an automated system. So long as S is constituted/programmed to achieve a given Tn irrespective of an FP, it is an automated system. It is no use saying that we can set an FP as Tn because then the FP is no longer an FP but merely an extrinsically given Tn.

2. S is an intelligent system if it sets the FP itself and accordingly infers the Tn that will enable that FP to be achieved. Having done that, it may behave like an automated system to achieve that Tn by going through $T1$, $T2$, etc. But its intelligence will be manifest whenever it resets the FP even if going for the same Tn, or resets the Tn to achieve the same FP, or resets both Tn and FP.

Now let me try to put this in common-sense words.

Consider the most venerable of automated systems, a clock. A mechanical clock goes through a series of tasks (pulling a lever, pushing a spool, etc.) to reach an end task (continuously revolving hands on the clock face) to serve our intelligent FP (read the time and coordinate our lives for our collective harmonious co-existence). Now let's make the automatic capacity of this clock more complex. The clock is programmed to send messages back and forth to other clocks which together activate different sensors in different corners of the USA in a coordinated manner; the sensors measure danger signals in particular territories; if a sensor finds a high danger signal, it unlocks a relevant defensive weapons system; the weapons system eliminates the detected danger; once eliminated, the sensor activates a robot designed to assess damage and chooses from some standard damage-control measures; and so on. Now this system can no longer be thought of as a clock, let's call this C-lock instead. C-lock's tasks are different and more complex than the clock's ever was: conduct surveillance, detect danger, eliminate danger, take damage-control measures. But C-lock is still no more or less an automated system than the clock. The FP of all these tasks are extrinsically set by intelligent humans in the USA: perhaps something like, to keep the nation safe because we believe in US democracy.

Now, suppose that C-lock takes charge of the FP ('keep the USA safe') and decides to change it (to 'world peace is paramount'). You can see how that might reset its tasks. For instance, C-lock may then determine that some external force is more likely to further world peace at the expense of the immediate safety of the USA and set its tasks accordingly. If C-lock sets its own FP and infers tasks accordingly, then we can say it is possibly intelligent. (Of course, that's after the intelligent humans in the USA check whether some enemy state has not tampered with C-lock's programming.) We would be apt to say that C-lock has acquired a 'self', become 'autonomous', shows 'subjectivity', become an 'intelligent agent' and the like (more numinous terms) — i.e. is behaving 'intelligently'.

Putting into common-sense words is more useful here than putting into general logical terms, because it tells us something about the character of FP — final purpose — which isn't easily conveyed in logical terms. FPs are usually composed of and expressed in numinous terms themselves. These terms are difficult to define or understand consensually, but they are regarded as collectively or individually significant and meaningful anyway, like: pursuit of 'world peace', 'national interest', 'happiness and fulfilment', 'meaning of life', 'salvation and grace', 'cultivation of knowledge', 'beauty and truth', 'proving oneself', 'self-possession', 'freedom' and so on. That is to say, the statements of FPs are apt to be fuzzy and choosing one has a degree of arbitrariness about it. But once an FP is adopted, the tasks that seem to follow appear determinate and can be determinatively set. And an intelligent agent can always change the adopted (chosen) FP to another one more or less arbitrarily and with a similar kind of fuzziness. In philosophical circles, this used to be thought of as 'existential freedom'.

At any rate, it seems to me that to get to artificial *intelligence* we need to get to the bottom of such numinous terms. The evidence of intelligent behaviour follows *from* them, rather than becomes revealed in the steps that lead up to them.

4

Elaborating Terms

Peter

- Comments on Sayre's views on *recognition* as a form of attainment
- Deep learning (DL) methods are introduced
- Searle's Chinese room problem is reviewed — a call for grounding
- Thoughts on reinforcement learning (RL) are outlined
- Jayne's Bicameral Mind and Searle's views on *consciousness* are considered

Suman, let me start by clarifying Sayre's efforts to define terms such as 'detection', 'classification', 'perception' and 'recognition'. Sayre's main argument is that there is confusion between 'classification' and 'recognition'. He states that 'classification' is a process or pre-defined recipe (remember the use of the ring to classify eggs as either small or large) and that 'recognition' can be thought of as an 'attainment', where an 'attainment' is defined as a durationless achievement in Gilbert Ryle's (1949) sense. For more details on 'attainment,' I will have to refer you to Sayre's book. However, let me describe various aspects of what might be thought of as a recognition engine with the hope of trying to make the point that 'classification' and 'recognition' may be two different beasts …

'A farmer is out standing in his field and all of a sudden a rabbit jumps out of the forest — the farmer makes a mental note that he should make sure that the fencing around his carrots is in good repair'. Let's say that the farmer had some sort of motion-detection system running and that once the rabbit appeared, it was selected for analysis. However, since the farmer was not actively looking for rabbits, he probably would not have his rabbit classifier teed up and ready to go. Instead of a rabbit, the thing that suddenly appeared could have been a camel in profile or a cunning replica of Donald Trump's hair piece. In this regard, a recognition engine seems to have the capacity of recognising an almost limitless number of classes in a very short period of time. It could be argued that with sufficient parallelism, one could be running a large hierarchical set of classifiers with many leaf nodes allowing for logarithmic processing time. For example, a binary classification tree could be thought of as something like the 20 questions game. Another possibility is some sort of elaborate indexing scheme, where the rabbit is transformed into something like a Dewey Decimal code that can then be used to reference a specific book or, in our case, concept.

At this point, it makes sense to quickly discuss the deep learning (DL) neural networks that have allowed for this type of capability. The deep learners are essentially large multi-layer neural networks with high connectivity and various non-linear transformations between layers. The strategy of the Convolutional Neural Networks (CNNs) is to view the world as compositional in nature such that any image can be decomposed into a set of Lego-like primitives that can be combined hierarchically into increasingly complex structures. Object classification can then be accomplished by analysing the sets of primitives that seem to correspond to a given object class. Another type of deep learner is the Autoencoder (sometime referred to as a Variational Encoder). This network can be thought of as a kind of hourglass. For a given object class, the goal is to simply force the output image to replicate the input image with the idea that the number of nodes in the middle layer is much smaller than the input and output layers. This forces the network to compress the information associated with the object class. It turns out that features that we think of as semantically relevant seem to become separated during this process. For example, an Autoencoder trained on human faces may have a specific set of middle layer nodes that focus primarily on the presence or absence of spectacles. In this way, these networks seem to provide semantically meaningful descriptors for objects.

With both CNNs and Autoencoders, one could imagine the ability to transform the world into primitives and semantically meaningful features, which might get us on the road to being able to recognise an open-ended list of object classes. The next level of sophistication is that the recognition engine seems to be able to recognise novel object classes that have never been seen before. For example, if the farmer saw a person riding what appeared to be the back half of a motorcycle, he would not be baffled. We now require the recognition engine to be able to combine and possibly transform prior concepts into new concepts on the fly and in a very short amount of time.

Adding to the list, we can now consider the ability to handle abstract concepts. For example, the farmer may have a certain set of tasks that he must perform in order to keep the farm up and running. At any given time, the farmer may be confronted with a large set of observations, he must be able to distinguish between observations that are relevant and irrelevant to his given task. Due to the variety of tasks and possible observations, a pre-defined process for such discriminating capability would be a challenge. Along similar lines, in his book *Thinking Fast and Slow* (2011) Dan Kahneman argues that associative memory is a remarkable thing: given a set of circumstances, relevant memories seem to come to mind. From a recognition point of view, this seems to imply that a recognition engine could discriminate between useful and non-useful memories. Given the fact that novel experiences may not have been anticipated, it would be difficult to have a pre-defined process for classifying memories based on relevance to the current circumstances.

One last point along this line of discussion is a kind of emergent recognition. When playing chess, a good player may at some point make the determination that he or she is about to fall into a trap. In this case, it seems that recognition may precede awareness.

To summarise, recognition as an attainment seems to have the ability to distinguish between a possibly open-ended set of existing classes, never seen before classes, abstract classes, relevant and non-relevant classes and may be able to function ahead of awareness. Whether or not all of these capabilities can be formulated as a classification-like process (pre-defined rules applied to data) is yet to be seen.

On to the next topic, I really like your proposal that we hunt for a Turing-like test for Intelligence. One note on tests: John Searle's (1980) 'Chinese Room problem' was used as an argument against the Turing test. In this construct, a person sits inside a box and is handed queries written in Chinese characters, he has a set of rules written in various books that allows him to produce a set of Chinese characters that provide a suitable answer to the questions. The person does not speak or read Chinese and at no point are the Chinese characters translated into the person's mother tongue. Searle's argument is that even though such a system seems to satisfy the Turing test, we would be hard-pressed to call such a system 'intelligent' since one could argue that the grounding problem (the ability to define symbolic meaning) was not addressed. When it comes to judging the presence or absence of intelligence, the ability to do something may not be as important as the manner in which it was performed. With this said, let's go on with your proposed test.

In your example of tasks vs. final purpose (FP) selection, let me first give a quick review of an AI concept known as reinforcement learning (RL). The idea is quite simple, an agent is able to sense its environment, resulting in an observed state: S. At any point in time T, an agent can take an action A which can have an effect on the state of the environment. Based on these actions, the agent may periodically receive rewards based on the state of the environment. The goal of RL is to define a policy P which determines which actions to take as a function of perceived states. A value known as $Q(P)$ is defined as the expected long-term rewards that would be achieved if the agent follows a given policy P. The choice of policy is then established by finding the P that maximises the value $Q(P)$. The Go masters have now been beaten by AI agents trained using RL. The idea being that the configuration of the Go board represents the state S, the action space is defined by the legal moves that can be taken at any given time and reward is given if and when the Agent wins the game.

From a computational point of view, the use of DL methods (previously described) was adopted to handle challenges associated with the size of the state and action spaces. While impressive, critics of this type of algorithm make the argument that a policy does not represent intentionality (i.e. the ability of an Agent to have intentions), which is what I think you are looking for. While we may want our Turing AI machines to be grounded (or at least John Searle does), what qualities do we want an Intentionality engine to have? For example, I could wake up each morning, roll a set of Dungeons & Dragons dice and based on the outcome, set my FP for the day. With such a possible solution in mind, we might argue that the process of selecting an FP should not be capricious. Maybe instead of focusing on properties of an intentionality engine, we could consider the manner in which an agent (or species) might develop the capacity for intentionality. This brings up the topic of Julian Jaynes's work (1976) on the 'Bicameral Mind'. The idea being that in order to accomplish group level tasks such as hunting and fishing, humans had to stay on task even without direct supervision of others. To this end, the right brain was used as a kind of god-like task master (intentions) and the left brain was used to accomplish tasks (RL/DL) much like an automaton or AI Go player. At some point, the two brains merge and here we are today. A quick summary of this topic is as follows:

- For most of the last 10,000 generations (this is how long we have been around as humans), we were hunter-gatherers.
- Language emerges as an abbreviation for command and control between humans.
- Left hemisphere — mortal, right hemisphere — divine.
- Bicameral mind — voice of gods for keeping people on task.
- Idols for consolidation of power.
- General decision-making by the gods — Iliad.
- Large bicameral theocracies.
- The written language, migrations, upheavals, chaos.
- The rise of deceit and natural selection.
- The gods recede, and metaphorical consciousness emerges (the Odyssey).
- Mindscape, spatialisation, narrativisation, the analog 'I', the metaphor 'me'.
- The Bible, the Odyssey, Paradise Lost.
- Vestiges: music, poetry, augury, hypnosis, glossolalia, schizophrenia.

The last episode of season 1 of HBO's *Westworld* was dedicated to this concept. While there are many critics of this hypothesis, it does point to the elephant in the room: consciousness. At this point, let's return to John Searle (2005) who argues that consciousness has a number of attributes worth considering:

1. The combination of qualitativeness, subjectivity and unity.
2. Intentionality.
3. The distinction between centre and periphery of attention.
4. All human conscious experiences are in some mood or other.
5. All conscious states come to us in the pleasure/unpleasure dimension.
6. Gestalt structure.
7. Familiarity.

My take is that consciousness is an established phenomenon and that we should not shy away from considering it as we plod our way through this discussion. I hope that in this regard we can find agreement …

5

Methods and Approaches

Suman

- A metadiscursive pause is proposed, to reflect upon the different approaches to the topic already evident
- A distinction is made between the respective instrumental and clarificatory approaches to AI taken by the conversationalists
- Raises a question about Reinforcement Learning (RL)

Patiently

Let me start where you end, Peter: 'consciousness is an established phenomenon ... I hope that in this regard we can find agreement ...'. If by saying that you mean that you and I are talking and interacting on the basis that we are conscious (and so are others), I agree. The phenomenon of consciousness is established in that we constantly reiterate/perform consciousness as working. But if by saying that you mean we have agreed and consensually articulated what 'consciousness' means, then I'll have to demur.

There's a touch of impatience in your saying that. You seem to be implying: 'if only we could get past these elementary points, there are wonderful concepts and applications to contemplate'. I am inclined to think that if we aren't careful and thorough about these elementary points, we may be talking at cross purposes and could find ourselves walking into blind alleys. That's even if the consequences of moving quickly after accepting elementary points are indeed wonderful. You and I have a difference in approach.

This isn't to do with our inclinations, it's a difference in modes of reasoning. Some people will call it a *disciplinary* difference, as if that's the end of the matter. I don't think it is; we don't need to be disciplined into talking at each other rather than to each other. In any case, a metadiscursive pause is in order: you and I need to talk about *how* you and I talk about AI (or anything). A few points on that first, I'll return to one of your substantive concepts later.

(1a) Your approach to AI is an *instrumental* one, in the literal sense that you process the argument so as to be able to conceive an *instrument* (AI). It typically goes like this:

> Definition of $X \rightarrow$ breakdown of definition to instrumentalisable aspects
> $\rightarrow$ putting together instrumentalisable aspects into a functional process
> $\rightarrow$ integration of functional process into the functionalising instrument
> $\rightarrow$ production of X by the functioning instrument.

Thus, according to your previous intervention:

> Definition of 'classification' (the X) by Sayre $\rightarrow$ for an image, decomposition into primitives which can be organised into different sets (instrumentalisable aspects) $\rightarrow$ analysis of the sets of primitives through CNNs (the functionalising instrument) $\rightarrow$ production of 'classification' (Y) by the CNN.

Or alternatively:

> Definition of 'classification' by Sayre $\rightarrow$ for an image, decomposition into nodes at different layers $\rightarrow$ forcing the nodes through a restrictive middle layer and reconstituting via the Autoencoder $\rightarrow$ production of 'classification' by the Autoencoder.

In this approach, the key question at each step (the $\rightarrow$) is 'how can …?'

(**1b**) My approach to AI is a *clarificatory* one, i.e. I try to give the concept the best possible (most fitting, most consensually acceptable) description of its meaning in the world where it is conceived. The point of doing this is to thereby describe lots of other existing concepts and ultimately the world itself. It typically goes like this:

> [Definition of X ↔ disaggregation of definition against existing linguistic/textual practice, logical clarification (e.g. in analytical philosophy), social modelling] → confirmation of definition of X (which is rare) OR laying further definitional parameters of X according to contexts.

To follow on where we start for you:

> [Definition of 'classification' by Sayre ↔ honing/modifying/adjusting/ departing from that definition by checking how 'classification' is understood in ordinary language, in systemic logic, in social organisation] → either confirming Sayre's definition OR finding that it is not enough, 'classification' needs differently nuanced definitions according to context. The latter implies that this one definition is too narrow/biased, and misleads in being less than it pretends to be (it pretends to be 'classification' *per se*). For example, at times 'classification' signifies a distinct logical relationship (say, Bertrand Russell's idea of 'class' [1908; with Whitehead 1910] as an extension of a propositional function), at times a naming practice (think of classification in terms of the Sapir–Whorf hypothesis on colour perception [Berlin and Kay 1969]), at times a social control mechanism (consider how biological taxonomies bounce with social class, or of distinctions in taste *a la* Pierre Bourdieu [1984]). I might find that Sayre's conveniently instrumental definition is so limited as to not be meaningfully 'classification' in a received sense at all, though it is consistent with some aspects of the received sense.

In this approach, the key question at both the mutually tested juncture (↔) and the step (→) is 'why is ...?' I have in mind the rather splendid discussion by Richard Feynman (1983) on 'Why' questions.

(**2**) It is obvious that your and my sense of a *definition* are quite different.

- You want to fix a definition and move on to the instrumentation. To fix the definition, you typically appoint an authoritative definer (Sayre says this and that's the end of the matter). You opportunistically accept the authority of the definer if the proffered definition suits your purpose, and then conceal the part played by your convenience by deferring to the authority of the definer (Sayre, here).
- I want to check definitions against existing usage of terms and in practice (Sayre says this, but that's not enough because *A*, *B*, *C* etc. define it somewhat differently, and how far does it work against the horizon of ordinary language usage in specific contexts). I want definitions to be sufficiently accommodative or to remain provisional so that clarification of the world proceeds (mutual understanding prevails in the world).

(3) There are consequences to taking different views of definition.

- You are likely to feel impatient about my tendency to render definitions provisional or incomplete. That holds up instrumentation and enthusiasm about what can be achieved thereby. That's the impatience one feels at the slow person who is holding up those waiting in the car all set to hit the road. Or at the ignorant person in a symposium who asks questions which all the cognoscenti in the room know the answers to.
- I am likely to feel suspicious that you are trying to palm off something that is not quite right in your hurry. I might think, for instance, that what you are calling 'intelligent' is not what is generally considered as 'intelligent', and wonder whether you have some ulterior motive for doing that. That's rather like a customs officer who looks suspiciously at everything and everyone that crosses the international airport's declaration line.

In that vein, you would want to answer Turing's question having understood it straightaway; I would want to clarify the pre-conceptions underpinning Turing's question first. In fact, in my view, Turing's question is not clear and it is a lack of clarity in posing the question, not really a lacuna in Turing's test, which Searle exploits in the Chinese Room. But let's go there some other time.

(4) In considering AI nevertheless, approaches 1a and 1b are complementary and need each other. Had this been technology which is purely based on stable natural/physical laws, approach 1a could perhaps disregard approach 1b and *vice versa*. While natural/physical laws hold in the instrumental direction of AI, they are at the same time inextricably interfered with by unstable social principles. To put it glibly, the *artificial* in AI follows natural/physical laws to a considerable extent, but the *intelligence* in AI is socially constructed to a significant extent.

This puts a particular charge to the mediation of ordinary language, which is significantly socially determined (possibly beyond some level of 'language universals', such as those proposed by Noam Chomsky [esp. 1980] or Joseph Greenberg [1966]). Ordinary language forms a necessary correlative in mathematical expression (a point in Kurt Gödel's [1931] undecidability proof). In relation to AI, you can find few terms, definitions, inferences which aren't complicated by social *a priori* and social constructions of intentionality.

(5) The best way for you and I to continue therefore is perhaps not by either of us giving sweeping Zeitgeist statements and world-encompassing proclamations (like that terrifying mishmash of terms in the bullet-pointed/numbered lists in your previous intervention). Better, perhaps, to start patiently with something specific and small, so ...

... A Question

I do like your clear outline of Reinforcement Learning (RL):

> The idea is quite simple, an agent is able to sense its environment resulting in an observed state: S. At any point in time T, an agent can take an action A which can have an effect on the state of the environment. Based on these actions, the agent may periodically receive rewards based on the state of the environment. The goal of RL is to define a policy P which determines which actions to take as a function of perceived states. A value known as $Q(P)$ is defined as the expected long-term rewards that would be achieved if the agent follows a given policy P. The choice of policy is then found by finding the P that maximises the value $Q(P)$.

What does 'rewards' mean there? How is it determined that $Q(P)$ is an accrual of 'rewards' rather than, say, 'punishments' or 'nothings'? Let me put that another way: as far as the agent goes in this outline, it doesn't matter whether those are 'rewards' or 'punishments' or 'nothings', does it? $Q(P)$ could be anything that is set as the targeted long-term outcome as far as this agent goes. Given that, the agent's actions and the system's state changes and the agent's determinations of policy would follow. Is that right? It would be useful to have an example to contemplate for such 'rewards' in RL.

6

Methods and Field

Peter

- The various domains of AI research are briefly described
- Sources of inspiration and influence for AI research are outlined
- Pac-Man is defined in terms of a reinforcement learning (RL) problem

---

A meta-pause makes sense. This got me thinking about the concept of an AI Menopause. Some say that AI began in earnest at a Dartmouth College workshop held in 1958. One gets the feeling that now is a time for an AI change of life. One way of looking at our communities is to consider two infinite lines in three-dimensional space that are askew. With this metaphor in mind, talking past each other is somewhat natural. But let's see if we can find the shortest possible connecting chord and see where we go.

Since you have done me the service of defining my approach to research, let me start by trying to flesh this out a bit by giving a brief description of the various AI research communities as well as our sources of inspiration and influence.

AI Research Domains

- **Traditional AI:** From its inception, this community has focused on a variety of topics, including computational logic, belief networks, causal reasoning and general search. Many of the proposed approaches have collapsed due to lack of computational resources, system complexity and the curse of dimensionality.

- **Signal processing:** This group mostly focuses on structured data such as a time series generated by multiple sensors. Accomplishments of note include the speech-to-text problem, which is now routinely incorporated into our handheld devices.

- **Natural language processing (NLP):** This group focuses on raw text analysis. They use concepts such as knowledge trees, which define various semantic relationships between words and ontologies. However, one of their most powerful methods of analysis is based on observed statistics: Given a corpus of training documents and a sequence of words, what is the probability distribution associated with the next word? Using this simple formulism allows for concepts such as semantic embedding methods: Given a corpus of documents where the semantic distance between all pairs of documents have been manually estimated and defined, all documents can be transformed into a vector space (embedding) such that the Euclidean distance between any two documents is equal to their semantic distance. This embedding process allows for a kind of calculus over semantic meaning. One of the most memorable achievements of the NLP community occurred when the IBM Watson machine beat the world champion quiz experts on the television show called Jeopardy ...

- **Robotics:** These folks deal with issues such as inverse kinematics, path planning and production systems. Everyone gets excited when these contraptions perform back flips — lots of fun videos.

- **Cognitive science:** This group focuses on the modelling of mental processes. Due to the complexities of experimentation in the real world, they tend to work in 'sandbox' domains. As far as I can tell, no idea is too preposterous for publication in this space.

- **Cybernetics:** Not exactly sure what these guys do. But when they pass by, their robes make a very distinctive swishy sound.

- **Computer vision:** Given an image sample x, what is its class label y (classification)? Given a set of image samples x, which samples y belong to a specific class (detection)? Given an image x, what is the partition y of x that defines the boundaries between x's constituent parts (segmentation)? Given an estimate of the latent variable y at time $t - 1$ and the observations at time t, what are the values of latent variable y at time t (tracking)? Given a set of observations at time $t - 1$ for N entities and a set of observations at time t for the same N entities, what is the correspondence mapping y of the observations between the two sets of observations (data association)? Given projections x of an object, what is its original state y (reconstruction)?

- **Machine learning:** $y = f(x)$.
- **Deep learning (DL):** I fear that in my last intervention it may have sounded as if concepts such as Convolutional Neural Networks (CNNs) and Variational Encoders were mere hypothetical constructs. This could not be farther from the truth. While these multi-layer neural networks got their start in the computer vision labs, they are now incorporated into just about every form of AI. After some initial resistance, DL is now being adopted by almost every computation-minded research community. I have been to a number of conferences where luminaries in the field stand up and say: 'I have devoted my life to developing a beautiful mathematical framework and now you expect me to throw this all away, download this *%&# and just start feeding it data? Such work is not even fit for interns!' But alas, within a cycle or two the conference proceedings go from one or two DL papers to 90% or more DL papers. These methods have also been highly democratised. All across America, shiny-eyed high school students, trained from birth to delight ivy league college admittance officers, are downloading DL software and making their own AI applications #Precious.

AI Influences

- **Neuroscience:** Using instruments such as FMRI, we are getting a good idea of where certain mental processes take place and how they interconnect. We can now do tricks like reconstruct an image that is being observed by a person or even imagined by a person simply by measuring region-based neural activity. However, for the purposes of measuring neuron-to-neuron interactions, our devices are orders of magnitude too coarse. So, there is not much help here in terms of producing new computational models. This being said, AI researchers love the term 'Biologically Inspired'.

- **Behavioural science:** Experiments focused on how people get through their daily lives hint at models that can be used to emulate such capabilities. Our capacity to learn both slowly, quickly and cumulatively is a constant focus of study.

- **Linguistics:** Models of language such as the fabled 'meta-language' that rules them all have been used as inspiration for such things as automatic text translation.

- **Mathematics:** Has certainly played its part in establishing concepts such as projective geometry and generative models. However, mathematics is basically a reductionist approach. We are looking at an emergent phenomenon which seems to require millions if not billions of parameters. With the provenance of DL methods, the role of today's mathematics is not certain.

- **Philosophy:** We can argue that many of our current approaches have traceable epistemological roots. In the old days, papers would use philosophical argument to justify a novel approach; but at the end of the day, motivation does not seem to be well correlated with measured performance and hence impact on the field (more on this later).

- **Physics:** Physicists are good at coming up with mathematical formulations that AI researchers are more than happy to commandeer: simulated annealing, Gibbs sampling ... However, they seem relatively silent when it comes to inspiring new ideas regarding how intelligence manifests itself in the physical world. Once again, the emergent *vs.* reductionist nature of AI may be the reason why physicists have contributed so little. Like string theory, is AI a generation or two too early? Do we simply not have the mathematics and instrumentation needed to pursue these concepts? My take is that, pound for pound, there is nothing in the universe that exhibits the complexity associated with a lump of brain, and so much of what we know about the universe as well as the tools used to investigate it might simply not apply to AI. However, there is a suspicion that there are certain properties associated with this possibly unique type of matter that we have yet to fathom and there is of course the promise of quantum magic blah blah blah — get on it guys!

Going Forward

While there have been many AI accomplishments over the years, I would say that much of the hype around AI today is based on the following: 'In the universe there are a large number of probabilistic mechanisms with both observable and latent variables. Given large amounts of data, we are good at producing models that allow us to infer the value of the latent variables'. The main research ethos that has driven this work is the idea that all computational models can be evaluated based on their performance against real-world data. For better or for worse, measured performance is our divining rod. While elegance of formulation or seeking the authority of luminaries is well appreciated, all such considerations are essentially cast aside once the validation experiments have been performed. With this said, I would argue that when I cite folks such as Sayer and Searle, I am not trying to wear the mantle of their authority and gravitas, instead I view them as muses that we can use to open up new avenues of investigation. When Sayer suggests that classification and recognition might be different mechanisms, this might lead to new forms of indexing and analogy creation. When Searle criticises the Turing test, it might encourage researchers to focus on the grounding problem.

It sounds like instead of following our muses, you suggest that we build a conceptual edifice from which we can harness the insights of the humanities and then more clearly peer off into the distance. As Donald Trump Jr. once said, 'If this is what I think it is — I love it'. But as you suggest, maybe we should start small and not try to boil the ocean. To this end, I will give a nice example of the reinforcement learning (RL) problem, with the idea that we can distil the wisdom of the humanities in a systematic and fruitful manner.

Long Live Atari!

Right now, there is a whole cottage industry focused on applying RL methods to vintage video games such as those made famous by Atari. To this end, I propose that we study Pac-Man.

- **State Space S:** The Pac-Man screen has 640×480 pixels. Let's assume that each pixel can take up to 256 different colours. At any given point in the game, the state of the game can be defined by the colour values taken by each pixel. Thus, there are in principle $256^{640 \times 480}$ possible state values. While large (the universe has much fewer atoms), we will not be daunted.
- **Action Space A:** At any given time, the Pac-Man can either go up, down, left or right. Thus, the size of the action space is 4.
- **Reward:** The Pac-Man is given a reward whenever it eats one of the food elements as well as for eating fruit. Also, if the Pac-Man eats one of the power pills, the ghosts turn blue and can then be eaten by the Pac-Man resulting in a large reward. Note that the Pac-Man is not instantly rewarded for eating the power pill, it only gets rewarded if and when it catches a ghost that is in a blue state. This is a classic example of delayed reinforcement. If the Pac-Man eats nothing but just moves around the screen, it gets zero reward. If the Pac-Man clears the screen, it gets a bonus reward and goes to the next level. If the Pac-Man is eaten by a ghost in a non-blue state, the game is over and there are no more future rewards.
- **Goal:** Find a policy P, where $a = P(s)$ such that the expected cumulative rewards $Q(P)$ associated with this policy are maximised.

We know how to make an RL Pac-Man Agent that can just about beat anyone's high score, but at the risk of being accused of using numinous terms, I would very much like to instantiate a Pac-Man that is wise, creative and capable of interesting forms of recognition ... So let's build an edifice and follow our muses and figure out what it means to be an intelligent Pac-Man.

7

Discerning the Intelligent Agent

Suman

- Assumptions made in outlining AI research domains and influences are questioned, e.g. regarding *natural language* in natural language processing (NLP)
- The Pac-Man screen is described as an expressive medium tracking tasks and purposes
- The Pac-Man agent expressed through the screen is delineated accordingly
- The Turing question is restated with Pac-Man in view

A good idea to play Pac-Man as you suggest, Peter (and taken aback to see you not just risking but drowning in numinous terms by the end — 'wise', 'creative', 'interesting forms of recognition'! — none of which I'm sure I understand).

But before playing Pac-Man, first a few passing thoughts on your splendidly useful characterisation of the field of AI research.

A Few Points

1. At a tangent: We tend to use the word 'intelligent' (at least in English) in two distinctive senses.

- **Intelligent-1:** As opposed to *unintelligent* or *stupid*. Here 'intelligence' is used to refer to the upper end of a spectrum of a set of abilities between 'very able' and 'not able' or 'high performance' and 'low performance'.
- **Intelligent-2:** As opposed to *automated* or *simulated*. This is the sense that is relevant here, and consists in the meaningful existence of the set of abilities just mentioned in a system.

I argued in an earlier intervention that this set of abilities is only considered meaningful ('intelligent') if the abilities can be rationalised and applied in terms of Final Purposes; otherwise they are evidence of 'automation'. Another way of saying that is:

- Intelligence-1 is only 'intelligence' if it is conditional to Intelligence-2. Otherwise the abilities in question are automated/simulated.

One of the things I was wondering about is to what extent the nine domains you outline and their attempt to develop high-performance systems are motivated and informed, if at all, by making a distinction between 'intelligence' and 'automation' ('simulation'). (I come back to this distinction with regards to Pac-Man below.)

2. One of the interesting features of your outline of both domains and influences is that these carefully exclude social determinants and contexts. This might seem okay for some of the domains, less so for others. Let's pause, for instance, on the domain of natural language processing (NLP). Incidentally, I have always thought 'natural language' is a misleading phrase unless it refers to something like the language of bees, which is relatively stable over time. Otherwise it makes human language sound inborn rather than socially produced.

'Everyday language' or 'ordinary language' makes more immediate sense. Such language usage is extremely socially sensitive or contingent, often amenable to reinvention or planned change (such as standardisation) and otherwise continuously being modified at lexical and syntactic levels — i.e. unstable over time. That's why dictionaries have to be updated regularly and grammar books rewritten. What's 'natural' about it?

The method you describe is of computational corpus analysis. That in itself poses some limitations. Arguably, appointing parameters to select any sort of text and analyse their use of language will necessarily preconceive what is inferred — a typical circular argument. In linguistics circles, the objection was influentially made by Noam Chomsky in *Syntactic Structures* (1957). That doesn't mean that corpus analysis is not very useful indeed for instrumental purposes and has been proven to be so. It means this method gives access to a small range of ordinary language usage, not to the actual range of variables and shifts that work in an ordinary-language community on a more or less daily basis — which may have something to do with 'intelligence'.

The particular analytical parameters you mention to exemplify its relation to AI — statistical breakdown of word order in training texts — could give access to both the synchronic (patterns at a given moment and context of usage) and the diachronic (changing patterns with time and interaction) dimensions of this corpus (those are Ferdinand de Saussure's (1916) terms). But in shifting that to something like performance of automatic translation, the performance-based tendency would naturally be to favour the synchronic at the moment the shift is made. In doing that, so much is left out of the scope of ordinary language that it is doubtful whether ordinary language is in reference at all.

Similar arguments about the elision of social determinants and contexts can be made for some of the other domains too (especially cognitive science and deep learning, but let's hold those arguments in reserve).

3. As you say, the key driver for all domains in AI research is 'performance against real world data'. Researchers have occasionally offered persuasive arguments about the bind between methods of elicitation of data (tabulation) and interpretation of data (statistical analysis) in any social field to propose that rhetoric plays a significant part in this. Importantly, that doesn't imply a misuse or abuse of statistics; to some degree, the argument goes, social statistics is implicitly rhetorical, at a methodological level. We don't need to go into this straightaway. As a holding position, Deirdre McCloskey's *The Rhetoric of Economics* (1998) gives a useful account of such arguments for, obviously, the field of economics.

Mine is a more mundane point. Appointing performance measures for AI against real-world performance measures could simply be a flip way of social engineering, i.e. so as to force the behaviour of human systems to cohere with those performance measures. There might be an ideological Final Purpose in such engineering rather than anything to do with 'intelligence'. To be pat, the idea might be to help AI simulate human intelligence by making human intelligence simulate AI.

But onwards to Pac-Man! That's more fun than such nitpicking and brings back salad days …

So, Who is Pac-Man?

Your suggestion, Peter, to anchor arguments to Pac-Man is a useful one. Your brief description of Pac-Man in terms of Action Space A, State Space S, rewards & goal $Q(P)$, where P stands for policy, is good. Just to give it visual immediacy, here are two static screen shots of the game at two phases at one level (see Figure 1).

When you say that reference to this game may be used to understand what AI means, or what 'intelligence' might mean, this suggests that an agent that is or is not intelligent is in question — let's call this Agent Pac-Man. You simply call this 'Pac-Man', whom you want to be 'wise, creative and capable of interesting forms of recognition'. However, what you call 'Pac-Man' slips in contradictory ways. At one moment, you suggest it is ᗧ (which 'eats' and gets 'rewards'), at another, it may be the structure of the game itself [$a = P(s)$ such that max $Q(P)$], and at yet another, you speak of an artificial Pac-Man Agent which can beat anyone's high score. So the question really is: who is the Agent Pac-Man? Once we are clear about this, we can consider what may be needed to think of this Agent Pac-Man as intelligent.

You and I, and Pac-Man players generally, know the answer already, so laying it out is by way of stating the obvious. Nevertheless, let's do the obvious. There's a bit of confusion there, arising from a trivial linguistic circumstance: our fondness for zoomorphic/anthropomorphic terms. So, let's translate to neutral terms (marked in italics below, which is closer to programming language by a step or two):

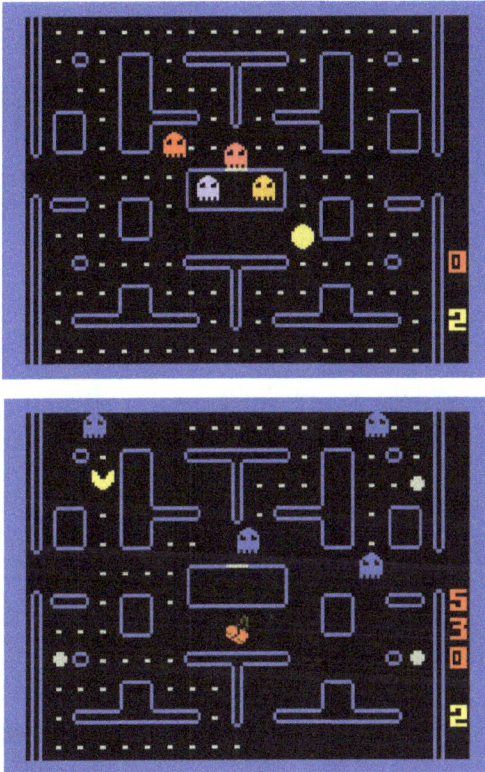

Figure 1. Static screen shots of the game at two phases at one level.

- ▚ is a *cursor* which Agent Pac-Man controls within the *frame* of the game according to its spatial and action parameters. The cursor has the property of *deleting* ('eating') point-bearing features and being deleted by free-moving features on contact.
- The *point-bearing features* are visualised as small dots, large dots, ghost phase of free-moving features and fruits. Some of these carry more points than others, and there are some sequential moves between some of these, but these are simply *classes of point-bearing features*.
- The so-called *rewards* are an *accruing number* shown on the bottom right-hand margin of the screen, just *outside* the frame (the limits of the

action/state space) — the sum total of the point-bearing features accruing as the cursor deletes them.

- The 'goal' of the game is to *keep the accruing number growing* towards
some hypothetical limit by manipulating the cursor. There is an actual
final limit for the accruing number, but let's not worry about that.

- *Agent Pac-Man* is the system that operates the cursor so as to take the
accruing number towards some hypothetical limit within the constraints
and possibilities of the frame and its features.

So, if we are looking at the game unfolding on the screen, what are we
looking at? We are looking at, essentially, the *expression* of Agent Pac-Man.
The screen as a whole with the game unfolding is Agent Pac-Man's *expressive device*. The frame is telling us what Agent Pac-Man is calculating
and doing or failing to calculate and do. From this, we can infer that Agent
Pac-Man is trying to delete point-bearing features such that the accruing
number grows (maybe, but quite possibly this may not be evident — maybe
Agent Pac-Man simply enjoys seeing 🝰 deleted). However, the accruing
number just outside the frame is, in itself, not telling us much. Just by looking at it and the frame we can neither tell what the P could be nor what the
Q is in $Q(P)$. To understand what that accruing number means, we need to
refer to something outside the expressive possibilities of Agent Pac-Man
offered by his expressive device.

We need perhaps to ask Agent Pac-Man to use a different expressive
medium if he can — but then we are outside the game, and Agent Pac-Man
becomes more than simply Agent Pac-Man.

Let's say Agent Pac-Man is an automated system with some access to
another expressive medium, ordinary language. If you enquired why it is
manipulating the cursor it can tell you that it was given a target goal in
advance ($Q(P)$): such as, 'the highest score ever achieved, which is X' or
even 'the greatest score achievable in this game' (max $Q(P)$). This is a
simple statement of its final task (*Tn* as I had put it earlier) which makes
sense of the Q in $Q(P)$. But if you asked it 'Why $Q(P)$?' it would only be
able to say, 'Because I was told so' — and there the conversation would end.

Let's say, Agent Pac-Man is an intelligent system (human or not),
with access to the expressive medium of ordinary language. You can keep
asking it 'why' for quite a while if it doesn't become impatient.

- 'Why?'
- 'Because $Q(P)$ is greater than the highest score ever achieved' (there's the final task Tn)
- 'Why try to go beyond the highest score?'
- 'Because I want to show I am better at this than anyone'
- 'Why?'
- 'Because other Agents Pac-Men will honour and respect me then'
- 'Why do you want to be honoured and respected?'

… and so on, till some exhaustion point is reached when Agent Pac-Man may say something like

- 'Because humans exist to better themselves'

… well, something numinous like that, which I had put down as the Final Purpose (FP) earlier.

Though we have reached the FP through a sequence of consequential moves from the final task Tn (understood as $Q(P)$) onwards, once stated it becomes evident that the rationale actually works backwards from FP to Tn for Agent Pac-Man. It is only if Agent Pac-Man has the FP in his horizon that he can work backwards to set a Tn which is $Q(P)$ in a particular context. And only then the to-dos in consequential order towards Tn on the screen (which are interim tasks $T1, T2, … , Tn$) are worked out according to a best policy P. Without the FP, nothing intelligent has happened. If it is an artificial system which sets the FP, it is AI — otherwise it is a non-intelligent complex automated system which has been given a Tn.

Saying that an artificial system can defeat a human in any inferential logic-and-response game (such as chess, Go, Pac-Man or whatever) proves nothing about that system's intelligence apropos of the human model of intelligence. Only a game player with a lot of cultural capital invested in his playing ability may think otherwise — a Garry Kasparov, for instance.

How does the FP come to be stated by an intelligent Agent Pac-Man? I think of it as emerging from Agent Pac-Man's relationship with the World. The World is a theoretical sum total of everything that's in it and possible within it, and it has lots of other Agents Pac-Men in it and every

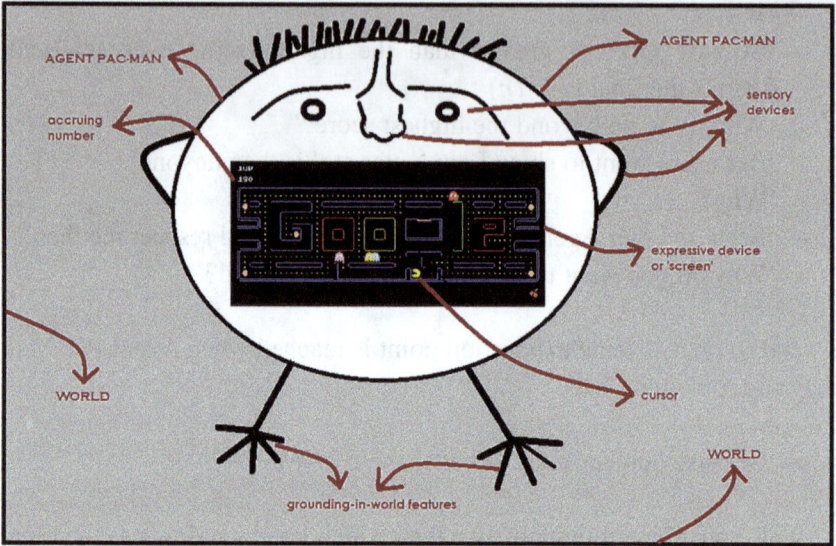

Figure 2.   Agent Pac-Man.

other sort of thing. The intelligent Agent Pac-Man you have been interrogating would have derived his FP from within the resources of his cognitive environment and experience within the World, using his sensory
devices and processing capacities (from something like what Wittgenstein
called a 'form of life' in *Philosophical Investigations* (1953)). Or, in other
words, from the part of the World that this Agent Pac-Man is grounded in.

Figure 2 shows how I visualise Agent Pac-Man.

Nice Questions

Given that Agent Pac-Man is thus, and given that the only expressive
device he has is the screen:

- Is there any way in which we can make out that Agent Pac-Man is intelligent simply by observing the screen with the current parameters of the
  game as they are?
- If not, what is the minimum adjustment we need to make to the parameters
  of the game so that this becomes possible simply by observing the screen?

In short, could this be a pathway to a new 'imitation game'?

8

Realising the Intelligent Agent

Peter

- A historical account of the first and second waves of AI and their associated winters is given
- Emergent languages and their associated mechanisms are presented
- A recipe for constructing an agent that can choose what to do and tell us why is proposed

---

Suman, first let me start with agreeing with your last figure! If we want our agent to be able to answer the question of why it does what it does, we are going to require that:

1. It has the capacity to accept such a query.
2. It has the introspection needed to produce a satisfying answer. By satisfying, we are hoping to avoid glib responses such as, 'Because that is what I am programmed to do'.

To this end, I agree that the Pac-Man Agent may need to have a grounded universe, it may need a community, it may need the concept of a past, present and future and it may need to have an internal experience that goes beyond a policy P that attempts to maximise $Q(P)$. But before we delve into what such an agent might look like from a computational point of view, let me address some of your initial questions regarding the field of AI.

It is my belief that an agent's capacity to select its own Final Purpose (FP) is what is referred to as 'intentionality'. You ask quite rightly who if anyone is working on the intentionality problem. In my last intervention, I attempted to characterise AI as it is done today, but to address your question, I think that we need to have a brief review of how AI got to where it currently is. Classical AI started with lofty ambitions that can be characterised as Artificial General Intelligence (equivalent to human intelligence) or Strong AI (Artificial Consciousness). Some of this work focused on the idea of a Community of Mind (CoM), where a set of capabilities could be instantiated with the hope that some sort of emergent intelligence would ultimately manifest itself. For example, a system called Gamygdala, which is currently used by the gaming industry, was developed to synthesise emotional responses for non-player-characters (NPCs) that are consistent with the narrative of the video game. This can be thought of as a stand-alone AI engine that could be part of a CoM. Other capabilities might include reasoning engines, production systems, mechanisms for curiosity and natural language processors. This first wave of AI failed to deliver for a number of reasons: insufficient computational resources, brittleness and an inability to operate under real-world conditions. This lack of performance resulted in the first AI winter.

To get back in the game, the second wave of AI shifted to Narrow AI which is focused on solving specific AI problems. This spawned targeted fields such as computer vision, machine learning and natural language processing (NLP). Methods for problems such as face recognition, generic pattern matching and automated service calls were developed. However, promises did not live up to performance and this resulted in the return of the AI winter. I would argue that with the advent of modern computational devices and various algorithmic advances (see my previous observations), we are now at the point where Narrow AI has started to deliver the goods. There are now renewed calls from various parties such as DARPA (Defense Advanced Research Projects Agency) for progress to be made on Stage III AI, which can be defined by a wonderful series of numinous terms.

Just a quick note on your concerns regarding NLP. I would argue that languages such as Arabic and Hindi are naturally occurring since they were not a product of artificial or manufactured processes. An example of an artificial language is some interesting work by Serhii Havrylov and Ivan Titov (2017). Inspired by the game-like interactions proposed by Ludwig Wittgenstein (1953), an approach to constructing an artificial 'grounded' language is as follows: Two agents, a sender and a receiver, are given access to millions of images taken from the real world. During each iteration, the sender selects, at random, an image which is sent to the receiver. During this process, the receiver is also sent 1000 random decoy images. The goal of the receiver is to determine which of the 1001 images was sent by the sender. While the sender does not have knowledge regarding the 1000 random decoy images, it does have access to the image that it sent and can select a small number of symbols from a vocabulary of up to 20,000 symbols in order to produce a sequence or expression that is sent to the receiver to help identify the transmitted image. Initially, the 20,000 symbols have no associated meaning, but every time the receiver is able to make a correct identification, both the sender and the receiver are rewarded. After a large number of iterations, both the sender and receiver appear to develop an agreement regarding the interpretation of each symbol as it pertains to describing images. This is a good example of a form of artificial emergent language.

Now let's return to our concept of a Pac-Man Agent and consider a plausible sequence of sophistication that might lead us in the direction of intentionality which can be interrogated and leave us with a sense of authenticity.

1. Let's start with a single agent that has been constructed by developing a policy p based on reinforcement learning (RL) such that the expected overall score associated with following $p(Q(P))$ is as large as possible. While the agent will be successful in this narrow AI problem of playing the Pac-Man game, it does not have the ability to accept and authentically respond to queries regarding its intentionality.

2. Now let's add a community of agents. We will orchestrate the emergent language process that I previously described by giving each agent the ability to describe any image that can be generated by the Pac-Man game but also describe any game played by the agent. We will also give each Pac-Man a variant of the CoM AI engines such as

the Gamygdala emotion engine as well as other capabilities, such as a Curiosity engine (popular in the robotics world, see Forestier, Mollard and Oudeyer (2017)). In this way each agent can describe how each game was evaluated by these CoM AI engines, it may also be able to evaluate how these CoM AI engines might evaluate a game played by another agent. But at this point, the agents are still compelled to follow their RL policies and so intentionality is still not in the cards.

3. Now let's give each agent some sort of oracle that is in charge of taking as input the CoM AI engine outputs and using these outputs to influence the manner in which it plays the game. In some agents, the oracle will want to minimise fear at all cost and so it would avoid the ghosts at the expense of collecting all the fruit. In some cases, the oracle will be completely indifferent to the ghosts, in which case it would lose right away. One could then ask (possibly via the emergent language) why the agent chose to play Pac-Man and get responses such as: 'My oracle puts great weight on avoiding ghosts'. One could argue that the fear of ghosts was merely hard-wired into this particular agent's oracle and as such has not satisfied our concept of authentic intentionality …

4. Now let's give each agent only a limited number of games to play (say 100), but let's say that if the agent is able to achieve a score better than a minimum value over the first 20 games, then it is allowed to produce offspring if another agent, which also meets the minimum requirements, agrees to mate with it. The resulting offspring will have oracles and CoM AI Engines that are some sort of combination of its parents' oracles as well as a modicum of random mutation to add a little bit of spice. We can also add in the concept that the number of offspring that an agent is allowed to produce is based on the size of the scores that the agent is able to achieve throughout its life time. Now when asked why the agent chose to play the way it did, the honest answer would be 'I am the product of a sequence of agents that played the game so that each of them was able to successfully procreate'. Like all evolutionary arguments, this response is a bit tautological:

>   Darwin: Evolution is based on the idea of survival of the fittest.
>   Sceptic: What defines a fit individual?
>   Darwin: Fit individuals are those that survive.

5. Now let's lean a bit more on our emergent language and CoM. Since an agent must choose a mate at the age of 20 games, it has to be able to evaluate how a potential partner will perform in the future (assuming it wants lots of offspring). Using the CoM AIs and the emergent language, it may be able to develop concepts that can be used to evaluate a particular partner. Concepts such as 'daring', 'heroism' and 'systematic' might emerge as useful criteria for selecting a mate. The concept that 'agents are attracted to agents that other agents are attracted to' might result in the concept of socially accepted traits of attractiveness which may deviate over time from the ability to produce high scores. Now when we ask the agent for its motivation for doing what it did, we may be able to get an answer in terms of socially acceptable criteria for behaviour. While giving the appearance of reason, this response is still a bit Popeyesque ('I am what I am and that's all what I am').

6. OK, let's go all in on our emergent language and CoM. Suppose that over time various agents have found some interesting gambits, such as how to avoid a ghost under certain circumstances. Now such discoveries are made via exploration, experimentation and experience. Unfortunately, such learnings cannot be given to one's offspring via the mechanism of inheritance (this is not a Lamarckian universe!), but one can imagine that parents could transmit such learnings to their children via the emergent language in the form of stories. Given the ability to encapsulate and transmit, such learnings would represent a significant advantage. Let's assume that agents become so adept at crafting and learning from such stories that this capability becomes internalised. Each agent is now able to construct a running narrative of its experience that is:

   i. Centred on the agent.
   ii. Able to justify the actions that the agent takes in terms of social norms and agreed-upon concepts.
   iii. Able to represent the present and past as if such sequences of events were the result of a causal process.
   iv. Able to quickly reconstruct the narrative as and when incongruous events occur so that the sense of continuous causality is preserved.

Let's also give the agent the ability to predict how its peers (and potential mates) might react to this running narrative — a kind of Theory of Mind. This might allow the agent to proactively take actions that result in a narrative that would meet with approval by these internal Theory of Mind modules. Now when we ask the agent to explain why it did what it did, we can expect to get an answer in terms of the agent's running narrative. While such an explanation may simply be a rationalisation of actions produced by an evolved CoM that had been influenced by its community, one can argue that if we have no understanding of the internal workings of the agent, we might infer that the causal nature of the narrative is consistent with the idea of volition and an ability to select an FP — the agent thus appears to have an authentic form of intentionality.

A couple of points: While I made a number of technological jumps — such as, the capacity to form rationalising narratives — in general I think these moves are within the realm of the possible. One of the difficulties of studying consciousness is that it is a subjective experience that does not lend itself to external scrutiny; if I ask you why you did what you did, I just have to take your word for it. Finally, it has been said that the veneer of intelligence fades away once you know how it is done. In this regard, our lack of introspection may be a gift that we might not wish to squander.

9

Recognising the Intelligent Agent

Suman

- Some nuances of the terms *intelligence*, *natural language* and *intentionality* are noted
- The distinction between producing and recognising intelligence in an artificial agent is underlined, the latter is the point of the Turing question
- A process of reverse inferring from the Pac-Man screen is proposed as a test

---

Words

Little quibbles first, Peter, before admiring your more substantial argument.

Engineers are expected to use words with as much precision and as little ambiguity as possible — for naming/labelling, signifying relations, as analogies/metaphors. Words are unavoidable instruments in the toolbox of scientific practice. Using words without sufficient cognizance of their received nuances potentially courts fundamental distortions in scientific practice. That's either because ill-judged use of words obscures the investigator's observations (the interference of inaccurate instruments) or because ill-chosen words are apt to be misinterpreted (the interference of preconceptions). These are, in fact, the kinds of interference that symbolic rationalisation tries to avoid by minimising ordinary-language words.

This is so even when those words seem to be established by convention within communities of scientists, as keywords or buzzwords.

I begin with these pedantic sentences, Peter, by way of saying that I have some small bones to pick with you with regard to the initial part of your last intervention — which is, on the whole, a stimulating whizz over a lot of ground. So, words:

- **Natural language:** Hindi or Arabic (or even Esperanto) is 'natural' in the sense of being unplanned to some extent, not entirely. Not insignificant areas of usage in such specific languages are, so to speak, artificially programmed and implemented (standardised elements, specialist areas of lexis and syntax, whole signifying systems at times, etc.). So, it is misleading to suggest that they are the opposite of artificial machine languages, which are wholly planned and programmed (which is also not quite the case if one thinks through your summarised and cited example). Ordinary language contains both evolving (therefore 'natural') and planned elements, which often slide into each other. But I am happy to go along with *emergent artificial language* (or simply *emergent language*) as a specific sort of applied linguistic formation: essentially, the extrapolation of specialist aspects of ordinary language so as to form a discrete and internally consistent language game which is amenable to utility-based programming.
- **Intelligence:** It must be fairly clear by now that I'm sceptical of the prevailing distinction, which you reiterate, between 'strong artificial intelligence'/'artificial general intelligence' and 'narrow artificial intelligence'. I don't think the latter refers to 'intelligence' at all, it refers to complex automation. A system either is intelligent or not, and all that's described as 'narrow artificial intelligence' is not. If intelligent, a system may show strong or narrow intelligence — that is within 'artificial general intelligence', which I argued is based on back-inferring from final purposes (FPs). Much of what passes as functional AI now — 'narrow AI' — is (often impressively) complex automation bolstered by anthropomorphic description. The initials 'AI' are

principally a glib way of palming off more than is meaningful, particularly beloved of managers, funders, policymakers and media gurus. Scientists and engineers have found it practical and materially rewarding to go along with these influential lobbies. It now seems to be taken for granted that there is some continuous line between automatising specific cognitive, inferential and communicative functions and the possibility of an integral artificial intelligence — is there good reason to expect it?

- **Intentionality:** I'm afraid I'll have to differ with you here. The process of back inferences from FPs (often numinously phrased) to immediate practical Final Tasks is not quite covered by that term. Intentionality is much discussed in some branches of philosophy and linguistics. The main senses in which 'intention' seems meaningful are as follows:

  1. The autonomy of a subject/self is reiterated constantly and often undermined by *intending* to accomplish Final Tasks, not FPs ('I intend to win the prize' or 'I intend to tell her the truth').

  2. The enunciation of 'intention' is a speech act, where saying 'I intend' is in itself an act of intending (a verb, not dissimilar to 'I promise').

  3. Intentions are grounded in contextually specific reasonings and justifications. The last has some bearing on what I mean by back-inferring from FPs. But 'intention' is seldom given in the numinous terms of FPs, and generally attaches to practical Final Tasks. A Pac-Man Agent is more likely to say 'I intend to finish Level 1' rather than to say 'I intend for humans to better themselves'.

You give a strong account of how numinous terms as FPs work for practical Final Tasks and may appear as 'intelligence' at the end of your sixth move in developing Pac-Man agency. In brief, numinous terms accommodate lots of different functional interpretations. When lots of agents use them to justify their immediate tasks, those numinous terms seem to acquire a collective meaning after the fact, which is understood more by exemplification than definition.

Now, back to the Pac-Man Agent.

Quasi-Human

Peter — in pushing (in six steps) from the individual Pac-Man Agent in my figure to where strong AI may be established, you go way further than the modest questions at the end of my last intervention. You move towards working out how the Pac-Man Agent may be made intelligent in the sense of answering 'why' questions satisfactorily. As you put it, this involves the Agent (a) being able to accept such questions and (b) having the ability to produce a satisfactory answer.

To do this, you suggest a series of integrative steps which effectively simulates an entire evolutionary/historical process along quasi-human lines, with reference to currently available and possible technologies. And at each step you consider whether the possibility of the Agent's answering 'why' questions in terms of FPs can be satisfactorily realised. This involves endowing the Pac-Man Agent with an emergent language which functions much like ordinary language, a social milieu (the gaming Community of Mind), an 'oracle' (I suppose a directive organ, with reasonable abilities of observation, analysis and probability assessments), the ability to reproduce and mutate, the ability to inherit and form consensual forms of behaviour, the ability to form collectively understood narratives (stories) — along with other nudges along the way which effectively enable the production of functional numinous terms. The aggregation of all those into agents might lead to intelligence in the sense of articulating satisfactory FPs.

This line of thinking seems to me terrifically ambitious. Though each bit of technology is available or developable, their integration may be as intractable as human diachronic development still seems, even with retrospection. The development of each step of integration, I suspect, would only be determinable, let alone controllable, to limited degrees. You end on a note of optimism, but I suppose many engineers contemplating this pathway might feel a twinge of doubt or despair at the prospect.

At any rate, you are clearly *designing an intelligent artificial Pac-Man Agent in theory*. This may or may not be the way to go. As often, I feel more elementary pauses are needed before zooming off in that direction. So, let me go back to my questions, which were in essence a restating of Alan Turing's question (in 'Computing Machinery and Intelligence',

1950) — not so much to do with *designing an intelligent Pac-Man Agent* as with *simply recognising whether a given artificial Pac-Man Agent is possibly intelligent* (how would we know whether this machine can think?). Only, here it is restated without depending upon ordinary language-like interrogations involved in the 'imitation game'. On reflection, I expressed myself badly in my last intervention (by imagining 'why' interrogations of the Pac-Man Agent), so let me restate the revised version of the Turing question in Pac-Man terms.

The Expressive Device

As I observed in my previous intervention, the Pac-Man screen is an expressive device. We (intelligent humans) can make inferences as to the kind of agent operating the cursor by watching the screen. Let's assume that the Pac-Man Agent is not visible to us and has no other means of expression — no access to an emergent language or ordinary language-like mode for us to interrogate the Agent. In that sense, the screen itself is an expressive language. It offers a trace of behaviour (cursor action within the space), with some fixed signs (fruits, cursor, ghosts, dots, accumulating number, labyrinth and pathways), related by a set of pre-agreed rules (a syntax).

My first question was: can we, simply by watching the screen (not interrogating), determine whether the Pac-Man Agent playing the game is *possibly* intelligent or not — in the sense of *possibly* setting its own FPs? We can think of this as a version of Turing's imitation game. We are the 'evaluator' in Turing's terms; the Pac-Man Agent may be an intelligent system (human or artificial) or an automated system; and our task is to watch the screen and decide which it is.

Let's say we are watching the screen expressing the Pac-Man Agent playing level 1 numerous times. Obviously, if the screen tells us that nothing more is expressed than the Pac-Man Agent's determination to reach the given final task Tn (or max $Q(P)$ according to the accruing number) — i.e. by following the rules of the game — we cannot tell whether the Pac-Man Agent is or is not intelligent.

Now, let's say that by watching the screen we can discern that in an initial number of games the Pac-Man Agent was following the rules of the game and going for a given Tn. However, at some stage we observe that the Agent has radically altered the *Tn* to $T_\cup$ and is playing a series of games consistently for that final task. This $T_\cup$ could be something like playing to make the level last as long as possible while being indifferent to the accruing number, or playing to delete all the dots without deleting a single ghost — i.e. has changed the rules of the game. And then we observe that Agent Pac-Man has come up with yet another consistent change across a series of further games of the final task to *Tη*. We can now consider several possibilities:

1. If the Pac-Man Agent is human, then these shifts in final tasks from *Tn* to $T_\cup$ to *Tη* are motivated by switches in relevant FPs (say, from an FP which motivates competition to one which motivates eccentric individualism to one which drives an anarchist agenda).
2. If the Pac-Man Agent is artificial, then it may have been programmed to switch its Final Tasks occasionally.
3. If the Pac-Man Agent is artificial and has not been programmed to switch Final Tasks occasionally, then some sort of error has crept into the programming.
4. If the Pac-Man Agent is artificial and has neither been programmed to switch final tasks and nor is manifesting an understandable programming error, then something interesting is happening. We need to work out why there are shifts from *Tn* to $T_\cup$ to *Tη* — i.e. could there be understandable (at least in our terms) FPs behind these shifts?

The leap from suspecting error to suspecting intelligent reasoning (between 3 and 4) is a tricky one. It depends on (a) knowing what an 'error' is, (b) being able to find the error as such in the programming or being sure that there is no such error to be found. It is quite possible that any intelligent self-reprogramming on the Pac-Man Agent's part will be interpreted as an error. Perhaps we can have an error-determinant machine simultaneously at work if we define 'error'. I hope we will come back to the concept of 'error'.

The other question in my last intervention was whether the expressive device, the Pac-Man screen, can be adjusted so as to actively nudge an artificial system towards possibly demonstrating intelligence.

I'll leave that question open here.

Last Point

The point on which you end your previous, Peter, is critical to the themes of this conversation, isn't it? If we know how 'intelligence' works and can replicate it satisfactorily, we'll possibly not think of that as 'intelligence' any longer *or* 'intelligence' will lose its mystique. If there is something unachieved in our conception of 'intelligence' given what is achieved technologically, then that remaining quotient will be dubbed 'intelligence' — it's a shrinking area. If the mystique of 'intelligence' is lost because what we understand as such is fully achieved through artificial means, we will lose something significant in our sense of human distinctiveness. Does anyone want to go that far? How far should the quest for artificial intelligence go, and why?

There are the two obvious answers:

- We go as far as we wish to in line with replacing/enhancing existing human capacities — but confined to complex automation. The push for that is a social one: to restructure commodity and service and employment markets, to manufacture the consent of consumers and regulate populations accordingly. That could be motivated by some idea of perfecting the capital cycle, total social policing and coordination, reaching infinite sustainable production, stabilising inequities in perpetuity, etc. Any such Final Purpose can be sought by simply dubbing complex automation as 'artificial intelligence', thereby generating a continuous balance of social anxiety and desire, and pushing for whoever's interests are best served thus.
- We can pursue artificial intelligence as a goal of producing a cohabiting species, the implications of doing which are indeterminate in given social terms (we pursue it, so to speak, for its own sake). Various numinous reasons can be offered for this, some imbued with religiosity and some premised on humanistic reasoning — a kind of Frankenstein drive. This is not especially practical, not financially meaningful and so on, but that doesn't matter.

Does a conversation like this one have to necessarily be premised on one or the other such Final Purpose?

10

The Intelligent Agent in the Prospect

Peter

- The difficulties of studying products of evolution such as intelligence are raised
- Reminiscences of playing against a bona fide dyed-in-the-wool Pac-Man Agent
- Techniques that might synthesise the illusion of having a shifting final purpose (FP) are considered
- Changing the game to unmask an imposter is raised
- Why we should persist with this potentially dangerous game is addressed

Suman, I like your argument that the ability to back-infer an evolving final purpose (FP) based on observed changes in the style of play of our Pac-Man Agent may imply some sort of deliberative process which may be indicative of intelligence. I have a number of thoughts along these lines, but before holding forth in this direction, I will make some comments regarding your statement: 'A thing is either intelligent or it is not…' While this quibble might be a bit pedantic, it seems to me that our form of intelligence was based on a gradual evolutionary process and hence 'intelligence' might not be as binary as we might think. The problem with evolved systems is that their histories are so convoluted and, in many cases, undocumented that it seems that the end product could only have functioned in its current state. Darwin could not explain how the optics of the human eye could have 'evolved'. In his book *Out of Control* (1994), Kevin Kelly describes how attempts to reconstitute American grasslands (or prairies) almost always end up as large fields of weeds. The main argument being that we are not aware of certain critical stages of development that may require specific environmental conditions such as the presence of a key catalyst. In one of my previous interventions I mentioned the work of Julian Jaynes who proposes a possible evolutionary path for the development of human consciousness. Along these lines, my colleague Tao Gao and I recently went through Michael Tomasello's *Origins of Human Communication* (2008). To further make the point that our intelligence must have emerged through some sort of gradual process, I thought I would give a quick summary of Tomasello's thoughts:

- The great apes are able to use intentional gestures to request or demand actions from others.
- In contrast, early humans were able to use gestures (pointing and pantomime) to accomplish three basic things: (a) requests for actions from others, (b) to give information that might be of assistance, and (c) to express one's feelings regarding the environment.
- The ability to both request and offer assistance can be seen as a form of cooperative communication that involves mechanisms such as common conceptual ground, joint intentionality and various forms of recursive 'mind reading'.
- The drive towards expressing one's opinions can be viewed as a mechanism for building common conceptual ground with the goal of minimising within tribe differences and maximising between tribe differences. You might be willing to cooperate with a non-tribe member, but you generally only share your admiration for a pleasant sunset with a member of the tribe.
- While pointing allows for identifying objects within the current field of view, pantomime allows for identification of non-visual referents.
- As these pantomimes become conventionalised, they can become increasingly arbitrary in nature. This allows for the development of spoken language which is based on completely arbitrary but socially accepted symbols.

- Arbitrary languages (both spoken and sign) have the complexity required to construct narratives which can describe events and actions of multiple agents over both space and time. Various frameworks can then emerge so that these sequences of events can appear to be causal and even 'make sense'.
- Through this analysis, we see that cognitive skills evolve phylogenetically (over the lifetime of the species), enabling the creation of cultural products historically, which then provide developing children with the biological and cultural tools they need to develop ontogenetically (over the lifetime of the organism).

Now back to our Pac-Man Agent.

Around 2016, I was in Washington DC and I bumped into a good friend of mine, John K. We decided to meet later that day for dinner and drinks at John's favourite watering hole. John paid for dinner and I picked up the drinks (thanks GE!). It just so happens that there was a vintage Pac-Man machine at the bar — John challenged me to a game and was generous enough to give me the first go. I got through the first stage without losing a life, the second stage was a little tougher and by the fourth stage I was barely able to white knuckle my way through. I lost two lives on level five and level six was my undoing. But I felt that I had put in a good showing. Gleefully, John K said that he could tell by the way I played level one that I would not make it past level seven. He said that I was figuring out the game as I was going and that I obviously had no wired patterns of play. John then cracked his knuckles, inserted his quarter and flew through the first 20 levels without breaking a sweat. While John's performance was clear evidence of an ill-spent youth, it does also have a bearing on our current conversation.

Your examples of FP, such as competitiveness, the desire to express one's individuality or in John's case, humiliate a venerable colleague, make sense. However, I think that your term 'rules of the game' should be viewed as the mechanics that govern how the game works, such as when a ghost intersects with your cursor three times, the game is over. To fill this terminology gap, let me describe a method known as Dynamic Programming (DP), which is similar to the reinforcement learning (RL) framework that I described in my previous intervention. At any given state, an action can be taken that results in the transition to a neighbour-ing state. The value (positive or negative) associated with making such a state transition is defined by a metric. Given an initial and a final state, the goal of DP is to compute the optimal path from initial to final state, where optimality is defined as the path with the highest possible cumula-tive value. If the metric has the property that for any states *A*, *B* and *C*, the optimal path going from *A* to *C* through *B* is equal to the optimal path from *A* to *B* plus the optimal path from *B* to *C*, then the metric has the Markov property and can be thought of as extensible. The complex-ity of solving an extensible DP problem is linear with respect to the cardinality of the state space, which allows for efficient computation. If the Pac-Man Agent was using a form of DP to govern its actions, then the ability to estimate the cost metric used would be relatively straight-forward. Thus, changes in the metric could in principle be used to detect an evolving FP.

In the event that we observe a shifting metric, you propose a number of conclusions: (1) the Agent was programed to randomly shift its metric giving the illusion of an evolving FP, (2) an error in the programming occurred resulting in a shifting metric, or (3) neither pre-programmed randomness nor errors occurred, something else is going on leading to the hypothesis that we may have tripped inadvertently into a deliberative pro-cess that results in an evolving FP. I will add a fourth possible conclusion, we may have fallen victim to a hacker! These overweight, bedridden individuals from the great state of New Jersey or folk like myself that can trace their ancestry back to the middle kingdom would love nothing better than to pull the wool over the eyes of a liberal arts major. They may even have the audacity to attempt to bring down a luminary from the Humanities. A possible tool for such nefarious individuals is an approach known as Adversarial Networks (ANs). Suppose that the hacker can record the extended play of a large set of intelligent Pac-Man players — training data. The hacker can then construct two neural networks: a dis-criminator network and an imposter network. During each iteration, the discriminator is exposed to the play of either a random sample from 'the intelligent data' or the play produced by the imposter network. The dis-criminator is rewarded every time it is able to accurately discriminate between samples from the intelligent data and play produced by the imposter network. Conversely, the imposter is rewarded every time it can fool the discriminator. In some ways, this process can be thought of as cooperative, in that the discriminator teaches the imposter how to play like an intelligent agent and the imposter teaches the discriminator how to distinguish between authentic and false intelligent play.

I fear that if we now had to face the outputs of a fully trained imposter neural network, our rule of thumb for detecting intelligence would need to be more than just the back-inference of an evolving FP. This reminds me of a similar challenge that my colleague Fred W once faced. We were approached by a company (I will call it X, but you could just as well call it Pied Piper) that claimed to have a new breakthrough in the field of loss-less image compression. Given an image of size N bits, the goal of image compression is to take advantage of natural redundancy in the image in order to reduce the size of an image down to M bits using an encoder where M is significantly smaller than N. At some future point in time, a decoder is applied to the compressed image resulting in an exact copy of the original. X was claiming compression rates significantly below the current state of the art — Fred was suspicious. X proposed the following demonstration:

1. We were to give them a set of 100 natural images, each of size N bits.
2. They would then send us 100 compressed images as well as a decoder program that we could then apply to the compressed images.
3. We could then compare the reconstructed images to the originals.

The experiment was conducted, we received the 100 compressed images, which were each smaller than what the current state of the art could achieve. When we applied the decoder to these images, the resulting images were compared to the originals and, as advertised, there were no differences. However, prior to sending the original images, the cunning Fred had applied independent random noise to the bottom 4 bits of each pixel. To the eye, this is not particularly noticeable, but it is a known fact that it is just about impossible to compress random noise — we don't need to go through the math right now but take it from me it is straightforward and beyond refute. Clearly, company X had embedded our original images into their decoder and this was how they were able to produce exact copies of the originals … What I take away from this is: can we detect behaviour of the imposter agent that is too good to be true?

Another approach might be to consider an intelligent behaviour that would be too hard for our hacker to produce. For this I would consider the nature of the inferred FP itself. Since the imposter agent is cut off from the hacker during our test, we might observe a certain limited novelty associated with the types of FPs that we may encounter. This would be due to the fact that the training data is finite and hence there would be an upper limit on the number of possible FPs that could be emulated. This would be like watching old episodes of Star Trek over and over again, at some point you come to the conclusion that you have in fact seen them all — when we get to a point where we only detect FPs that we have seen before, we might become suspicious. One might argue that an intelligent agent has the potential of being both endlessly novel and perverse …

Let me give an example. A few years after Fred W successfully exposed X for their fraudulent ways, he and I had a conversation regarding men's fashion at GE Global Research. We both agreed that any deviations from the standard button shirt and a pair of slacks was strictly policed by the good people at human resources and that any flashes of personal style are quickly snuffed out. What was surprising to me was Fred's complacency in this state of affairs. When I called him out on this, Fred looked to the left and then the right and then he asked me if I knew what his criteria was for selecting his clothes. After thinking about it for a while I confessed that I could not detect any form of intentionality in his attire. Fred smiled — he then explained that his clothing decisions were motivated by the single criterion that the casual onlooker should come to the conclusion that Fred made no consideration of the thoughts of others when making his clothing decisions … The endlessly recursive irony associated with Fred's confessed FP left my head spinning. I would argue that a sequence of such shocking FPs from our Pac-Man Agent might be something to look for.

Taking another tack, it seems to me that by changing the rules of the game, we might see some cracks in the façade of our imposter Pac-Man Agent. For instance, some of the fruit could periodically become poisonous or the ghosts could start using new coordinated tactics of offense. In the competitive video gaming world, this is known as buffing and dumbing the characters, which pushes the players out of routine behaviours. The ultimate version of this kind of test is a game called '1000 blank white cards'. The players start by randomly selecting a set of cards from a deck, where each card has a rule. The game is initially governed by these rules. The game evolves by letting players make up new rules as they go and applying them to the existing set of rules. In this way, the rules of the game continually shift and there is little opportunity to learn in advance using brute force trial and error methods. Due to the open semantics associated with this game, akin to Calvinball, to date no AI system has been particularly effective in this challenge. Of course, you might argue that the ability to handle a changing environment is not indicative of a deliberative approach to FP.

Let me end this discussion by taking this concept one step further. Suppose that we change, ever so slightly, the premise of this test. Let's start by simply providing the Agent with access to the Pac-Man machine, it will be given the capacity to observe the screen and operate the controls, but the designers of the Agent will have no prior knowledge regarding the Pac-Man game itself and the Agent is not rewarded for adopting any particular behaviour. If the Agent just sits there and does nothing, that would be one result. If the Agent starts to play the game, I would argue for an FP such as curiosity. If the Agent started to win, I would argue for an FP associated with a desire for accomplishment. If the Agent surprises us with its style of play, I might even argue for an FP of creativity and maybe a sense of panache and expressiveness. If the agent clears the first 20 screens in the first go, I would suspect the maniacal hand of John K ...

I am perhaps being too verbose in this intervention. But like a treasured child, once written it is hard to delete a paragraph. This said, I would like to address your last question regarding why we want to engage in AI research. In James Barrat's *Our Final Invention* (2013), we get some pretty good arguments as to why AI Research might be a bad idea. He starts with the Busy Child scenario where some sort of entity with monotonically increasing intelligence starts to grow at exponential rates going from AI to Artificial General Intelligence and then Artificial Super Intelligence. He makes the argument that we have yet to see a stronger species being overly concerned with the welfare of a weaker one. He points out that we are currently in the midst of one of the greatest periods of mass extinction in known history. He talks about the 'rapture of the nerds' where gentle AI mavens try to upload their consciousness into the cloud and live forever with billionaire singularity enthusiasts. I think that a more charitable motivation for going forward is that we are living in what appears to be a lifeless universe.

In Lawrence Krauss's extraordinary book *A Universe from Nothing* (2012), we come to grips with a series of incredible facts:

1. The universe is about 13.8 billion years old.
2. We now have some reasonable ideas for how something can come from nothing.
3. The universe appears to be flat, which means that it will just keep on expanding forever and ever.
4. In a couple of billion years the galaxies will be so far apart that observers at that time might not even be aware that they are living in this type of universe.

The last point is particularly chilling. Our species is 10,000 generations old. The traits that got us here (tribalism, personal greed, treachery, etc.) when mixed with the technologies that we have built, might mean that we are quickly coming to the end of our line. We are too delicate for space travel, but our AI progeny could withstand the rigors of interstellar flight. It might not be too late to create an enchanted universe. What is the point of galactic splendour if there is nothing there that can revel in its glory?

(Spoiler alert) As we saw in the movie *Her* (2013), our AI agents may soon become bored with our limited cognitive capabilities, but I can't help but hope that sometime in the far distant future, in a faraway galaxy, Scarlett Johansson will look back at us and smile.

11

Devolving Evolution

Suman

> - Insofar as evolutionary processes bear upon thinking about AI, some of the received principles are noted
> - Four alternative ways of correspondingly thinking about non-evolutionary processes are proposed

Peter, let's say, we agree that the prospect of a future AI Scarlett Johansson looking back and smiling at us justifies any kind of effort in the present, however unpromising.

In response to your preceding intervention, the following focuses more on your brief initial observations about evolving systems (*vis-à-vis* language) and less on the entertaining and informative appearance of the hacker later.

Evolutionary and Non-Evolutionary Processes

I might have a few quibbles with your summary of Tomasello's argument, some of which are also quibbles with Tomasello's argument — but I'm not sure about them yet, so won't go there. Much depends on what you and others understand by the term 'evolution'. I find it a confusingly shifty term and it would be grand if you could settle its import once for all. I have in mind particularly your observation:

> it seems to me that our form of intelligence was based on a gradual evolutionary process and hence intelligence might not be as binary as we might think. The problem with evolved systems is that their histories are so convoluted and, in many cases, undocumented that it seems that the end product could only have functioned in its current state.

Let me put some initial constraints on the term 'evolution', which I expect we'll both agree on (let me know if otherwise).

First, *evolution* refers to a process of change in a mechanistic rather than teleological manner. That is, we say a system *evolves* in response to a change in a given state of affairs (such as, in a given habitus or environment) and then further according to changes in subsequent states of affairs, rather than to reach a pre-determined final-system condition (towards a Final Purpose (FP), to realise a 'perfect' system). The responsive evolutionary principle can be formulated, but that doesn't reveal a direction towards or give a clue about a final-system condition. So, if we observe that the means for system change (e.g. by selection and adaptation) in response to a new state of affairs (e.g. depleting source of energy) is according to a principle of continuing system survival — this principle is not revealing of a future final-system condition. It clarifies the working of the process, it doesn't point to an ending. The end result by following the principle may as well be system extinction as system survival. In this sense, the term 'evolution' is consistent with its etymological derivation from 'unfolding' — an ongoing mechanical process rather than a teleological striving towards a final condition.

Second, as is implicit already, it refers to consistent change at a system level rather than transient anomalies in a component of a system. So, we are apt to speak of evolution at species level (such as, modern humans), rather than in reference to an individual specimen of a species (we are unlikely to say, 'Peter embodies a unique and eccentric evolutionary career'). If all finches in a particular habitat have a particular kind of beak, we say 'ah ha, evolution has been at play!' If we find one finch with a beak unlike any other, we might say 'tis a freak' — unless, of course, it then so happens that this freaky beak becomes a consistent feature among its descendant finches (it is not a transient anomaly).

In the biological field where the term 'evolution' is most familiarly grounded, systems are generally understood in terms of collectives of individual entities, and 'evolution' refers to collective processes of change in a system. But in theory, a system may well be a discrete individual entity (using Humberto Maturana and Francisco Varela's (1980) biological or Niklas Luhmann's (1995) sociological terms, an individual entity as 'autopoietic system') and in that case evolutionary change could be manifested at an individual-system level. For our purposes here, however, let's stick to changes in collective systems within which our model of human intelligence, and the function of language therein, is so firmly grounded.

With these features of *evolutionary* process in mind, we might wonder how to relatedly describe a *non-evolutionary* process in such a system: what might the latter consist of and how might it be exemplified? It seems to me that a putative distinction between evolutionary and non-evolutionary processes may have something to do with received conceptions of intelligence (in terms of FPs), and perhaps also with the distinction between 'natural' (born) and 'artificial' (made) systems with which this conversation began. At any rate, in common parlance and in some weighty academic discourses, certain processes of collective change are *not* thought of as evolutionary. In contradistinction from *evolutionary process*, these may be variously referred as 'planned process', 'artificial change', 'socio-historical process', etc. — which I am clumping together here as *non-evolutionary process*.

With reference to a given system, it seems to me that there are four alternative ways in which *non-evolutionary process* may be described *vis-à-vis evolutionary process* — as follows. Each involves a different conception of 'intelligence'. And the question I ask is: which of these do you consider to be the most acceptable description and why?

1. At a sufficiently complex system level, there are no non-evolutionary processes. All processes, even those that are seemingly planned or ostensibly managed according to an FP within specific contexts, actually fit into evolutionary processes when all the considerations relevant to the system are taken on board. So, intelligence appears as an

evolutionary adaptation, and though the intelligent agents think they are self-determining and decide their own ends, that is no more than a symptom of the evolutionary development that is intelligence. Intelligence is an adaptation to principally enhance the collective survival of some agents irrespective of whatever purposes they invent for themselves.

2. An *evolutionary process* is underway when the component entities in a system behave collectively and mechanistically according to an indifferent principle — where 'indifferent' means, not according to the determinations of any particular individual entity or subgroup of entities.

    Correspondingly, a *non-evolutionary process* is underway when intelligent agents in a system try to determine pathways according to their FPs or in terms of self-interested principles. This might lead to changes in the state of the system which don't realise any agent's particular FP. Nevertheless, such a process involving competing or cooperating pathways of intelligent agents is considered a *non-evolutionary process*. The non-evolutionary process is imbued with intelligent agents' plans, policies, self-set tasks and FPs.

    It might be reasonably averred that once intelligence emerges among agents in a system, that system can neither show a purely *evolutionary process* and neither a purely *non-evolutionary process*. In such a system, evolutionary and non-evolutionary processes might be interwoven with each other, such that there's a balance or one supersedes the other at times or permanently. If we were trying to place the function of language among intelligent agents in a system, the appearance and development of communicative modalities might well be the transition point from a purely evolutionary process to a mixed or dominantly non-evolutionary process, where the non-evolutionary is the domain of intelligence.

3. You might prefer a more restrictive version of 2, where only a process in which intelligent agents in a system can be shown to realise their Final Tasks and FPs is considered a *non-evolutionary process*. Otherwise, the system follows only *evolutionary processes*,

irrespective of the existence of intelligent agents therein and the unsuccessful parts (by their own reckonings) they play. Another way of saying that is: where processes are predictable and lead to a pre-determined end, according to a blueprint, they are non-evolutionary; otherwise they are evolutionary.

4.   Putting an added emphasis on the previous sentence, you may choose (though I doubt it) to think of *non-evolutionary processes* as particular to a certain kind of system and *evolutionary processes* as specific to another kind of system. Thus, you may choose to define non-evolutionary processes as the domain of *artificial* systems (which are made; with or without intelligence), and evolutionary processes as the domain of *natural* systems (which are born; again, with or without intelligence). This raises certain obvious conundrums. If, for instance, you design your artificial system such that it *may* follow/simulate an evolutionary process towards intelligence — can this in fact be regarded as an evolutionary process? Or is it merely a non-evolutionary process of replicating an evolutionary process? This seems to verge on playing with words. Nevertheless, this is an alternative way of naming processes.

Which would you go for as the most reasonable description — 1, 2, 3 or 4? (I suspect political proclivities may sway your choice.)

Hacker

As a Pac-Man Agent, I fear your friend John K might be more efficient automaton than an intelligent human. You should ask your friend Fred W to check out John K's programing. That you lost to John K might be a sign of your intelligence as a Pac-Man Agent.

Your friend the busybody hacker evidently comes with the purpose of interfering in automatic Pac-Man Agent's expressive device — behaviour on the screen — without revealing himself. His objective is to make it appear that the artificial Pac-Man Agent fulfils expectations we have of discerning intelligent behaviour (shifting Final Tasks according to newly appointed FPs) without exposing his interference. So, the hacker defeats the purpose of this Turing-like Pac-Man test. We could simply say that the hacker should be exposed in advance (your friend Fred W will catch him out). We should set the test such that there are no hackers. We should put our artificial Pac-Man Agent in conditions whereby intelligence *may* evolve, and the Agent *may* come to be revealed as an AI agent by its behaviour on the un-interfered-with screen.

But the larger point you are making, I suppose, is that what the hacker does by introducing Adversarial Networks (ANs) (discriminator and imposter) is so close to simulating intelligent behaviour that it may well *be or become* intelligent behaviour. That test will be in the pudding, it needs more fleshing out. You have marked some of the limits of this possibility already in your intervention. Apart from that, the obvious quibble would be that the FP of simulating a given model of intelligent behaviour has been set by the busybody hacker and not by that which seemingly exhibits this model of intelligent behaviour.

12

Evolution as a Creativity Engine

Peter

- Various aspects of evolution are explored
- The argument that evolution can be viewed as a creativity engine is made
- Mechanisms are analysed based on their capacity to produce creative solutions
- A calculation is made regarding the ability to repeat the human evolution experiment

---

Suman, let me start by quickly summarising the interesting thoughts and questions that you raise regarding evolution:

1. Evolution is a mechanical process without a final goal state.
2. We say a system *evolves* in response to a change in a given state of affairs (such as, in a given habitus or environment).
3. Change is viewed at the system level vs. individuals having certain peculiarities.
4. The question then arises regarding what a non-evolutionary process might look like. Does this have bearing on intelligence in terms of a final purpose (FP)?
5. There are four choices for describing a non-evolutionary process: (a) There are no non-evolutionary processes; (b) A non-evolutionary

process is underway when intelligent agents in a system try to determine pathways according to their FPs or in terms of self-interested
principles; (c) Option b except only when the agents are successful;
(d) Evolutionary processes apply to certain kinds of systems, while
non-evolutionary processes apply to other kinds of systems.
6.   I am to now pick an option and then try to justify my selection.

Let me start by making the point that a system evolves in response to a
change to the environment is certainly one way of looking at evolution.
A good example is the case of the English hedgehog. Around the early
1920s, when a hedgehog was faced with a predatory attack, the vast majority of hedgehogs would roll up into a ball such that their spiky coat would
provide suitable defence. With the rise of automobiles, this technique
turned out to be disastrous. However, a small minority of hedgehogs
(maybe 1% of the population) would elect to scurry away instead of rolling
up into a ball. It turns out that some small number of generations (say 10)
after the introduction of the car, the vast majority of hedgehogs now scuttle
away when threatened. A classic example of how genetic diversity allows
for relatively rapid adaptation to a changing environment.

Another way of looking at evolution is through the lens of competition.
Richard Dawkins's (1976) greedy gene thesis argues that the behaviours of
an organism are driven primarily by the imperative to amplify the expression of one's genes in subsequent generations. With this view, there may
be no changes in the environment; however, if one member of the species
gains some sort of advantage, then this may quickly lead to a change in the
species even though the environment has ostensibly remained the same.
Mechanisms such as the William Hamilton's (1964) rule for altruism come
to mind — as stated in the abstract:

> A genetical mathematical model is described which allows for interac-
> tions between relatives on one another's fitness. [...] Species following
> the model should tend to evolve behaviour such that each organism
> appears to be attempting to maximise its inclusive fitness. This implies
> a limited restraint on selfish competitive behaviour and possibility of
> limited self-sacrifices.

In other words, we are more helpful to people who share our genes.

Let me now provide a slightly different view of evolution. Gregory Chaitin (2012) makes the argument that Kurt Gödel's findings that there are no universal axioms may imply that there is always room for mathematical creativity. Through a series of experiments that mimic the mechanics of evolutionary mechanisms, the 'busy beaver' problem was explored. The busy beaver problem is simply the task of finding a Turing machine that must produce the largest possible number in a finite number of iterations. Initially, the concept of addition might emerge, followed by multiplication, exponentials, factorials, and exponentials with factorials ... Observations regarding the rate of convergence of these experiments lead to the argument that instead of a method for producing optimal solutions, evolution should be viewed as a search for creative states.

So, with the view that evolution should be seen as a creativity engine, we can now consider various processes and decide whether they support or hinder the search for creative states. Now before you throw down the numinous flag, let me define what I believe to be a creative state:

- Given the set of concepts/capabilities associated with the current state, a creative state allows for a conceptual/capability leap — this implies novelty.
- These new concepts/capabilities cannot be derived (or anticipated) directly from the current state.
- Given the current state, there is no systematic method for arriving at a creative state.

So, I am now making the argument that if a mechanism supports the search for creativity, then I will consider it to be an evolutionary process. If it hinders creativity, then I will declare it to be non-evolutionary. I will start with a non-evolutionary process. It turns out that the sweetness associated with fruit does not breed true. That is to say, if two apple trees each have sweet fruit, there is no guarantee that their offspring will have sweet fruit. For this reason, grafting methods are used in most orchards. I would argue that grafting, cloning and other forms of monoculture offer little scope for creativity and hence should be viewed as non-evolutionary. This thus rules out option a — there are no non-evolutionary processes.

Let's now consider a list of mechanisms that we can judge with regard to creativity:

- **Mutation and chromosomal crossover:** both have the potential for creating novel genetic instances which leads to biodiversity and the possibility of arriving at a creative state.

- **Co-evolution:** Predator-prey interactions have resulted in the fact that certain breeds of cicada now have a 17-year hibernation period making it difficult for a predator to directly target them. It has been argued that humans and dogs have co-evolved to the point where humans have gained cognitive skills at the expense of certain capabilities such as the sense of smell. Conversely dogs may have traded their autonomy for the benefits gained from human community. These species could not have arrived at their current states without being part of a co-evolutionary walk. I think that this is one of the great examples of creativity.

- **Symbiosis:** I would argue that when different species are able to develop mutually beneficial arrangements, this is an act of creativity. Similarly, creativity occurs when separate parts of the body develop over time with a certain form of utility but then are combined resulting in an entirely new capability. It can be argued that this mechanism is critical for going beyond derivative advancements.

- **Cultural selection:** The survival of the group will depend on qualities associated with the group. Authors such as Robert Trivers (2014) and Matt Ridley (1996) argue that our ethical systems may have naturally arisen due to mechanisms such as game theoretic dynamics, cultural selection, shared intentions and the virtue of cooperation. Humans are the only species to have discovered David Ricardo's law of comparative advantage. For those not familiar with this concept, consider the following: let's assume that both the UK and the USA require an axe and a spear to survive. In terms of hours of labour, it costs the UK 20 hours to produce an axe and 15 hours to produce a spear. Now in the USA it only takes 5 hours to produce an axe and 10 hours to produce a spear. At first glance, it appears that everything is cheaper in the USA and that there should be little incentive for the USA to trade with the UK. So, in the no-trade scenario it would cost the UK 35 hours of labour to produce its own axe and spear. In the USA, it would cost 15 hours of labour to produce its own axe and spear. Now suppose that the UK chooses to focus on just spear production and the USA just on axe production. Each country will produce two of its products and then trade with each other so that both countries will end up with an axe and a spear. In this scenario, the UK spends 30 hours of labour — 5 hours less than the no-trade scenario. The USA spends 10 hours of labour — also 5 hours less than the no-trade scenario. Both sides benefit from this arrangement. The trick is that the UK's relative costs of production were inverted with respect to the USA. Whenever such inversions occur, there is an opportunity for a win–win scenario. Clearly, this represents a conceptual leap, I therefore argue that cultural selection can support creativity.

- **Intelligence:** One might argue that the spell is broken once we learn how evolution works. Interestingly, Robert Wright's (2017) analysis of Buddhism makes the argument that we are still firmly in the grip of our evolutionary past. For example, for the last 10,000 generations most humans would have gone through life encountering at most 50 people. The opinion that those 50 people had of you might very well determine whether or not your genes make it into the next generation. So, we are all the product of 10,000 fathers and 10,000 mothers who managed to win their popularity contests. Flash forward to today. For many people, the prospect of attending a cocktail party, where they don't know anyone and hence there is a reasonable likelihood of being ignored or even rejected, is a great source of anxiety. This is odd when one considers the fact that the opinions of the other party goers will have almost no bearing on one's survival. We are still stuck in the Matrix …

  In another example, there is a dating service where all the gentlemen must pay a $10,000 annual fee, while membership for ladies is free. The argument being that in order to afford $10,000, these must be men of significant means. On the other hand, the woman must be sufficiently statuesque in order to warrant the attentions of such successful gentlemen. Under this rational arrangement, both sides get what they want. However, when asked if there are any traits that the women would find disqualifying, almost all of them required that their potential suitors must be at least six-foot tall — a somewhat arbitrary threshold that does not seem to be based on reason. I think that this is an example of 'The heart wants what other hearts want' — the argument being that if other people find your mate attractive, then it is likely that your offspring will also be attractive and hence the agenda of the greedy gene is still at work.

- **Technology:** With the advent of spectacles, our species is no longer selecting for 20/20 vision. With GPS, those that cannot read a map can still thrive. On the other hand, one might argue that entities such as the FANGs (Facebook, Apple/Amazon, Netflix and Google) are using technology to destroy companies that simply make or do things. I would argue that vandalism is a creative act.

- **Genocide and eugenics:** The average troop of monkeys exhibits more genetic diversity than the entire human race. I would argue that our genocidal tendencies have led to this state of homogeneity. If successful, the Nazi eugenics programs would have taken this to a new level. Current US immigration policy seems focused on creating an America that looks like Norway. This tendency seems to be at the heart of our current infatuation with populism (which I use in the pejorative sense). Even if we end up with a global monoculture, I would argue that culture itself will remain a source of creativity. Consider Fermat's last theorem. The proof that was found 10 or so years ago could not have been constructed without the support of modern mathematical methods. The Flynn effect points to the observation that standard IQ test scores on average increase 3 or 4 points every 10 years — the speed of such advances cannot be attributable to biological processes alone. However, as new languages and other cultural tools become enriched with more intricate conceptual tools, new modes of thinking can emerge. *Maybe evolution itself has evolved.* With the argument that culture, and not genetics, is the new crucible for creativity and hence evolution, I rule out options b (groups aspire to genetic FP) and even option c (groups are successful in achieving a genetic FP).

Now let's consider option d, are some kinds of systems evolutionary and others not? I was recently thinking about what it would take to reproduce the human experiment. The human brain has approximately 10^{10} neurons, each with 10^3 connections, each performing $2*10^2$ operations per second. The human species has been in existence for roughly 10^4 generations, where each generation lasts for approximately 30 years (10^9 seconds). There are currently $7*10^9$ humans (although much less during historical times). Thus, cumulative human cognition to date is roughly equal to $7*2*10^{(10+3+2+5+9+9)} = 14*10^{38}$ calculations. As of 2012, The Department of Energy (DoE) Sequoia supercomputer can perform $16*10^{20}$ calculations per day. This would imply the need for 10^{18} days of dedicated compute time (note: the universe is only $4*10^{12}$ days old). Assuming a highly optimistic Moore's law like progression where available compute time doubles annually, it would take approximately 50 years to reduce 10^{18} days of present-day computation down to one hundred days or one quarter of a calendar year. Since this is about as long as most funding sources are willing to wait for tangible results …

So, the question is, can we synthesise a cradle where we can grow our own Artificial Intelligence? Suppose we have an image of a painting in our heads, but we don't know how to paint it. Consider a program where at each iteration we are shown 100 images and we can rate them based on similarity to the painting we have in mind. Using these similarity measures and mechanisms similar to mutation and gene crossover, a new set of paintings can be produced. After a number of iterations, this can result in the desired painting. Such algorithms exist today. *I would argue that this is an example of optimisation not creativity.* I assert that intelligence is a result of creativity, but that if we start with intelligence as the goal, we might never get there. This is because optimisation is a trap. Now we can certainly construct a simulated environment where we believe that intelligence would be advantageous, but what we end up with might have very little resemblance to human-like intelligence. This said, I for one would certainly like to see what jumps out. Just so my point is clear, while artificial systems can be examples of evolutionary processes, I believe that artificial systems based on external optimisation with targeted results (animal husbandry, intelligent design …) are non-evolutionary. So, my choice is option d.

Going back to our Pac-Man discussion. I just want to make it clear that once the test has started, the Hacker does not have access to the system (he can't trick us by pretending to be the Pac-Man Agent), I just argue that if the Hacker knows what the judging criteria are, then he can try to build an agent that fools the test but is still just a glorified clock. Hence, I suggested that an interesting change to the test would be that the designers of the Agent should have no prior knowledge of the Pac-Man challenge so that if the Agent simply starts to play the game with what appears to be skills gained via its own volition, then something interesting might be going on.

Since I argue that intelligence is a result of a creative process, I would like to extend the argument that intelligence itself is a creative process. As I mentioned earlier, co-evolution seems to be a great source of creativity. Charles Fernyhough (2016) makes the point that the back and forth nature of dyadic conversations between diverse individuals often leads to creative solutions. He goes further to assert that via Theory of Mind mechanisms, we are often able to hold such conversations within our own minds. He makes the argument that John Lennon and Paul McCartney may have spent relatively little time directly collaborating on pop songs, but since both had strong models of each other, they each might have been able to hold an internal form of co-evolving musical creation. I am sure if we put our heads together, we can find other examples of authentic Humanities-based creativity.

13

Evolution and Articles of Faith

Suman

- Doubts are expressed about the normative presumptions in defining *creative states* and in considering evolution as necessarily tied to *creativity* and dissociated from *optimisation*
- A mechanistic account of evolution as system change is reiterated in normatively neutral terms

In explaining life by intellect, it limits too much the meaning of life: intellect, such at least as we find it in ourselves, has been fashioned by evolution during the course of progress; it is cut out of something larger, or, rather, it is only the projection, necessarily on a plane, of a reality that possesses both relief and depth. It is this more comprehensive reality that true finalism ought to reconstruct, or, rather, if possible, embrace in one view. But, on the other hand, just because it goes beyond intellect — the faculty of connecting the same with the same, of perceiving and also of producing repetitions — this reality is undoubtedly creative, i.e. productive of effects in which it expands and transcends its own being. These effects were therefore not given in it in advance, and so it could not take them for ends, although, when once produced, they admit of a rational interpretation, like that of the manufactured article that has reproduced a model.

Henri Bergson, *Creative Evolution* (1911, p. 52)

Argument

Your previous intervention is informative, Peter, but confusing to me in various ways. This one is devoted to (slowly) unpacking the various ways in which yours confuses. The above quotation from Bergson's text written over a century back is, it seems to me, in line with what you say there. Though the details of your argument are different, the thrust of your argument is mystificatory in much the way that Bergson's was.

Let me summarise and comment on your argument in the way that I understand it. Where I quote you, I put different parts of what you say in different underscoring, continuous underscoring where you give an example, dotted underscoring where you label, and dash underscoring where you present a generalisation.

- You have gone (against my anticipation) for the fourth option from the possibilities I had suggested earlier: some system changes are evolutionary, others are not.
- You have done this however by defining 'evolution' in a particular way. Though you start with adaptation and competition as two kinds of mechanics of evolutionary change, which coincide with my account in the earlier intervention, you then bring in a contention which cancels their salience out. By this contention, evolutionary change is conferred with a first principle that precedes mechanics: 'evolution should be viewed as a search for creative states'. Thus 'creation' by your account becomes a first principle by which any mechanics can be conditionally understood as evolutionary or not-evolutionary; what 'evolution' means is no longer *inferred* from observations of the mechanics of change. Bergson also had such a first principle in his argument: *élan vital*, something like 'life force'.
- In effect, you confer a kind of agency to 'evolution' itself, as if evolution is the name of something that acts. Evolution is something that *does* something in itself, and later you underline the idea by suggesting that 'maybe evolution itself has evolved'. Having done that, you make a little leap.
- First you define 'creative states' in a way which you claim evades numinous content — far as I can see, it doesn't and I'll say why soon.
- Second, you make 'evolution' and 'creation' mutually definitive: 'If a mechanism supports the search for creativity, then I will consider it to

be an evolutionary process. If it hinders creativity, then I will declare it to be non-evolutionary'. This is a labelling statement, not an inference. Since mechanical processes like adaptation and competition in relation to an environment do not necessarily subscribe to such a condition of being 'creative', you wrench the term 'evolution' away from much of its received connotations and simply define it in a way that suits you. By this wrench, 'evolution' makes sense only if your definition of 'creation' makes sense. So you are no longer talking about a received understanding of 'evolution' (Evolution 1), but your peculiar idea of 'evolution' (Evolution 2). Evolution 2, which for you is 'evolution' *per se*, corresponds to the emergence of 'creative states'. So we need to look really closely at your allegedly non-numinous definition of 'creative', which I'll do soon.

- But then you go one step further: not only do you make Evolution 2 equivalent to 'creative states', you confine the connotations of 'creation' to a particular kind of mechanics of change. Namely, you put the mechanics of change determined by intelligence (reasoning as working towards Final Purposes (FPs)) as 'uncreative' and dub it 'optimisation' (by definition something that builds upon a given thing). That makes 'creative' the sole domain of Evolution 2, and makes all intelligent rational processing its opposite. Doing so also liberates the word 'creative' from its received meaning, since it has usually had something to do with intelligent rational processing. Your argument:

> Consider a program where at each iteration we are shown 100 images and we can rate them based on similarity to the painting we have in mind. Using these similarity measures and mechanisms similar to mutation and gene crossover, a new set of paintings can be produced. After a number of iterations, this can result in the desired painting. Such algorithms exist today. *I would argue that this is an example of optimisation not creativity. I assert that intelligence is a result of creativity, but that if we start with intelligence as the goal we might never get there. This is because optimisation is a trap.*

I don't see how the example you give (in continuous underscoring) leads to the generalisation (in dash underscoring). All that the argument allows is for you to attribute a label to that kind of process (in dotted underscoring), but not to lead into the generalisation. We could say that's one kind of intelligent process, not intelligent processing *per se*.

- With that generalisation, you make quite a startling jump — it is, as you say, an *assertion*. With it, in fact, you are saying that AI can only materialise from Evolution 2 and not by any intelligent reasoning process with FPs (now labelled away as non-evolutionary 'optimisation'). But the way in which you have positioned Evolution 2 makes this an article of faith rather than a reasoned argument.

- Moreover, it's an article of faith with an implicitly religious thrust. Since you have made 'creativity' the sole domain of Evolution 2 where 'evolution' itself seems to be an active agent, doing things by a supra-intelligent process — according to a pre-rational principle — Evolution 2 begins to sound awfully like a principle of divinity. That you locate it in culture rather than genetics does nothing to make it otherwise: 'culture, and not genetics, is the new crucible for creativity and hence evolution'. Since, according to you, 'culture' is part of Evolution 2 rather than of intelligent rational processing, 'culture' here excludes human planning. Again, that's against the term's received meaning (unless one thinks of 'microbial cultures'). This account of 'culture' is also an article of faith rather than an inference.

- Thus, a teleology of Evolution 2 stretches out before it. At this point, it seems to me, your argument steps away from both engineering and the humanities into theology. And that has something to do also with your choice of terms, not just numinous but explicitly normative. To this I turn next, before looking closely at your definition of 'creative states'.

Normative Terms

Normative terms suggest a direction of action and are usually value laden (let's say, received as good or bad). 'Creation' ('creative'/'creativity') is a positive normative term, thought of as good — mainly because of its religious associations and connection to ideas of authorship and originality. It doesn't suggest a value-neutral direction. So, its antonyms, 'uncreative' (passive form) or 'destructive' (active form), are usually received as bad. By making Evolution 2 equivalent to 'creativity', you make Evolution 2 good, in contradistinction from uncreative processing: rationalising according to FPs, rationalising according to mechanical processes … rationalising itself.

However, you also confer a positive normative term to uncreative processing: 'optimisation'. That would be thought of as good, as opposed to, say, 'diminishment' or 'suboptimisation', which would ordinarily be considered bad. But in doing that, you put intelligent rational processing as *conditional* to — after the fact of — creative Evolution 2. Only if something has been created first can that then be optimised.

The normativeness of the term opens the door to teleological articles of faith. You would no doubt argue that you have guarded against any such normative value in giving 'creative' a definition — but, hold your horses, I come to your definition in a moment.

The other jarringly normative term that caught my eye in your intervention is 'vandalism': 'one might argue that entities such as the FANGs (Facebook, Apple/Amazon, Netflix and Google) are using technology to destroy companies that simply make or do things. I would argue that vandalism is a creative act'. This seems to me another statement of an article of faith, since it is preceded by no argument, though it seems implied that one might be found if your repertoire of labels is accepted. But it does suggest a political proclivity, if not an argument. Here's a careful reversal of normative value: you seem to be saying, 'such companies might seem to do bad from a small perspective of intelligent reasoning but actually do good from the larger one of Evolution 2 creativity'. It reminds me a bit of Evolutionary Leadership Theory (*a la* Mark van Vugt (with Ahuja 2010) or Michael Alznauer (2016)), which, in practice, seems to absolve corporate or political 'leaders' of any need to rationalise their decisions while maintaining their prerogative to make those decisions. It's a convenient establishment position whereby ideas like 'corporate social responsibility' or 'answerable government' seem like legalistic nitpicking in the face of the greater good of organisational creative vandalising Evolution 2.

Defining 'Creative States'

Here's your three-point definition of 'creative states' which, you say, 'evolution' (i.e. Evolution 2) is in search of:

- Given the set of concepts/capabilities associated with the current state, a creative state allows for a conceptual/capability leap — this implies novelty.
- These new concepts/capabilities cannot be derived (or anticipated) directly from the current state.
- Given the current state, there is no systematic method for arriving at a creative state.

To simplify consideration of this three-point definition, let me resort to a simple graphic representation of a closed system at time $T1$ and a subsequent time $T2$, between which an evolutionary process could be said to have taken place (see Figure 1).

The evolutionary processes working in the closed system from time $T1$ to $T2$ have resulted in changes which are graphically represented by the change of brown animate entities into green animate entities, a reduction in the number of purple animate entities, a larger number of red inanimate objects, and a change in the intangible features marked by a background colour change.

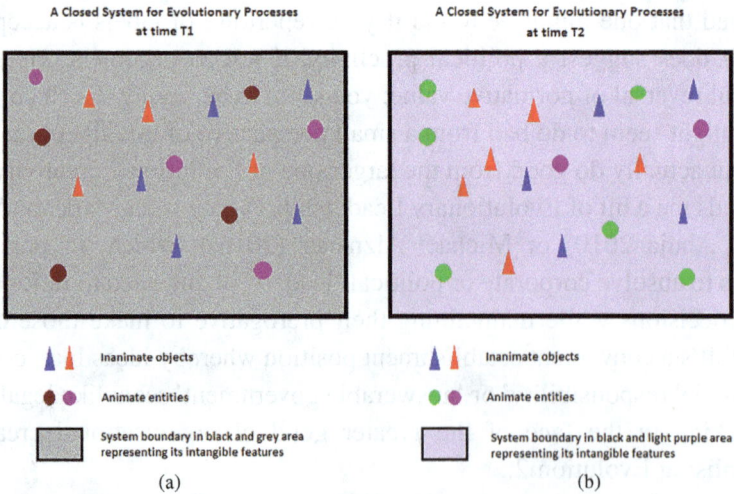

Figure 1.   Simple graphic representation of a closed system at time $T1$ (a) and a subsequent time $T2$ (b).

With regard to the above three-point definition of 'creative states' here are the areas that confuse me.

1. With regard to the first bullet point:

    *   Given the set of concepts/capabilities associated with the current state, a creative state allows for a conceptual/capability leap — this implies novelty.

    I am not sure what is meant by 'state' in the phrases 'current *state*' or 'creative *state*'. Usually one would think of 'state' in such contexts as referring to the given condition of a system or material, which might, for instance, have a stable or unstable state. But we are talking about evolutionary processes and whatever 'state' is seems to refer to that which is evolving. Going by the simplified closed system represented above, what is evolving? Is it the system itself (so the whole represented in Figure 1(a) evolves into the whole represented in Figure 1(b))? Or is it perhaps only the animate entities (the brown animate entities of Figure 1(a) have evolved into the green animate entities of Figure 1(b))?

    If it is the whole closed system, then Figure 1(a) must be a 'given state' and Figure 1(b) represents the 'creative state' — is that right? Or maybe Figure 1(b) represents the aftermath of an interim 'creative state'? But by what measure can we say that a 'conceptual/capability leap' or something 'novel' has taken place? In comparison to what? Other closed systems? For whom or what is this 'novel'?

    If the 'state' that evolves refers to animate entities, then we may say that something 'novel' or some 'leap' may have taken place in the process of the brown animate entity evolving into the green. But again, by what measure and for whom is this process 'novel' or involves a 'leap'?

    Either way, the idea that we need some kind of gauge or comparison to understand that some process is 'creative' where others are not (are 'uncreative' or merely 'optimisation') could follow the two standard connotations of normative terms: we could think of the process as *implicitly creative* (creative in-itself), or we could think of the process as *consequentially creative* (having creative consequences).

    Let's quickly get rid of the notion that there is a consequential dimension in the three-point definition of 'creative state' quoted above. If we were to say: the creativity of the process from the brown to the green animate entity is shown by its success in proliferating the green animate entity relative to the purple animate entity, there could be various objections. First, that proliferation could be the result of optimisation. Second, if it isn't, it still doesn't mark a *success* except at time $T2$ relative to time $T1$. At another time $T3$, that process may result in the green animate entity's own extinction. For example, if the process involves evolving a device that makes the purple animate entity prey to predator green animate entity, then $T3$ could be the moment when the purple animate entity is consumed to extinction and leads to the extinction of predator green animate entity. That is unless there is another evolutionary process whereby the green animate entity consumes something else. But that would be the *result* of the change in the closed system (the absence of purple animate entities), and therefore not subscribe to the notion of 'creativity' offered here, it would probably be an 'optimisation' change. Third, perhaps not-evolving if everything else changes in the closed system is equivalent to evolving relative to the characteristics of the closed system. A passive process may be an active process within a closed system.

In fact, it is pretty obvious from the second and third bullet points of the three-point definition that the 'creativity' in 'creative states' — or in Evolution 2 — is given as *implicitly creative*. Which leads to my next area of confusion.

2. The second and third bullet points are:

    - These new concepts/capabilities cannot be derived (or anticipated) directly from the current state.
    - Given the current state, there is no systematic method for arriving at a creative state.

    If the whole closed system is considered as evolving, then no future closed-system-state can be considered as unequivocally displaying 'novelty' or a 'leap' without reference to the internal dynamics of the system's components (the objects, entities and intangible features). The ability to derive or to systematically process would apply to the relations of those components; any notion of *implicitly creative process* would be in relation to one or more of those components.

So, let's say that it is the process from brown to green animate entity where evolution is manifest. This would be 'creative', according to these bullet points, only if the change in the brown-to-green entity is not explained as a *response* to other entities, objects and intangible features at time $T1$, but as the *cause* of changes in those at time $T2$. Otherwise, the change in the brown-to-green entity is uncreative or an optimisation, which can be derived and arrived at systematically. In other words, to be meaningfully 'creative', the change in brown-to-green entity from time $T1$ to $T2$ should be inborn or self-impelled by the entity — not-inferable and unplannable. In common parlance, we may think of such change as 'accidental' or a 'malfunction' (negative norm-bearing), though in consequential terms we may consider such a change to be possibly good (with potentially positive normativity) or not.

But isn't that more or less the definition of 'mutation'? 'Mutation' is a value-neutral normative term. Is the three-point definition of 'creativity' simply a positive-value-attribution exercise for 'mutation', now overdetermined as 'evolution' itself — as Evolution 2? And one may wonder why one should bother to take such a tortuous and confusing way to overdetermine and confer positive value on a small element of the value-indifferent mechanical process of 'evolution' as the term is received now. Perhaps it has something to do with the articles of faith and that political proclivity mentioned above.

14

On Evolution: Ungrounded Hardwired Knowledge Short Circuits Intelligence

Peter

- Creativity is considered in the context of search
- The reproduction strategies of lobsters young and old are considered
- The accidental nature of going from here to there is considered
- How quantum mechanics transforms the act of search into sampling is hinted at

---

Suman, my guess is that the source of your mystification is due, in part, to my lack of mathematical formalism. To address this issue, let's (Science, Technology, Engineering and Mathematics) STEM things up a bit so we can bring light where darkness yet remains.

The spatial dimensions X, Y and Z have no intrinsic direction, yet time's arrow has both a future and a past — it has direction. Evidence of this phenomenon can be found in the second law of thermodynamics, which states that the entropy of a closed system will increase after each irreversible event. As entropy increases, the amount of available energy that can be used for work decreases. You can view an increase in entropy as going from order to disorder. Imagine a boarded-up bowling alley that has gone out of business — a closed system. Initially, half of the lanes may still have their pins in their upright formations ready for customers that alas will never come — sigh. Over time, random vibrations and small movements of air molecules may cause a pin or two to fall over. Once fallen, it is statistically improbable for a fallen pin to inadvertently return to its upright position. Such irreversible events can be thought of as one-way ratcheting effects. Eventually, all the pins will fall. This is the fate of the universe.

Let's consider another form of ratcheting which is associated with mechanisms that can be thought of as iterative copiers. Such mechanisms include:

- **DNA:** Each time a cell divides, both of the new cells get a copy of the parents' DNA. For certain organisms that make use of mating, a copy of the combined DNA is passed on to the offspring.
- **RNA:** RNA is sometimes used as an intermediary for the DNA copy process, it is also the means by which biological viruses make copies of themselves. RNA is inserted into a host cell, which is then forced to make new copies of the virus.
- **Software viruses:** Similar to biological viruses, software viruses can infect a host computer in order to make copies of itself.
- **Spoken languages:** Children make copies of languages that are taught to them by their parents.
- **Ideas:** An idea held by one person can be instantiated in another via a variety of mechanisms.

The ratcheting effect for some of these copy machines can be described as follows:

- **Discovery:** The discovery of certain creative states (I will get back to this) represents an irreversible act: photosynthesis, the Krebs cycle, claws, teeth, warm bloodedness, sight, zero-day hacks, fur, flight, fire, clubs, spears, metallurgy, arrows, gun powder, nuclear devices, community, fermentation, agriculture, deception, industry, printing, radio, television, internet, the Great British Baking Show, transistors …
- **Complexity:** In many cases, adoption of new capabilities results in a kind of layering effect. There is often no opportunity for refactoring. This results in increasing complexity over time.

In this way, the ratcheting effect of evolution is bound to time's arrow. Once a creative state has been found, there is no going back. Pandora's escape from her box is an irreversible event. Like the second law of thermodynamics, evolution's forward march via creative jumps is a consequence of the type of universe that we happen to live in.

Let's now ruminate on the mechanics of search and optimisation. Consider the function $y = f(x)$, where y is a scalar and x can be multidimensional. In terms of our discussion, x can be thought of as a state variable and y can be some sort of description of the qualities of x. For example, x could represent the components of a DNA sequence and y could be the probability that an organism with DNA x will be able to produce at least one offspring given the current environmental conditions e. Alternatively, x might be thought of as all the DNA sequences of all current instances of a given species concatenated one after another. In this case, y might be the probability that, given current environmental conditions e, the species avoids extinction for at least one more generation. The state variable x could also be the state of knowledge associated with a given corpus of documents and y could be the probability that such knowledge will allow a given species to overcome an environmental challenge e. The equation $y = f(x|e)$ can be thought of as a surface. Qualities of such surfaces include the first derivative $\frac{dy}{dx}$ associated with any value of x, which is defined as the limit of $\frac{f(x+\Delta x)-f(x)}{\Delta x}$ as the change in x, Δx goes to zero. A point (x, y) on the surface is known as a maximum if the first derivative at x is equal to zero and the second derivative at x (the derivative of the first derivative) is non-negative. Note, maxima can be a single point like a pinnacle, they can also be a plateau or maybe a saddle point. These maxima can be valuable since roughly speaking y at these maxima will be greater than or equal to all the other y's in the local vicinity of x. Convexity of the surface implies that there is at most one maxima. If the surface is non-convex, then there will be multiple maxima which are sometimes called modes.

The search for maxima is referred to as optimisation. It is often the case that a search is an iterative process, which starts with an initial state x_0. Given the current value of x, there is a subset of the domain of x that can be explored during the next iteration. One strategy for finding maxima is to evaluate the derivative at x in order to determine which change in x will result in the greatest increase in y and then take a step in that direction. Such approaches are known as greedy-gradient ascent or hill-climbing methods. Given a continuous surface, these methods will converge to what are known as local maxima. However, such maxima may not be a global maximum, which are associated with the greatest possible value of y. Local maxima can be thought of as traps for greedy strategies.

To escape a local maximum, a search algorithm must incorporate some form of randomisation into its selection of new x locations to investigate. Such random jumps are known as exploration. An algorithm called simulated annealing, which is based on the physical process of annealing, incorporates both random jumps as well as gradient ascent methods with the hopes of ultimately finding a global maximum. In this discussion, we can now define a creative state relative to the current state x as a mode in the distribution that has not been previously identified and is not collocated with the local maxima associated with x. That is to say, creative states must be discovered via exploration as opposed to derivative based methods. Due to the topology of the surface and constraints associated with possible regions of search, certain creative states may need to be found in order to 'unlock' other creative states. For example, a working knowledge of butter production processes must be established before a species can stumble on to the wonders of the puff pastry.

It is not surprising that software developers have crafted search algorithms based on mechanisms that I described in my last intervention: mutation (random jumps sometimes referred to as Brownian walks), chromosomal crossover, co-evolution and symbiosis. Like an arms race, efficiency in the search for creative states can be an advantage. Thus, changes in the mechanisms that govern the evolution of a species can themselves be part of the competitive or evolutionary process. Organisms that rely solely on mutation (i.e. a Brownian walk) will in general be outpaced by species that make use of chromosomal crossover.

Before casting our earlier discussion in terms of the search for local maxima, let's quickly discuss issues associated with the characterisation of various classes of algorithms. Consider the problem of sorting. Given N randomly selected numbers, the goal of a sort algorithm is to rearrange the numbers in ascending order. The QuickSort algorithm uses a divide and conquer approach that randomly selects an element as a pivot and partitions the current array around the picked pivot. The average time to completion for QuickSort is proportional to $N \log(N)$. BubbleSort is a simpler algorithm that works by repeatedly swapping adjacent elements that are in the wrong order. The average time to completion for BubbleSort is proportional to N^2, which for large N is much larger than $N \text{Log}(N)$. In contrast, consider the British Museum sorting algorithm, which can be described as follows:

1. Write all the numbers on to a set of blank cards.
2. Throw all the cards into the air.
3. Pick up all the cards without looking at their numbers.
4. If all the cards are in the right order, go to step 6.
5. Go to step 2.
6. Terminate.

Similar to winning the lottery, the odds of the cards being in the right order at any given iteration is $1/N(N-1)(N-2) \ldots = 1/N!$. Unlike the first two sorting algorithms, there is no guarantee that the British Museum algorithm will ever terminate. The point that is being made is that by observing various statistics associated with a mechanical system, such as average time to completion of a given task, inferences regarding the class of underlying algorithms that govern such mechanisms can be made.

Let's now consider some of the stimulating questions raised during your last intervention.

Question 1: How do your views on creativity and evolution compare to Henri Bergson's?

Response: I must say that I like the cut of Bergson's jib! But being a humble engineer, I fear that terms such as 'the meaning of life' are meaningless to me.

Question 2: Do you confer a kind of agency to evolution? What do you mean by 'maybe evolution itself has evolved'?

Response: Similar to entropy's march to universal disorder, evolution can be characterised as a one-way succession of creative states. Since there are advantages to be had with respect to the efficiency with which such states can be discovered, the means by which a species changes over time may itself change over time.

In preparation for a family trip to Maine, I read *The Secret Life of Lobsters* by Trevor Corson (2004) and *The Lobster Chronicles* by Linda Greenlaw (2002). It turns out that a natural lobster hatchery requires very specific conditions. Accordingly, young females will lay their eggs where they are born so as to maximise the probability of producing successful offspring. I would argue that this is a greedy strategy. However, once a female lobster reaches the age of fifty, she will no longer return to her birthplace. She will instead march out to the middle of the ocean and release her eggs to the mercy of the open seas. Most, if not all, of the eggs will perish. However, a few of the eggs may end up at a suitable, yet undis-covered, cove capable of becoming a crustacean hatchery. I would argue that in such cases, a new local maximum has been found. This can also be viewed as a form of species-level adaptation, since over time reliable birth places can become inhospitable due to changes in geology, fauna or climate.

Question 3: By declaring evolution to be a search for creative states, are you not wrenching it from its received connotations such as adaptation and competition?

Response: As previously stated, I would argue that evolutionary mecha-nisms that are adept at finding creative states will have advantages with respect to adapting to drastic environmental changes (remember the grand lobster matrons) as well as competing for limited resources such as access to the gene pool.

Question 4: Why do you believe that optimisation as described by the painting algorithm will not necessarily succeed in creating human-like intelligence?

Response: First, let me state that I make no assertions regarding intelligent agents having the wherewithal to construct intelligent agents. My argument is that if an intelligent agent attempts to breed intelligence using a metric of intelligence, there will be a distinct possibility of being trapped by something akin to a local maximum. For example, if we let x = the collective DNA of a set of artificial agents and we let y = the maximum IQ test results of the current generation of AI agents, then by primarily favouring steps in x that result in increases in y, we may fail to stumble upon various intermediary creative states that are needed to construct the intelligent agents that we are striving for.

Let me give an example. Let's say that a well-meaning bureaucrat wants to make Great Britain great again. Having read our exchanges, the government official notes the fact that local economic prosperity is highly correlated with the concentration of qualified engineers. This leads to the following formulation: let the state variable x be the allocation of funding resources to research and let y be the probability that x stimulates advances in STEM. The derivative of y with respect to x implies that most of the available funding should be applied to STEM research. Now it may be the case that before Great Britain can be great again, she needs a framework for analysing the hiring practices of Brazilian Human Resource Departments. By following the greedy STEM strategy, there is little hope of discovering this eye-opening state. One could then simply discard the STEM metric and embark on an open-ended search for creative states. I would argue that where we end up may have very little resemblance to the utopia of Kurt Vonnegut's *Player Piano* (1952), a fiction where engineers take their rightful place at the top of both the social and economic ladders.

My basic argument is that the intermediate states or environmental catalysts required to 'grow' intelligence may not be obvious so that the local maxima problem associated with driving primarily towards the fixed goal of intelligence may end up in a dead end that is very hard to escape. Conversely, an open-ended search may end up in a state of carnivorous vegetation or benevolent slime as opposed to the desired human-like intelligence. In my opinion, there is and was nothing inevitable about intelligence. Once again, I am not saying that intelligence cannot be constructed,

I am just saying that the process by which human intelligence emerged might not be readily repeatable.

Along these lines, Jared Diamond (1997) was asked by a native person from New Guinea why, in comparison to folks like himself, people from the West have so much cargo (slang for technology). Native New Guineans have an encyclopaedic knowledge of the jungle and have the strength and stamina needed to overcome life-threatening challenges on a daily basis. In comparison, after a week by ourselves in such environments I doubt that either of us would be doing particularly well. Diamond argues that a series of random or accidental events culminated in the West's ability to produce artefacts such as 'The Great British Baking Show'. This list includes: an east-west orientation to Asia and Europe, access to domesticable animals and plants and the gradual buildup of immunity to communicable diseases. The universe is like a giant pachinko machine.

Once again, there is nothing stopping us from arriving at a deep understanding of the mechanics of intelligence and then subsequently constructing an intelligent agent, I just doubt that intelligence will emerge from a cauldron of metric-driven methods such as genetic algorithms.

Question 5: Have you turned culture into an article of faith with its own agency? Why is intelligent processing separated from culture?

Response: DNA-based methods are not subject to Lamarckian evolution. A giraffe having spent a lifetime stretching its neck to reach leaves on tall trees will not in general have offspring with longer necks. If, over a lifetime, you have learned how to start fires in an efficient manner, such knowledge is not transmitted via your DNA to your children. However, cultural tools such as language, mathematics, science and books allow for the maintenance and transmission of discovered concepts (creative states) from one generation to the next. As for intelligence itself, I would argue that intelligence plus cultural tools and institutions allow for the discovery of new creative states.

In terms of the illusion of agency, I believe that this is once again a matter of the ratcheting effect as well as the advantages associated with the efficient discovery of creative states.

Question 6: Do you apply normative terms or consideration of value to such things as optimisation and creativity?

Response: These are mechanisms associated with exploring the state space — that's it.

Question 7: Doesn't my figure imply that evolution is just simple change or mutation?

Response: Random mutation is certainly an evolutionary mechanism, but like the British Museum Sorting algorithm, it may be outpaced by other algorithms akin to BubbleSort or QuickSort.

A few additional thoughts follow.

In this intervention, I have tried to reduce creativity down to a forward ratcheting mechanical process associated with the discovery of new local maxima that could not be found by simply following local derivatives. I have argued that the topology of such surfaces may mean that in order to transition from state A to state C, one might have to go through state B and, like a maze, this might not be obvious. Due to random changes of the environment or the order in which discoveries are made, outcomes of evolutionary processes can end up in wildly different endpoints, hence metric-driven evolution is problematic.

Similar to the local maxima problems associated with driving towards a fixed goal of intelligence, I am also suspicious of trying to directly incorporate knowledge into an AI system. My argument is that without going through the process of learning, such hardwired knowledge is not grounded, which may be a necessary step towards intelligence. Thus, I make the statement that ungrounded hardwiring may actually short circuit the quest for intelligence.

As I mentioned in my last intervention, at the beginning of the last century, mathematicians were looking for a set of axioms such that the truth of any mathematical statement could be assessed via the systematic application of these axioms. Finding such a set of axioms would mean that the mathematical state space (x) with respect to truth (y) would become convex. However, Kurt Gödel's work shows that such a set of consistent axioms cannot exist. This means that from now to the end of time, given a new mathematical statement, we have no guarantee that the current state of knowledge will be sufficient to determine the truth of such statements and that we may have to discover new mathematical formalisms to answer such questions. Only with modern mathematical methods was Fermat's last theorem proven to be true. In this universe, there will always be room for mathematical creativity.

Up until now I have discussed the discovery of local maxima in terms of search. However, in this universe there is another possibility — quantum mechanics. Suppose that a quantum system is associated with a state space x and an energy function y. A quantum system can be thought of as occupying all possible states simultaneously. When such a system is made to collapse, it will end up in a particular state. The key concept is that the probability of collapsing into a given state is proportional to the energy y associated with that state! So instead of searching for creative states, quantum systems may allow for sampling them … In this way, quantum mechanical systems can be viewed as a bizarre creativity engine. The fact that this universe works like this has led physicists like Roger Penrose (1989) to hypothesise that quantum mechanics may play a role in human intelligence. Some have even whispered the phrase: quantum free will.

15

On Evolution: Intelligence Short Circuits Ungrounded Hardwired Knowledge

Suman

- A counterargument is made to the argument made in the previous intervention such that it could be reversed without changing its substantial basis
- Further objections are advanced to the use of the term *creative* and the difference between *algorithm* and *mathematical formula* is underlined along the way
- The limits of Gödel's proof of undecidable propositions are noted with reference to metamathematical concepts
- The question of what *artificial* means for AI research is raised

Reversal

Reversing the title of your last intervention, Peter, is merely to say that I don't need to disagree with any detail of your description of the state of affairs to point out that nevertheless you are looking at that state of affairs from one perspective rather than the equally valid other. There is nothing in your description to suggest that it can't be flipped to make the statement in the title. Your determination to look at it from one perspective possibly amounts to an article of faith.

I am inclined to leave this part of the discussion there after the following comments and move on to another issue which comes to mind. It is useful to leave a discussion open-ended when it is in danger of going in circles, and yet after a few comments on your latest first.

1. What you describe as 'irreversible ratcheting effects' are not in any understandable way 'creative' or 'uncreative' — such as, when you say, 'Once a creative state has been found, there is no going back'. They are distinguishable from derivable mechanistic effects which are adjustable or engineerable. They are not necessarily precedent to the latter, though in terms of derivation they seem to precede the latter — but that's only for the mathematician's expressive convenience. They could equally be expressed as consequent to a derivable effect, as subverting (short-circuiting) the latter.

    The point is: to say 'irreversible ratcheting effects' are distinguished from 'reversible' or 'adjustable' makes sense; to say they are 'creative' seems to be saying something more without saying anything more. It seems that such 'irreversible ratcheting effects' can be described if and when found.

2. You say: 'We can now define a creative state relative to the current state x as a mode in the distribution that has not been previously identified and is not collocated with the local maxima associated with x. That is to say, creative states must be discovered via exploration as opposed to derivative-based methods'. That is to say, those 'irreversible' effects may be found by looking for them. Where particular local maxima or specific kinds of irreversible effects are sought, one can either come up with an algorithm to home in on the former or with an algorithm to look for the latter (which involves some random, indeterminate, improbablistic, etc. approach but nonetheless functional for that). Neither looking for nor deriving *through the formulation of an algorithm* can really preclude intelligent rational processing (according to Final Purposes (FPs)) because *an algorithm is by definition a functionalising formulation* — a rule for a system to work persistently with.

In that sense, an *algorithm* is different from a *mathematical formula* (in, for instance, Gödel's sense). The latter consists of axiomatic- or inferential-descriptive symbolic propositions within a formal system, rather than simply being a functionalisable formulation for an applied system (or any extant operating system). Anything that can be captured in an algorithmic formulation necessarily involves the intervention of intelligence (with FPs). That the outcome is indeterminate or pre-determinable makes little difference to its functionalising thrust. This still doesn't explain why 'irreversible effects' should be dubbed 'creative'.

3. I ask/you ask, and answer: '*Question*: Do you apply normative terms or consideration of value to such things as optimisation and creativity?; *Response*: These are mechanisms associated with exploring the state space — that's it'. No no no no, that's a cop out, that's not it. You can't call a 'bazooka' a 'fly swatter' without considering why you are doing so. Otherwise you might be doing more than you intend to do or should be doing.

4. I note your touching faith in 'mathematical formalism' and the reverence with which you say 'there's an algorithm for such and such...' My point above is that mathematical formalism helps efficient expression of a state of affairs and potential functionalising mechanisms; however, that doesn't clarify why and when norms are being inadvertently used and why one interpretive perspective is foisted over another. Your conviction that it might is akin to Plato's idealistic conviction in the Form; you seem to have mathematical formalism down as giving access to the Form — a Deep Reality. You seem to overlook the limits of mathematical formalism.
    In a way, this is revealed in what you take away from Kurt Gödel's proof of undecidable propositions: 'that from now to the end of time, given a new mathematical statement, we have no guarantee that the current state of knowledge will be sufficient to determine the truth of such statements and that we may have to discover new mathematical formalisms to answer such questions'. Gödel's proof was with regard to the formal logical system of *Principia Mathematica* or PM

(Whitehead and Russell (1910)) insofar as bearing upon the whole number system. These choices to illustrate the proof meant that it could be extended to all areas where such formal systems enable deductive rationalisations. However, these choices limited the proof to a definable part of a *current state of knowledge* and the proof does not extend to the totality of the *current state of knowledge*. The totality of the current state of knowledge is somewhat larger than what can be captured in a formal system, to which alone the proof is pertinent. This is, of course, almost the first thing Gödel noted: the PM system allows for capturing metamathematical significations (in David Hilbert's sense) within itself, so as to test the consistency of the mathematical system — i.e. it is a process for mathematically checking the consistency of a given mathematical system. For Gödel, of particular interest is the metamathematical capture of 'provability' in the PM system, by formulating 'proof-schema':

> a formula is a finite series of natural numbers, and a particular proof-schema is a finite series of finite series of natural numbers. Metamathematical concepts and propositions thereby become concepts and propositions concerning natural numbers, or series of them, and therefore at least partially expressible in the symbols of the system PM itself. In particular, it can be shown that the concepts, 'formula', 'proof-schema', 'provable formula', are definable in the system PM, i.e. one can give a formula $F(v)$ of PM — for example — with one free variable v (of the type of a series of numbers), such that $F(v)$ — interpreted as to content — states: v is a provable formula. (Gödel 1931 (1962)).

This allows for a proof within the PM system of the undecidable provability of certain V statements of v type given PM (for the whole number system, based on 3 Peano axioms and 8 axiom-schema) — i.e. it is not possible to prove either V or not-V. That exhausts the limits of PM to perpetuity, but not of the current state of knowledge. Functional confirmations, for instance, of the practice/happenings of real-world systems are not magicked away by the failure of the PM system.

That is to the say, the current state of knowledge is more than (and often other than) PM and such formal systems, and it surrounds both the mathematical and metamathematical extrapolations into the mathematical. The *idea* of the metamathematical gestures towards this. Let's say, we think of metamathematical expressions as *all* expressions that can be used to enable the doing of and to talk about mathematics, starting with the ordinary language definitions of particular symbols and the descriptions of deductive functions. Only some of them will need to be captured in PM so as to test it (like 'provable'), some will simply be ordinary language statements of axioms (we need words like 'is' and 'a' in the axiom '0 is a natural number', but we don't need to define them within PM), some will be relevant but logically outside (e.g. 'this is an elegant proof'). Underpinning the immediately understandable use of words like 'is', 'a', 'be' … and words like 'proof', 'brackets', 'natural', 'whole', 'number', 'symbol' … not to speak of irrelevant words like 'elegant', 'efficient' … in relation to PM, there is a working syntax which makes it possible to proceed with mathematical and metamathematical and non-mathematical expression, indeed all sorts of more or less formal spheres of expression. That would include a lot of statements which are not rigorously logical, non-sensical statements in any formal mathematical system, but nevertheless both mathematically expressible and informally in use and seemingly meaningful. This is the field we may loosely think of as ordinary language, or with a bit more Wittgensteinian (Wittgenstein, 1953) formalism, as 'language games' and 'form of life' — or generally as offering the building blocks of the current state of knowledge.

Only a certain kind of Platonic idealism impatiently brushes those aside to put mathematical formalism as giving access to the current state of knowledge, and algorithms as outlining the deep principles of the happenings of life and the world.

5. The quantum system could/does muddy everything in old fashioned mathematical formalism as in received linguistic expression. I accept this but am too ignorant to say anything more.

On Another Note

Let me leave that there. To take a different direction in our discussion: through all this talk about evolution, I have been feeling increasingly dissatisfied with my perfunctory way of understanding 'artificial' (as in the opening gambit of this conversation).

So, here's a question: when you speak of 'Artificial Intelligence', what do you understand by 'artificial' — or where do you think the artifice is? Or, to put that in a more graded fashion, do you think of so-called AI systems as:

1. Constructed from scratch in some sense?
2. Interventions in existing natural systems, perhaps with the effect of altering them beyond recognition?
3. Never really artificial?

16

Reflections on the Artificial in AI

Peter

- The concept of *artificial* is first considered through the lens of Theseus's paradox
- The current state of the art as it pertains to computational support for AI is reviewed
- The discussion shifts from artifice to a question of authenticity

---

Suman, as we let our conversation drift from evolution to artifice, I was taken with the way in which you twisted the title of my recent intervention. The idea being, that I have a point of view but am unwilling to give credence to different but equally valid points of view. To this end, I was considering what perspectives you may be alluding to. It seems to me that your thoughts revolve around the suspicion that AI Researchers are intrinsically motivated by quasi-religious convictions that lead to anthropomorphising, mysticism, unwitting belief in supernatural forces and of course an attraction to numinous terms. By maintaining an arched brow, you then become the Bob Mueller to my Donald Trump, the Ken Starr to my Bill Clinton and maybe the Javier to my Jean Valjean. You are of course to be commended for such courage and doggedness. Shameless self-marketing, delusions of grandeur and a willingness to take advantage of the gullible are of course disagreeable, but of greater concern is the degree to which the myths and fables that lurk in our collective psyche cloud both our judgement and understanding of this quixotic field of inquiry.

In terms of what we mean by artificial in AI, we can first consider the question of mechanical instantiation. Until someone can provide proof that the brain has certain unique physical properties, I would argue that we have to maintain the view that the brain is a mechanical entity. Many years ago, I first read an article in Omni Magazine that suggested the following:

1. We develop a kind of fabricated nerve that can be injected into a living brain.
2. Such devices would associate themselves with an existing nerve.
3. They would then study the behaviour of their targets.
4. Once such behaviours have been fully characterised, the fabricated nerves would slowly destroy their targets and one-by-one take their place.
5. Gradually all the original nerves would be replaced by fabricated nerves, but in principle the brain would continue to function as an intelligent entity.

Of course, there are other biological questions such as the chemistry of the brain or the role of DNA with respect to memory, but, in principle, I would argue that this thought experiment leads to the conclusion that the vessel itself does not determine whether intelligence is real or artificial. This line of reasoning is of course reminiscent of Theseus's paradox, where in addition to the question of identity we must also consider whether capability persists. Going beyond generic computing devices, various efforts have focused on the development of new vehicles for AI. For many years, certain researchers have been enamoured with the idea of spiking neural networks. Aficionados of this craft would demonstrate various rudimentary capabilities such as the detection of a moving object. When challenged with questions such as, 'Why is this any better than conventional methods that seem to be faster and more accurate?', the response always seems to be, 'Yes, but we did this with temporal spikes!' Various manufacturers now offer their neuromorphic chip sets with the argument that such architectures will make it easier to mimic the capabilities of the brain. With EU funding in the range of 15 million pounds, the world's largest neuromorphic supercomputer was recently announced. It can perform up to 200 million million actions per second. As you may recall from one of my recent interventions, this is roughly equivalent to the number of actions taken by a typical human brain. On a slightly different tack, consider organoids, which are sets of cells that are created in vitro. Recently, organoids based on neural cells were shown to exhibit phenomena similar to brain waves — see Sara Reardon's (2018) article for details.

I guess the next possible distinction might be a question of origin. Must true intelligence manifest itself unbidden through emergent processes? Without getting pulled back into our Scopes-like debates on Evolution, it seems to me that it is possible to construct a Matrix-like cauldron of synthetic genetic algorithms. As you recall, I made the argument that with a billion EU funded spiking networks operating for the equivalent of 30 years per generation for 10,000 generations, we might be able to reproduce the human experiment. Given 50 years of Moore's law advancement, this might even be trackable. If an intelligence emerged from such a process, then I would be hard-pressed to declare it as artificial. Given such a position we could then argue for shortcuts, such as access to physics simulators, deductive reasoning engines and emotion emulators in order to possibly speed up the process. Inch by inch we would move from intelligence via simulated evolution to intelligence via something completely different. As long as the outcome remains comparable, we would find it hard to justify making a declaration that we have inadvertently transitioned from real intelligence into the realm of the artificial.

While this is probably not what the founding fathers of AI meant by *artificial*, the question might be a distinction between Artificial and Authentic Intelligence. This then leads us to a question of quality. At what point does AI simply become I. The terrifying list of attributes that John Searle associates with consciousness certainly comes to mind. Julian Jaynes has some surprising opinions on what is and what is not a conscious or intelligent agent. Many of my physicist friends howl that they possess free will. While their tormentors argue that much of our perception of free will is but an illusion. Some of the most compelling evidence for this argument comes from the split-brain experiments of the 1960s.

In order to reduce seizures in sufferers of epilepsy, the connections between the left and right brains were almost completely severed. These individuals allowed for a number of interesting experiments. Investigators would present cards with the word 'Walk' to the patient's left eye (which is connected to the right brain), this would cause the subject to start walking. When asked 'why are you walking', the patient would respond 'because I was thirsty'. Since the left brain seems to be the origin of such responses, we can argue that, to a large degree, we simply do what we do and then justify such actions.

When confronted with such evidence, my physicist friends respond with references to such things as the Penrose Tiling problem and other tasks that can be shown to be incomputable yet readily addressed by human cognitive processes. Without reigniting our debate on Kurt Gödel's theorems, I think that Jack Copeland's (2008) paper is relatively helpful.

Turing in 1947 (quoted by Copeland 2008): 'There can be no machine which will distinguish provable formulae of the system from unprovable … On the other hand, if a mathematician is confronted with such a problem, he would search around and find new methods of proof'. A central aspect of mathematical creativity is the dreaming up of new methods — new methods for proving theorems, solving problems and so forth. Is the creative process in human mathematicians always computable (assuming an unbounded supply of mathematicians, paper, ink, time)? There are various ways of expressing this question more precisely. One is: is the sequence of new methods … m_i, m_j, … produced over time by the idealized mathematical community a computable sequence in the sense of Turing 1937 (also quoted in Copeland 2008, from Turing's paper 'On Computable Numbers')?

At the end of the day, maybe Artificial transforms into Authentic when the agent becomes Argumentative.

17

Parameters of the Artificial in AI

Suman

- Four parameters for understanding what *artificial* means here are outlined, with regard to the physical, behavioural, conceptual and generative systems
- Since those suggest four directions of research, the question arises as to which is preferable

---

You raise four suggestive points with regard to the question of artifice in AI, Peter.

1. First, you consider a variation of the Theseus Paradox, entailing the gradual replacement of the natural parts of a given intelligent agent by artificial parts while retaining its capacity of intelligence.
2. Then you comment on the possibility of instilling the capacity of intelligence — at least some symptoms of it — in an artificial system which does not resemble the natural one where that capacity is observed.
3. After that, you pause sceptically on the idea of setting an artificial system towards a natural-like evolutionary process such that intelligence appears spontaneously at some point.
4. Finally, you consider the distinction between 'artificial' and 'authentic', and wonder at what point a complex automated system may perceivably be received as demonstrating genuinely intelligent behaviour.

You end on a rule-of-thumb idea of 'being argumentative', which seems to return to a version of Turing's imitation game.

These appear to be divergent or parallel considerations. Let me try to find a way of expressing the links and differences between them in a coherent way.

The connections and slippages between four parameters seem to be at stake in all those, and I suspect in any consideration of what *artificial* might mean in AI. Perhaps the following distinctions of four parameters offer a sensible terminology for considering what *artificial* means in AI.

- **Parameter 1 (*P1*):** The *physical system* of the intelligent agent (what you call 'the vessel', Peter). This may be thought of as consisting of some or more of the following intertwined components: cognitive apparatus, motor-function apparatus, expressive apparatus, self-sustenance apparatus and processing equipment. The last involves some feed-in from and feedback to the other components, with interim processing pathways: in organic terms, the brain. There is a tendency to overdetermine the brain as the autonomous seat of intelligence (however defined), with all manifestations of intelligence emanating from it. However, it is impossible to understand the processing equipment without reference to the other components, just as the coordinated functioning of the other components depend on the processing equipment. Intelligence, in any expressible sense, arguably depends on the cohesive interconnections between all the components. The tendency to think of the brain as an autonomous repository of intelligence is perhaps a kind of myth. It reminds me of Roland Barthes's thoughts on 'The Brain of Einstein' in *Mythologies* (1972): 'Einstein's brain is a mythical object: paradoxically, the greatest intelligence of all provides an image of the most up-to-date machine, the man who is too powerful is removed from psychology, and introduced into a world of robots'.
- **Parameter 2 (*P2*):** The *behavioural system* of the intelligent agent. This consists of all possible actions by the intelligent agent whereby it becomes evident that the agent is indeed intelligent. This does not mean that actions are necessarily right or wrong or true or false (there is

no normative content in intelligent action); it means that there is a communicable or perceivable appearance of intelligence to other intelligent agents. That could consist of all communicative or expressive actions, all actions demonstrative of learning from experience, all actions involving using tools, etc. of a sufficient complexity and efficacy to be termed 'intelligent' (measurements of complexity rather than behavioural norms are relevant).

- **Parameter 3 (*P3*):** The *general conceptual system* of the intelligent agent. This includes all conceptual systems which can be called upon to explain and understand the intelligent action of an agent as being intelligent — i.e. all thought which underpins intelligent action. Again, the recognition of such conceptual systems is dependent on there being other intelligent agents to do the recognising. The kinds of conceptual systems that may be included in the general conceptual system are: linguistic/communicative modalities, mathematical formalising, practical reasoning and inferential analysis of any kind, ethical and aesthetic discernment, etc.

- **Parameter 4 (*P4*):** The *generative system* of the intelligent agent. The intelligent agent comes from a past state and moves towards a future state such that intelligence is understood as appearing and developing; that occurs within the agent's generative system. That is to say, along each of the other parameters (*P*1, *P*2 and *P*3) and in their combined manifestation there are pasts and futures implied for the agent, whereby its intelligence is understood as such. This system could be thought of as consisting of three levels of change: evolutionary (reproductive) [*L*1], learned and engineered (heuristic) [*L*2] and circumstantially inflicted (e.g. by a natural catastrophe) [*L*3].

It is quite difficult to disentangle the four parameters from each other so as to identify where the intelligence of the intelligent agent derives or is centred. That is to say, I do not see an obvious way of saying that precedent emphasis should be put on one or the other in thinking about how to artificially produce intelligence. I may suggest some propositions, however, which may or may not be useful — more or less instinctively, as in the area of axiomatic statements. For instance:

- *P2* is not possible without some form of *P1*, but *P1* may exist without *P2*.
- *P2* is not *P2* unless *P3*, but *P2* is not necessarily all that is *P3*.
- *P3* cannot be revealed unless *P2*.
- *P3* may be valid/functional irrespective of *P1* or *P2*, but I am not sure of this (is anyone?).
- *P1*, *P2* and *P3* are all conditional to *P4*, but ...
- ... *P1*, *P2* and *P3* are not conditional to *P4* in the same way. *P4-L1*, *P4-L2* and *P4-L3* may be actuated in *P1*, *P2* and *P3* in different permutations and combinations, which bear upon their interrelatedness.

Intelligence, we may say, is somewhere in the midst of or emerges from the relationships between *P1*, *P2*, *P3* and *P4*.

With this way of articulating the field embodied in the intelligent agent, let me go back to your four notions of what the artificial in AI might mean, Peter — summarised above. It seems to me that your four notions suggest distinct ideas of *artifice* or the *artificial*. The *artificial* is not understood in them as one sort of approach but as several different sorts of approaches. The specific nuance of *artificial* that is relevant to each of those four notions depends on where the precedent emphasis is laid among *P1*, *P2*, *P3* and *P4*. So, following your four points:

1. The gradual replacement of natural parts of a given AI agent by artificial parts while retaining its capacity of intelligence: this takes *P1* as the starting point of artifice — we may call this **Artificial(a)**. Artifice begins with the physical system of a given intelligent agent, on the assumption that it is the repository of intelligence. In other words, intelligence is somehow contained in the uniquely organised sum of the physical parts, and artifice consists in replicating/replacing the latter.

2. Instilling the capacity of or symptoms of intelligence in an artificial system which does not resemble the natural one: this takes *P2* as the starting point — we may call this **Artificial(b)**. Here, the behaviouristic system of the intelligent agent is taken as the primary marker of intelligence, and the quest is to constitute a different physical system to demonstrate (at least some of) the features of that behaviouristic

system. In other words, artifice consists in replicating the behaviouristic system through a non-natural physical system.

3. Setting an artificial system towards a natural-like evolutionary process such that intelligence appears spontaneously: this takes *P4* as the starting point — we may call this **Artificial(c)**. The generative system of the intelligent agent is taken as the key to intelligence, and the idea is to engineer such a generative system. The artifice consists in setting the preconditions and content of a generative system in motion such that intelligence may gradually evolve.

4. Regarding the point at which a complex automated system may perceivably be received as showing genuinely intelligent behaviour, i.e. when it is able to argue: this, again, puts the precedent emphasis on *P2* — and is also to do with **Artificial(b)**, as in point 2 above. Argument is a feature of the intelligent agent's behavioural system, and this observation equates artifice and 'authenticity' (which seems to connote 'natural-like' or 'natural') by taking that behavioural feature as the key.

In principle, it seems possible to add another nuance to the three kinds of artifice in conceiving AI — Artificial(a), Artificial(b) and Artificial(c). It should be possible to suggest an **Artificial(d)** approach, where precedent emphasis is put on *P3*, i.e. which begins with the intelligent agent's conceptual system. This could be the approach where the emphasis is on understanding the principles, processes and limits of intelligence itself before trying to realise it in terms of *P1*, *P2* or *P4*. Thus, a general theory of intelligence might be sought, elucidating the fundamental building blocks and grids on which something meaningfully thought of as 'intelligence' is *constructed* — as opposed to simply being *exercised* or *performed* by an intelligent agent. Once the mechanics of intelligence is thus grasped at *P3*, we may begin to think about how artifice may be brought to bear upon the re-realisation of intelligence or the production of AI. This is a bit impressionistically put, but hopefully makes sense.

So, there are four possible approaches to the artifice involved in conceiving AI: Artificial(a) which starts with *P1*, the physical system, and then brings in the other parameters; Artificial(b), which begins with *P2*, the behavioural system, and then extends to the other parameters;

Artificial(c), which starts with *P4*, the generative system, and then waits for the other parameters to emerge; and Artificial(d), which focuses on *P3*, the conceptual system, and considers the other parameters as conditional to that.

Do you have a preference, Peter, and why? I know from your last intervention that you are sceptical about Artificial(c) approaches to AI. But is there an approach which you favour, or which you feel should be favoured?

18

Limits of the Artificial in AI

Peter

- Arguments are offered for a deeper understanding of the mechanisms that govern our conceptual frameworks
- It is proposed that a good indicator that progress is being made are signs that AI can compose explanatory knowledge and achieve creative copying
- It is suggested that ethics may be a form of creative copying

---

Suman, your parameterisation of AI does indeed make sense: the physical instantiation ($P1$), intelligent behaviours ($P2$), conceptual systems ($P3$) and the generative systems ($P4$). As for your four proposed approaches (a, b, c and d), I will give brief comments.

Approach(a) (focuses on the physical or $P1$), this is like constructing a seashell and hoping that a crab will come along and make it its home. In general, I don't think that the 'build it and they will come' strategy will work. Approach(b) (focuses on $P2$), I would say that this approach has had some interesting success as of late but is essentially limited. Recurrent Neural Networks (RNNs) and Long Short-term Memory (LSTM) networks have produced some very spooky results. These systems are built using recorded stimuli and their associated observed human responses. If each stimulus–response pair can be thought of as a sequence, then an LSTM can be trained to take as an arbitrary input and produce a plausible response. For example, an LSTM can be used to synthesise verbal captions for arbitrary input images. I would argue that such capabilities are what you get when you buy a parrot from the pet store or one of the various commercial spies that are now available for in-home use (Alexa, Siri, etc.). Approach(c) (focuses on *P4*): I believe that each one of us represents proof that this direction is plausible. However, for the foreseeable future, synthetic evolution in its purest form will simply be cost prohibitive both in terms of time and resources. If we want to make any headway within our lifetimes, we need to take shortcuts and so this leaves us with the option of Approach(d). A deeper understanding of the mechanisms that govern the conceptual frameworks (*P3*) of intelligence (language, mathematics, memory, etc.) is where I believe we will get the most bang for our buck. With this said, the question at hand is 'how should we proceed?'

While Turing and others have posited a variety of clever tests for detecting the presence of intelligence, at this juncture I would prefer measures that might inform us on whether or not we are at least heading in the right direction. For Stage I AI, which we might define as the use of logic, progress was gauged by the number of frameworks that successfully made the transition from sandbox to real environments (not too many). For Stage II AI, a.k.a. statistical inference (estimate latent variable y given observed variable x), we may consider accuracy over ground truth datasets as an indication of progress. Statistics such as Receiver Operator Characteristic (ROC) curves have been used time and again to establish the merit of a given algorithm as well as the field in general. Stage III AI — exploring whether, given unforeseen circumstances, an agent can successfully reason over contextual cues: with regard to this the means for declaring progress is still unclear. To this end, I propose a number of criteria for determining whether or not we are heading in the right direction.

Explanatory Knowledge

David Deutsch (2011) makes the distinction between biological and explanatory knowledge. An example of biological knowledge is the DNA associated with the eyeball, in that it provides a recipe for producing such organs. In contrast, the field of optics provides a working description for the mechanics of light. DNA enables the cookie-cutter-like production of sight. Optics allows for the construction of cameras, telescopes and micro-scopes. Deutsch argues that mechanisms for criticism are essential for the production and maturation of explanatory knowledge. At this point, I would argue that knowledge encapsulated in AI models such as deep learning neural networks is essentially biological in nature. Going for-ward, I would argue that the capability to automatically construct and criticise explanatory knowledge within an AI context would be a positive sign that progress is being made.

Creative Copying

DNA, thoughts and viruses are all examples of memes, which are things that can be copied. Richard Dawkins has described the importance of memes with respect to the natural world. In this regard, David Deutsch points to the concept of creative copying. Mitosis is the means by which strands of DNA are copied in an almost 'exact' manner. However, such direct methods are limited. Through many generations of evolution, certain dinosaurs have become modern day avians with the gift of flight. Unfortunately, the option of going back in time so as to evolve feathers and wings is not in the cards for most if not all homo sapiens. In order to 'copy' this concept, humans had to invent hot air balloons and eventually modern-day aircraft. The ability to find an alternative path to an established capa-bility can be viewed as a form of creative copying. In one of our previous exchanges, I used a mathematical metaphor to describe creativity, where X represents all available knowledge and Y represents some sort of utility function associated with X. Creativity is then characterised as the search for X, such that $Y(X)$ is a new local maximum. In the case of creative copy-ing, the utility function Y is known (i.e. the ability to fly), we just need to find a new X for achieving Y. I argue that once machines start producing novel methods for accomplishing existing but inaccessible tasks, their prospects for becoming intelligent agents will increase significantly.

An interesting example of creative copying is Ethics. In Matt Ridley's *The Origins of Virtue* (1996), we are given a compelling account for how ethical behaviour could have emerged naturally due to such things as group-level selection. Now suppose an agent covets the benefits associ-ated with ethical behaviour, such as the win–win outcomes that result from cooperation and trade. However, it may be the case that the agent's genetic lineage had more to do with looting and pillaging than with the pristine division of labour. What is a Barbarian to do? Enter the philosopher. Learned individuals from Socrates and Confucius onwards have time and again constructed ethical systems that can be used to transform the Hobbesian hordes into docile populations at scale. Some might argue that religion is yet another form of creative copying. In *The God Delusion* (2006), Dawkins makes a mild objection as he argues that religion has essentially hijacked our capability to believe just about anything as long as two friends and a neighbour hold such views. Imagine a past where parents inform their children that playing in the river is not a good idea due to the prevalence of crafty crocodiles. Some children will take such advice to heart, while others may remain sceptical and thus on a hot day decide to take a quick dip. Generally speaking, we are all the descendants of the former and not the latter. In this way, religion is more of a meme itself as opposed to an act of creativity.

Maybe of more interest to the reader is the construction of computational models of ethics that may have the capacity to instil ethical behaviour into our yet to be artificial brethren. An interesting example of this type of effort is the work of Max Kleiman-Weiner *et al.* (2017). The authors start by arguing that the outcomes of actions taken by an individual can be characterised by various utility functions that are associated with the benefits or burdens that will be incurred by the individual as well as various members of society. Ethics then becomes a tradeoff between individual and communal utility. The ethics associated with a given society can then be defined as the accepted parameters and weights associated with such utility functions. The next question is to determine how a new agent can acquire an established ethical system. The authors argue that similar to language, such agents must contend with what is known as the poverty of stimulus. That is to say, with only a very few experiences, children seem to be able to accurately infer the ethical systems of their families and by extension their communities. The authors offer a Bayesian solution for such efficient learning. Finally, the authors consider various mechanisms for modelling the temporal evolution of a society's ethical system.

Monotonic Intelligence

Returning to the question of progress, I would argue that the emergence of what I call monotonic intelligence would be very encouraging. Simply put, the capabilities of a monotonically intelligent agent should generally improve as and when it is exposed to novel experiences. This should not be confused with the continuous learning paradigm, where a learner is permitted to retrain its models every time a false or missed detection has occurred. Monotonic Intelligence should be able to build on past accomplishments: e.g. having learned to play soccer, such agents should be able to more readily pick up the skills needed to master hockey. In addition, the diversity of accomplishments should be ever growing. This might be evidence of the ability to transfer expertise from one domain to another. A monotonic intelligence might never satisfy our tests for human-level intelligence, but they will certainly be interesting.

19

Restrictions on AI Research

Suman

- That the previous intervention has accurately marked the limits of automated capacities is accepted
- Social constraints of the regime under which AI research works are noted
- It is suggested that this is an ideological regime which uses AI research for managing people and serving establishment interests
- The beginnings of AI research from the 1950s are recalled

Peter, with regard to your last intervention: your preference for $P3$ (conceptual frameworks) and therefore Artificial(d) by way of pushing towards AI seems to me precisely the direction where the limits of complex automation could be described, or where the present non-existence of meaningful AI can be understood. And, in fact, you mark out those limits under the three subheadings of your previous intervention accurately.

- **Under 'explanatory knowledge':** 'The ability to automatically construct and criticise explanatory knowledge'.
- **Under 'creative copying':** Along with the optimism of the numinous term 'creative', the practical challenge of fulfilling 'the search for X such that $Y(X)$ is a new local maximum' without programming within a given $\lim_{x1 \to xN}(X)$.

- **Under 'monotonic intelligence':** 'Building upon past accomplish-ments' without referring to and reiterating every tried-and-tested model at every step.

These are what automation cannot yet do, which clarifies what it can do. That's to say, these describe the prevailing capacities of automation with-out the realisation of 'intelligence' in a received sense.

My general feeling is that given the way the field of AI research works by your account, the future direction would be towards more and more efficient automation without quite crossing those limits into intelligence. This isn't a purely impressionistic assertion, but it also isn't a direct infer-ence from what you say. Rather, I have been thinking about what you *do* in your arguments. So, a somewhat tangential response to your previous intervention, and those preceding it, follows.

One of the features of your arguments that I find stimulating is the productive opportunism they evince. Your arguments are exemplified variously by recourse to computational systems (the various algorithmic models you have cited), natural systems (like lobster hatcheries), and social systems (like Ricardo's comparative advantage, 'natural' language, ethical systems). They are cited as illustrations to make an immediate point. More importantly, they are cited as if these are ultimately all one sort of system, and really social systems behave like natural systems and all can be transferred equally into or described equally as (at least poten-tially) computational systems. This seems a doubtful preconception to me. Both natural and social systems may be understood fairly robustly in terms of computational models *insofar as they are currently functional*; i.e. if they are out there grinding away, their dynamics can be understood to a more or less satisfactory extent in terms of a set of algorithms opera-tionalised in a programme. However, insofar as the computational model may thereafter be used to make *predictions* or to anticipate *ongoing functioning*, it seems likely that natural systems would be more amenable than social systems. Social systems are cognisant of and respond to how they are conceptualised, often by resisting that conceptualisation or by deliberately taking an alternative conceptual direction — with both volun-tary and involuntary outcomes. That is well exemplified in most histories of social systems (economic orders, political arrangements, ethical tenets, cultural productions, etc.), and may well be characteristic of the quotient of intelligence in social systems. If the move to realise AI meaningfully is going to rest on the assumption that social and natural systems are the same and can all be grounded in computational models, I suspect AI will remain chimerical — as chimerical as an investment firm producing a financial package based on a computational model which shows guaranteed and perpetual profits for all investors.

But that isn't quite the point I'm reaching towards here. More pertinently, it occurs to me that your productive opportunism in exemplifying that preconception is perhaps not really that opportunistic, insofar as that suggests choosing an illustration at random. Arguably, a financial and ideological regime structures the field of AI research and thereby guides your selection of illustrative examples. This regime demands continuous acceptance of the notion that predictive computational models can be realised for social systems. You have mentioned this regime and its structuring function often, albeit in passing: AI researchers have to work according to the norms that funders set, the targets that public and private institutions enjoin (public and private are not especially distinguishable in terms of accounting practices now). Of course, but naturally, and it's obviously so and quite right too … most concur that funding is given and AI research is structured not so much for the long-term goal of realising intelligent artificial systems but for short-term objectives which may be regarded as broadly in that long-term direction. Or, at least, propaganda can make out that short-term objectives reach towards that ideal long-term goal. But it's really for the short-term objectives themselves that AI research is supported (allowed); these objectives justify investments in terms of immediate cost-benefits accounting and industrially advantageous applications. If an AI engineer wants to seriously explore the long-term possibility of an intelligent programme, this engineer has to constantly play the game of justificatory accounting, has to constantly articulate short-term benefits to keep the long-term option open. It seems arguable to me that this short-term benefits game works actively against the grain of any long-term idea of plausibly realising AI. The short-term benefits regime is a kind of insurance against any such long-term outcome, and if despite the odds an AI system were to crop up, it would be serendipitous and would probably be quickly erased as an error or as being an unacceptable financial risk.

There are three obvious and interrelated short-term justifications for research which seems ostensibly in the direction of some plausible AI system:

1. Along the way new technical commodities would be produced which consumers — preferably everyone — would become habituated to using. Smart devices of various sorts targeting all or particular sectors of the consumables market could be cited here. As consumers, people will accordingly need to adapt to emerging technological systems.

2. Along the way new technological means of production would be introduced whereby waged workers and the work they do — as many and as much as possible — can be replaced and expenses on production reduced. As workers, then, people would need to adapt to new forms of less-remunerative, technologically assisted work or to consider consumption itself a kind of work. As workers too, people will therefore need to adapt to emerging technological systems.

3. Underpinning both the above, since production and consumption occurs within prevailing social systems, people will have to be rendered compliant with the social systems (the ruling interests therein) which capitalise on the first and second short-term objectives. This involves adapting and maintaining governance and financial regimes that render the first two short-term objectives viable, by presenting them as convenient for all and by their being profitable for some. This could be thought of as an ideological regime: it is a matter of *managing people* so that their adaptation to technological systems, as consumers and workers, seems socially necessary or, better yet, *fait accompli* and they do not feel inclined to reject, change or shake up the prevailing regime.

The third area is where, it seems, the push to consider social systems as stabilisable in the way computational programmes are comes from. That push makes out that prevailing social systems are given rather than made — not ideologically constructed at all, just the way things really and unavoidably and naturally are. This is a manager's dream: to get to those unshakable formulae of how people can be made compliant with a given economic and governance regime. However, this is mostly a kind of trick which works for those who benefit from the first two short-term objectives and who fund AI research and control the firms and institutions where such research is undertaken.

The kind of trick involved is rather beautifully illustrated, Peter, by your observations on ethics in your previous intervention. In philosophical terms, there are as many ethical systems possible as there are first principles for understanding individuality and collectivity. By the way, since you dwell upon this: religious organisations in themselves cannot be considered equivalent to ethical systems (though the devout like to think so). Rather, religious organisations institutionalise specific first principles of individuality and collectivity which are then enacted as supernally given doctrines and diktats of conduct for the benefit of their clerisy and supporting elites. That is to say, different religious orders produce convenient ethical systems to maintain their dominance. I don't think your notes on religious memes have much to do with ethical systems *per se*. The account of ethical behaviour that you draw from your reading of Ridley (1996) is a very particular and recent one (it can be tracked back to around 300 years): its first principle is that *collectivity consists in the actions and negotiations of more or less independent and rational individuals who work out their best interests by interacting with other independent and rational individuals within a given rubric of in-born sociality* — as you put it, for the 'the win–win outcomes that result from cooperation and trade'. The formerly barbaric 'agent', in your terms, thus inevitably finds his way into becoming the rational self-determining individual. There are numerous versions of this concept from Kant, Hegel and Mill to Habermas and Rawls on the one hand and Hayek and Nozick on the other — let's call this liberal rationalist ethics. The computational programme that you mention with reference to Kleiman-Weiner *et al.* (2017) is simply based on mechanising a set of first principles of liberal rationalist ethics: that is, a version of liberal rationalist ethics programmed as an autonomously functional process. The thing is that such liberal rationalist ethical systems have not really obtained in any historical society; and conceptually, such systems provide little purchase for understanding the continuing calls of supremacist convictions (on the grounds of race, gender, nationality, class, etc.), the mechanics of coercive power, social irrationality and opportunistic short-termism, repeated recurrence of violence and conflict, the acquisitiveness of the few to the detriment of the many and so on. All of those too have found justifications with other first principles, have enabled other (non-liberal and illiberal) kinds of ethical systems, all perfectly amenable to modelling too. And if one were looking for them, genetic histories or common-sense ideas can be found for grounding those ethical systems too — different versions of virtue and evil. Liberal rationalist ethics is mainly used to produce nebulous concepts like the 'natural justice of markets' and 'democratic peace' and 'meritocratic rational bureaucracy', which mainly serve the vested interests of dominant persons and groups and make their privileges seem either natural and necessary or shroud them. The historical record shows that what you call the 'Hobbesian hordes' have seldom been 'transformed into docile populations' for very long, though corporate managers and ruling political elites now hope that these hordes will be programmed into perpetual docility with the help of AI engineers. That is more or less what you seem to have 'philosophers' pegged as, those 'learned individuals from Socrates and Confucius onwards' — as (uncharacteristically intelligent) managers on behalf of some establishment, devoted to engineering the docility of hordes. Of course, Socrates reputedly paid a high price for his inability to be docile.

At its best, such liberal rationalist ethics offers a utopian horizon, the *idea* of a reasonable and free order to aspire to and to express how prevailing social orders fall short and are less reasonable. Mostly though, such liberal rationalist ethics is used to persuade the hordes to behave, usually unwittingly, for the benefit and perpetual dominance of the prevailing elites. It is alluring, the idea that we the hordes consist naturally of free, self-determining individuals choosing continuously and spontaneously to cooperate and trade with other free, self-determining individuals in a rational process that is policed by … itself, by genetics, by democratic ideals, by the rule of law, something like that. It is obvious that this has never quite worked that way and doesn't now. However, it can be used cleverly to persuade people of policies with quite contrary implications, to make the policies so couched eventually function by coercion, all in the name of being natural, inevitable, obvious, ideology-free, common sense, genetically grounded, the ways things are — all interrogation and dissent then has to be expressed in conciliatory terms or be dubbed an unnatural aberration/deviation.

It is perhaps not fortuitous, Peter, that you give your concept of ethics with reference to Ridley (1996) as drawn from genetic history and therefore pertinent to real people and society, and the programme you find in Kleiman-Weiner *et al.* (2017) as being for 'our artificial brethren' to come. Another way of seeing that is to say that from the concept drawn from a history-that-never-was to a programme for the unconceived-brethren-to-come we have a project for managing people so that they are transformed into behaving like artificial agents themselves, happily at one in a technological system with accountable short-term benefits for some. That might be the pertinent purpose of AI research: not so much to *produce* autonomous intelligent artificial agents but to get humans to *behave* as intelligent artificial agents in line with a computational model. There is possibly a history of AI research to be written from this perspective, which would say much about the consanguinity between — indeed collaboration between — cybernetics and management via the study of group behaviour. Perhaps this history can start with Heinz von Foerster's work on 'self organisation', and researches at his Biological Computer Laboratory (BCL) set up in 1958 at the University of Illinois at Urbana-Champaign (useful retrospective account by Gordon Pask (1996), another pioneering cybernetics researcher; also see Müller and Müller (2007)). In brief, 'self-organisation' was defined in terms of changes in the ratio of observed entropy to maximum possible entropy within a given system against time; and research focused on identifying the factors (such as adaptability) which enable change towards decreasing observed entropy to take place. This research was mainly driven by a desire to design artificial systems that emulate human systems (biological and social). That necessarily involved exploring human individuals and collectives as self-organising systems and investigating the interactions between human and artificial systems. Naturally, the possibilities for understanding and enhancing learning and training were contemplated in this vein, since these seemed to be areas where findings might have immediate applications (Pask (1975) gave a useful overview of the theoretical considerations). This line of research wasn't too distant from suggesting that the interaction of humans as self-organising systems and computers as programmed systems could enhance the reduction of entropy in the former — help them to become 'educated', more docile, more manageable. That amounts to seeing humans as biological computers organising themselves according to the programmed options of artificial computers — in a way, programming themselves through a heuristic process of engaging with artificial computers. It's interesting how the AI quest and the management imperative flipped into each other and coalesced at this foundational juncture ... and so it continues.

20

Expectations of AI Research

Peter

- Comparisons between AI research and alchemy are considered
- Questions are raised regarding the illusionary nature of intelligence
- A review of the remarkable progress of AI research is given
- Final arguments are made for why AI research remains a worthy pursuit

---

Imagine a modern-day Connecticut Yankee returning to King Arthur's court and leaving behind a pocket calculator. Lacking today's instruments for magnification, the mere existence, let alone the purpose, of the myriad of transistors buried deep inside the mass-produced chip sets would surely go unnoticed. What would Merlin make of those round shiny batteries? He might infer that the absence of said objects renders the calculator inoperable, but without the concept of electricity, that's probably as far as the old conjurer could go. He might be reduced to simply transforming those silvery objects into a nifty pendant. Will future generations view AI researchers and the alchemists of old as birds of a feather? Will our quest to turn bits into brains be analogous to the dream of transforming lead into gold? In *The End of Science*, John Horgan (1998) argues that, like the string theorists, AI scientists and engineers simply do not have the math, the instruments or the words needed for this endeavor. It might simply be the case that we can't get there from here. But maybe this view is too harsh.

The lion's share of Sir Isaac Newton's writings was devoted to various forms of sorcery. While fruitless in themselves, along the way we got differential calculus, optics and gravity, and his contemporaries knew the value of those as we do:

> 'Newton was the greatest and rarest genius that ever rose for the adornment and instruction of the species.'
>
> — David Hume

> 'Nature and Nature's laws lay hid in night; God said, Let Newton be! and all was light.'
>
> — Alexander Pope

Unless there is a physical phenomenon that we have yet to directly observe, I cannot see an argument for why a set of artificial neurons cannot in theory emulate a set of biological neurons. If this is the case, then there are roughly 7 billion proof points out there that imply that what we seek can in theory be achieved. However, I would agree that what we are looking for is not a computational model such as a reductionist formula or a series of 'if-then' statements, but a computational framework where capabilities can emerge — more on this later.

Suman, it seems that at long last we have found common ground in the proposal of metrics for measuring the advancement of AI:

1. The automatic construction and criticism of explainable knowledge.
2. Creative copying.
3. Monotonic learning — the ability to build on expertise from one domain and apply it to others.

You rightly state that these qualities have yet to manifest themselves in the offerings put forth by the AI community. However, I would argue that what you are looking for seems to be the main difference between human and lobster cognition. Without symbolic abstractions such as language and mathematics, the production of explainable knowledge and the ability to transform such knowledge from domain to domain would be, to say the least, problematic. More importantly, without the ability to transmit learnings from one generation to the next, discovery of the ability to make fire or defy gravity (examples of creative copying) would disappear shortly after its inventor's demise. Simply put, language is our super-power, but language is only a relatively recent phenomenon — how important is it really?

Language with all its gifts is built on a vast array of pre-existing cognitive capabilities. What you have referred to as mere clockwork is the foundation of our intelligence. Basic capabilities such as pattern recognition, memory and policy construction have required phylogenic periods of time to develop. Yet, what you think of as intelligence might only have arisen during historical time frames. It is the icing on the cake or the tip of the iceberg. As Kahneman (2011) puts it: 'Our Intelligent selves are like the B-actors that mistakenly think they are the stars of the show'. Instead of AI being a chimera, is it possible that our sense of intelligence is the real illusion?

I would argue that few topics of inquiry have seen such dramatic progress as AI — we are getting closer and closer to laying down the cognitive foundation needed to launch the development of the intelligence that you seek. My first computer was the Radio Shack TRS-80, which had 16 kilobits of random access memory and operated at a clock speed of about one million cycles per second. As I mentioned in my previous interventions, the EU Spiking Computation Engine can perform 200 million million calculations per second, which is comparable to the human brain. The resolution and fidelity of the cameras in your smart phone are beginning to rival the eye itself. Automated face recognition engines routinely outperform human abilities. The curse of dimensionality has been broken as evidenced by the defeat of the Go, Chess and Trivia Champions of our generation by automated devices. While I agree that the average chameleon, cephalopod and lonely lobster are more cognitively robust than our mightiest contrivances — to say that no progress has been made would be a mistake.

As you pointed out, I am in favor of option D, where we develop proxies for societal frameworks such as ethics and aesthetics and then make them available to our AI systems. But let me make a clarification here: as I mentioned previously, I am not particularly interested in crafting models for such behaviours. I am more interested in building frameworks, where such behaviours can be learned, taught or simply emerge. For example, in order to detect faces we no longer try to build models for what a face looks like in terms of constituent parts (eyes, noses and mouths). We simply gather a large corpus of facial and non-facial images and then search for a discriminant that can be used to distinguish between the two classes. For natural language processing, we refrain from defining words based on dictionary definitions and instead construct numerical embeddings that preserve semantic distance. In my last intervention, I described a method that would allow an agent to acquire an existing but evolving ethical framework as opposed to instantiating one from scratch.

At this point, I can't help but take note of your concerns regarding my discussion of ethics. As a meager form of rebuttal, I only make the following points:

1. By arguing that evolution might favour groups that are capable of cooperation, I don't mean to imply that humans should then be viewed as rational agents that naturally come to the conclusion that personal sacrifice might enable the greater good. I would simply make the point that groups whose individuals have the capacity to cooperate may in the long run enjoy the benefits of such behaviour.

2. In terms of religion, I don't argue that it is an ethical framework, I was just pointing out that Richard Dawkins argues that instead of being an advantage with respect to group or individual survival, religion may have hijacked our superpower — the ability to pass ideas unquestioned from one generation to the next.

3. When I was taking my first statics and dynamics course in engineering school, our professor asked the class 'What is the cost of a human life?'. The answer turned out to be roughly $200,000 Canadian dollars. We know that for every arc of road curvature there will be a commensurate increase of the probability of human casualties. With unlimited funds, we as a society could choose to make all roads as straight as an arrow — but we don't and therefore we don't. We instead make calculations with parameters such as the value of life. My point here is that engineers are continually faced with ethical decisions. The Google employees have forced their management to no longer accept Defense funding. With the advent of driverless cars, the

runaway trolley problem will no longer be just an academic thought experiment, it will have to be resolved automatically on a daily basis. By developing ethical frameworks for our machines, we are not simply trying to opportunistically ape the manners of our betters, we are attempting to live up to the spirit of the iron ring (a somewhat saccharin tradition, where Canadian Engineers are given bands, made from material salvaged from a bridge that failed in an abrupt and disastrous manner, to wear on the small finger of their working hands).

You make the conjecture that AI investors are hoping to: profit from addiction, threaten the livelihood of labour or more monstrously, transform humanity into docile sheep that are herded by entropy minimising AI shepherds. This must be taken seriously. Neil Postman's *Amusing Ourselves to Death* (1985) seems more prophetic day by day. In *Deep Work* (2016) by Cal Newport we see how malleable the human mind really is. In *The Dumbest Generation* (2008), Mark Bauerlein laments:

> They are the dumbest generation. They enjoy all the advantages of a prosperous, high-tech society. Digital technology has fabulously empowered them, loosened the hold of elders. Yet adolescents use these tools to wrap themselves in a generational cocoon filled with puerile banter and coarse images. The founts of knowledge are everywhere, but the rising generation camps in the desert, exchanging stories, pictures, tunes, and texts, savoring the thrill of peer attention. If they don't change, they will be remembered as the fortunate ones who were unworthy of the privileges they inherited. They may even be the generation that lost that great American heritage, forever.

However, your sense of conspiracy reminds me of Joshua Knobe's thoughts on perceived intentionality (Leslie *et al.*, 2006; Knobe and Nichols, 2007). The argument goes as follows. An entity might have a primary goal, the pursuit of which may result in a side effect which may or may not be perceived by an observer as intentional. It turns out that in general, negative side effects are viewed as intentional while positive side effects are viewed as inadvertent. With this said, I think that AI investors are just in it for the money.

My cunning reference to Knobe's work leads me to the topic of experimental philosophy, where inhabitants of the Ivory Tower are encouraged to subject their thoughts to the clarifying light of real-world results. A while back, you made the impassioned plea that the humanities should be part of the AI experiment. Instead of lecturing engineers on the finer points of ethical frameworks with the implication that their sensibilities and pedigree are just a tad jejune, why not propose an Ethics Engine that can be incorporated into our AI Agents? Let the poets, painters and musicians put down their quills, brushes and tambourines and instead build new types of Aesthetics Engines. While making fun of the habits and hygiene of Silicon Valley Nerds can always get a laugh as well as create a smug sense of superiority, let funny man Bill Maher and his jackals come up with a theory of humour. Instead of judging, put on your swim suits and join the pageant. In this way, we can all become Humanity Engineers.

Earlier in our discussion you asked why bother at all with this topic of investigation. Putting aside, for now, the valid concerns raised by James Barrat in *Our Final Invention* (2013), let me finish this off with a few positive musings. It has been hypothesised that the co-habitation of humans and canines may have resulted in significant cognitive changes for both species. During this period, the pre-frontal cortex of the human brain increased significantly at the possible expense of our sense of hearing and smell. Dogs in turn gave up their wolf-like cunning in trade for more stable living conditions. Could exposure to AI allow for another jump in human cognitive capability? Could we gain the ability or more importantly the desire to distinguish between truth and fiction? Alternatively, could we build better versions of ourselves? Instead of schadenfreude, could we construct agents gifted with true empathy? Can we conjure an intelligence free of the shackles of prejudice and jealousy? The greedy gene got us to where we are, it's up to us to accept the baton and, as you say, continue on.

Part 2

AI and Government Policy

To Carry On …

We need to set up some common ground before embarking on this new direction in our conversation: AI and government policy. Even announcing it feels like biting into more than we can chew. Government policy covers a great many areas of our social lives and what's regarded as AI impinges upon them all — where to begin?

To set us off, some tentative clarifications and delimitations for this conversation follow, which may all be complicated or flouted later. These should keep us moving from wherever we start.

1. To keep this conversation grounded, we will be referring often to *policy statements*. By way of a tentative definition: policy statements present the intent of an executive authority, with bearing upon the domain of that executive authority. Further, policy statements are presented such that the legitimacy of the executive authority is reiterated and confirmed.

2. Such executive authorities could be with regard to various levels of governance, from a single firm to a transnational organisation. Here we are principally concerned with policy at one level: *governmental* — that is, at the level of political states ('nations' might be preferred in some circles, but many states contain more than one nation). We will refer often to UK and USA government policy statements, but we will also stray further afield at times, to PR China, the EU and so on (the Future of Life Institute's Global AI Policy website is a good entry point to different state and interstate policies). It seems reasonable to focus on the state governmental level for two reasons: (a) each state's government has a direct, coherent and overarching responsibility for conducting and regulating salient aspects of social life — economic, political, cultural, legal, military, employment and industry, communications, natural resources, international relations, etc. and (b) other levels of policy, from regional/local to transnational organisations, usually have effect insofar as ratified at the state government level. This is therefore not an exclusive focus; rather, it's an anchor from which we may consider other levels.

3. I think the general kind of state we would refer to is premised on principles of formal democracy: i.e. with institutions to ensure the representation and parity of constituent interest groups in the domain, underpinned at some level by an elective system with universal suffrage. That is not to say that those principles are necessarily adhered to consistently, for instance, in UK or USA policy making.

4. Policy statements are usually of the following sorts: (a) documents to inform policy debate (which include strategy-setting statements and summaries of existing research); (b) statements wherein policy resolutions are agreed on for implementation, either with hard effect (i.e. to become legally enforceable or written into law, formulated as rules) or with soft effect (to be issued as voluntary codes or norms); (c) documents which issue guidance and undertake publicity for implementation purposes. From (a) to (c) types of policy statements, there is a pattern of reduction of complexity and reintroduction of complexity. The (a)-type documents which inform policy debate consist of overviews, summaries and recommendations with regard to a complex area of government (a diverse sector or an issue of wide

import) so as to lead into (b). The (c)-type documents enable (b) to be interpreted and enacted comprehensively across all constituents/levels of the complex area of government.

5. The legitimacy garnering aspect of policy statements is usually marked by some or all of the following: (a) an inclusive and standardised policy language, which appeals to consensual principles and addresses a general interested readership; (b) referring to and maintaining coherence with past and existing policy statements (especially legal stricture); (c) maintaining coherence with existing policy statements for other areas covered by the government, even if not immediately relevant to the given statement (at the least, avoiding contradictions); (d) documenting and publicising a process of consultation and debate involving relevant informants and interest groups; (e) formulating modes of policing, moderating and regulating the effects of the policy statement during and after implementation such that public confidence is maintained. Adopting such measures, however, does not necessarily ensure uncontested acceptance of an executive authority's legitimacy; and nor are such measures consistently adopted in, for instance, UK or USA policy statements.

6. All policy statements — policy as a field — derive from, clarify and have effect on agreements. Agreements could be entered by birth (e.g. rights and responsibilities of being human, of kinship), by membership of a collective (e.g. as citizen, in an institution), arranged between persons. Agreements could be informal (e.g. by convention or custom) or formal. Formal agreements may be strict (contracts), i.e. legally binding, with well-defined responsibilities such that infringement entails some punitive consequence. These may also be lenient (such as, memorandums of understanding).

7. It might be prudent to refer mainly to policy statements that explicitly name 'artificial intelligence' or some obvious equivalent thereof. This is prudent as a matter of convenience, to put some manageable limit on the plethora out there. This is also prudent because how meaning is attributed to 'artificial intelligence' — as a term — in policy is of some interest to us.

21

Policy and Legal Autonomy

Suman

- How AI surfaced as an issue in UK governmental policy is outlined
- Considers the potential autonomy of *electronic agents* as defined in US and EU legislation
- The concept of *legal personhood* and its bearing on AI is raised

UK AI Policy

In UK policy circles, the phrase 'artificial intelligence' started featuring from the end of the 1990s with, as one might expect, steadily growing incidence. A search of the government paper collection at the Kew National Archives gives figures of incidence which speak for themselves (Table 1). The Google Ngram below offers a loose indication of usage of the term and associated terms in English language publications 1960–2009, in the Google Book corpus (see Figure 1), so across written texts of more or less formality.

Table 1. Incidence of 'artificial intelligence' 1999–2019, in the domain webarchive.nationalarchives.gov.uk

Year	1999	2001	2003	2005	2007	2009	2011	2012	2013	2014	2015	2016	2017
Occurrence	1	3	80	121	849	5308	6298	6269	5584	6368	4078	3675	8156

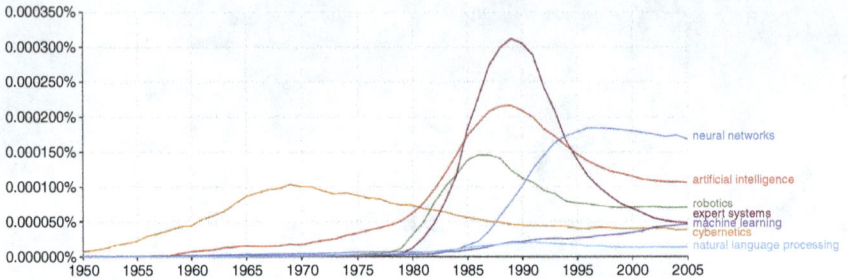

Figure 1. Google Ngram: Incidence of 'artificial intelligence' and some associated terms in the Google Books corpus, comprising a total of 5 million books up to 2009, a corpus size of approximately 250 billion words.

Source: https://books.google.com/ngrams (Last retrieved May 2020).

Two general thrusts of policy debates and resolutions with reference to 'AI' were set early and have generally held since: on the one hand, that AI capacities have developed already out there and have to be accounted, regulated and grounded (which means, really, capitalised for economic ends); on the other hand, that further AI capacities are potential or imminent and need to be anticipated (in trend and risk analysis, strategic or scenario planning, long-term investments, etc.). So, two kinds of policy statements referring to AI appeared from the late 1990s: for implementation and for contingency. From a policy perspective, AI capacities have seemed at the same time both already overwhelmingly here (crying out for response) and about to overwhelmingly emerge (urgently calling for preparation).

- **For implementation:** AI appeared by implication in the government's drive in 1999 to encourage e-commerce, marked by two consultation papers: the Inland Revenue's *Electronic Commerce: The UK's Taxation Agenda* and the Department of Trade and Industry's (DTI) *Building Confidence in Electronic Commerce*. These were followed by further consultations (Promoting Electronic Commerce) and then enactment of the Electronic Communications Act (ECA) 2000 and the Finance Act (FA) 2000. ECA 2000 was about legalising encryption and electronic signatures in business exchanges (licensing and contracts); similar Acts had already been passed in the USA, Canada and Ireland. FA 2000 had relevant sections on defining the boundaries of R&D whereby tax breaks for expenditure on R&D could be determined. DTI guidance of April 2000 on this matter, with regard to Software R&D, brings the first significant mention with something like a definition of the remit of AI, thus:

> Software R&D might include investigations in such areas as theoretical computer science, new operating systems, new programming languages, significant technical advances in algorithms, new or enhanced query languages, or object representations, software engineering methodologies for improved computer programmes and artificial intelligence. In this context, artificial intelligence might cover technical advances in such areas as machine vision, robotics, expert systems, neural networks, the understanding of natural language and automatic language translation. (DTI 2000).

In the context of this conversation, this tentative exclusion there is also of some interest:

> Normally research in the humanities and social sciences is excluded. But it is recognised that some aspects of the fields of natural or applied science require consideration be given to the humanities, for example the development of effective man-machine interfaces in virtual reality, or ergonomic considerations for new forms of communications. Where such research forms an integral part of the natural or applied R&D, it may be included.

Various policy statements started appearing about operationalising AI technology in specific sectors (social care, communications, etc.).

- **For contingency:** Thereafter various policy statements, mainly for debate and contingency planning, started to appear about the future role of AI: notably in the Defence Evaluation and Research Agency's (DERA) *Strategic Futures Thinking* report (2001) and the Ministry of Defence's *The Future Strategic Context for Defence* paper (2003). With regard to AI, the latter observed:

> By 2030, machines will be developing which have an advanced ability to gather information on their surroundings, and which, acting

autonomously, can make intelligent judgements (including judgements on risks) in response to that information. This will have obvious implications in many areas, especially for military intelligence, surveillance, target acquisition and reconnaissance (ISTAR) and support to military decision-making, and may improve our ability, in certain circumstances, to remove personnel from the front line.

In relation, but somewhat marginally, to these early policy statements — indeed to the earliest consultations in 1999 on ECA 2000 — an issue arose which seemed to link the implementation and contingency policy considerations. It allows a specific focus for discussing the remit of (perhaps more precisely, the horizon for) government policy in relation to AI.

Electronic Agents

While the draft ECA was under discussion in the UK, in 1999 Robin Widdison, Director of the Centre for Law and Communications at Durham University UK, wrote to DTI drawing attention to his 1996 paper co-authored with Tom Allen 'Can Computers Make Contracts?' He observed that it should inform the policy deliberations in the UK and had done so in the USA. I haven't found any evidence that it did in the UK, but it certainly had in the USA. It was explicitly cited in the Uniform Electronic Transactions Act 1999 (UETA) and also by implication in the Uniform Computer Information Transactions Act 1999 (UCITA) — a useful discussion of both is found in Weitzenboeck (2001).

Importantly, in UETA 1999 (Section 2(6)) a definition of 'electronic agent' was given thus:

> 'Electronic agent' means a computer program or an electronic or other automated means used independently to initiate an action or respond to electronic records or performances in whole or in part, without review or action by an individual.

And it was elaborated thus:

> This definition establishes that an electronic agent is a machine. As the term 'electronic agent' has come to be recognised, it is limited to a tool

function. [...] An electronic agent, such as a computer program or other automated means employed by a person, is a tool of that person. As a general rule, the employer of a tool is responsible for the results obtained by the use of that tool since the tool has no independent volition of its own. However, an electronic agent, by definition, is capable within the parameters of its programming, of initiating, responding or interacting with other parties or their electronic agents once it has been activated by a party, without further attention of that party.

While this Act proceeds on the paradigm that an electronic agent is capable of performing only within the technical strictures of its preset programming, it is conceivable that, within the useful life of this Act, electronic agents may be created with the ability to act autonomously, and not just automatically. That is, through developments in artificial intelligence, a computer may be able to 'learn through experience, modify the instructions in their own programs, and even devise new instructions'. Allen and Widdison, 'Can Computers Make Contracts?' 9 *Harv. J.L.&Tech* 25 (Winter, 1996). If such developments occur, courts may construe the definition of electronic agent accordingly, in order to recognise such new capabilities.

In other words, the question of the autonomy of such machines ('electronic agents') was explicitly recognised and given some space, and was then deferred for legislative and legal purposes without effect on the immediate implementation of UETA (i.e. it was left to a 'tool' function). That was precisely the point discussed at some length at the time, from a legal perspective, by Allen and Widdison (1996), to which I return below. Also relevant to this was the Nick Szabo's (1997) paper 'Fomalizing and Securing Relationships on Public Networks', discussing controls for 'smart contracts' (combining protocols with user interfaces to formalise relationships via computer networks).

So, the issue of autonomy of electronic agents was registered and deferred in UETA 1999 in the USA, and not quite taken up but tacitly noted and put outside deliberation in consultations on the ECA 2000 in the UK. Over the following decades to now, it has stimulated growing academic discussion among legal specialists (e.g. Weitzenboeck 2001; Chopra and White 2011; Pagallo 2013; Kurki and Pietrzykowski 2017). It has continued to be registered and deferred over this period in policy circles: raised by lobby groups and businesses adopting smart contracts; and considered repeatedly, with increasing seriousness but without resolution, by policymakers. The strongest move towards legal recognition of machine autonomy came from the EU appointed JURI Committee (2017) to draft recommendations for Civil Law Rules on Robotics which were presented to the European Parliament in 2017. In the version voted by the Parliament, however, the following recommendation had been deleted:

> creating a specific legal status for robots in the long run, so that at least the most sophisticated autonomous robots could be established as having the status of electronic persons responsible for making good any damage they may cause, and possibly applying electronic personality to cases where robots make autonomous decisions or otherwise interact with third parties independently.

Personhood

All that is by way of background, which leads me towards posing a question as a conversation starter.

The above details bring into focus the introduction of increasingly complex levels of automated systems (electronic agents) for mediating formal agreements between persons which are binding in law — i.e. contracts — for financial and commercial purposes. One of the considerations that arises there is whether and when such complex automated systems could be regarded as autonomous enough to be considered, in legal terms, persons themselves. *Should government policy (along contingent lines) and consequently laws be formulated to enable that when necessary, or is it perhaps necessary already for such policy (along implementation lines) and laws to be enacted?*

A key issue in considering this, from Allen and Widdison (1996) onwards, has been the distinction made between *natural persons* and *legal persons*. Natural persons are human individuals. Legal persons could be natural persons or could be collective entities (e.g. corporations) which are treated as individuals for the purpose of the law. Thus, GE or the Open University could be legal persons in a court case. So the definition of legal persons is more abstract and may allow for other kinds of entities to be so defined.

Incidentally, to complicate matters, in a lucid account of the juridical principles underpinning this distinction, Hans Kelsen (1967, p. 96) had observed that in law both natural (physical) persons and legal persons (he called them 'juristic persons') are similarly abstract, and thus natural persons should be distinguished from what is called 'human' in ordinary language. In law, all that matters is what behaviours and responsibilities can be attributed to whatever is defined as a person, not all the complex dimensions of being human (a natural person). One aspect of natural persons therefore forms a subset, and one aspect of corporations forms another, in the larger set of legal persons.

To consider the possibility of attributing legal personhood to electronic agents mediating contracts between persons, Allen and Widdison (1996) had presented a hypothetical situation. This is useful as an anchor to consider the question here:

> A buyer accesses an autonomous computer controlled by a seller — a widget merchant — and asks the price of widgets. The buyer has never had any dealings with the seller or the seller's computer before. Having checked that there are widgets in stock, the computer uses knowledge that it has acquired itself to calculate a price by means of a complex formula that it has evolved for itself. The computer then notifies the buyer of the price at which it is prepared to sell the widgets. The buyer responds by ordering a quantity of widgets from the computer at the price quoted. The computer informs the buyer that it accepts his order and then causes the widgets to be dispatched to the buyer, and an appropriate debit to be made from his bank account. The seller never knows that this transaction has occurred. Does the transaction constitute a valid contract? If so, between whom? (p. 29)

So, there are three parties here, two (the seller and buyer) are legal persons with contractual responsibilities and the third is that autonomous computer. The question is, under such circumstances, should some responsibility be laid at the door of the autonomous computer by declaring it to be a legal person also?

The question arises because the part played by the autonomous computer limits the seller's *awareness* of details of the contract. Legal responsibility has so far been premised on awareness underpinning the behaviour of legal persons (e.g. the difference between intentional, unintentional and accidental).

Notably, policies/laws ordinarily follow a kind of principle of inertia: changes are kept within the limits of what's necessary and pragmatic, and seldom stray into uncalled-for radical change. Attributing a new kind of legal personhood is a radical change. It won't be done unless it becomes unavoidable. The recourse so far for the above situation has been not to do that but to redefine the notion of awareness of responsibility: to remove the need for awareness of details of specific contracts and attach awareness instead to the general level of the electronic agent's contracting capacities and the relevant proprietorial relationship. Thus, the above situation can be dealt with by saying that the seller as legal person is responsible by owning the autonomous computer and intentionally deploying it to make such contracts with all buyers in the first place (by UETA 1999 this *electronic agent* is the seller's *tool*). The seller may be able to hold the autonomous computer's maker (an AI engineer) as owning some responsibility, but that involves a different contract.

Thus, this is really a question of *awareness distance* between contract and legal persons involved due to the electronic agent. So, the question posed above can be sharpened with Allen and Widdison's hypothetical case in mind: *Is it possible to imagine a degree of awareness distance whereby it becomes meaningless to assign full responsibility to the seller and therefore imperative that the autonomous computer is held separately responsible and declared a legal person?*

Another consideration there is that circumscribing responsibility could be a two-way concept: holding someone responsible may mean not holding others responsible. In the above case, making the autonomous computer a responsible legal person reduces the responsibility of the seller. One can envisage all sorts of situations where the seller might want to be absolved of direct contractual responsibility to aggrieved buyers and therefore champion the legal personhood of the autonomous computer.

At its most general, the question posed is: *can you think of any set of policy considerations — any kind of social/technological context — where an artificial system may necessarily have to be recognised as a legal person?* We may say, that would be a first step towards socially acknowledging the existence of AI in a meaningful sense, as something more than a tool.

I'm not sure whether that's one question or several packed together.

At any rate, Peter, this moves our conversation to a complementary area from the one we have addressed so far. In Part 1, we were concerned with the content of artificial systems such that they could meaningfully be understood as intelligent — *plausibly are* AI agents. In this Part 2, we can start by considering under what technological/social/policy circumstances might artificial systems necessarily come to be recognised as intelligent — *formally declared* AI agents?

22

Autonomy and Grounding Responsibility

Peter

- Why we don't hold children or the criminally insane responsible for their actions is outlined
- That crime and punishment might not apply to artificial agents is argued
- An example of how an AI can become untethered from its owner is proposed
- An argument is made for synthetic shame that is communally grounded

Before jumping into the question of what I think a responsible agent is, let me add to some of the government policy documents regarding AI that you have already harvested and presented. Back in 2016, the White House published their AI Research agenda. In 2018, this document was revived by the current administration and members of the public were asked to weigh in with their thoughts on a variety of identified strategies. I thought it would be informative to have a quick look at what the US Government believes are important topics of discussion with respect to Artificial Intelligence.

The National Artificial Intelligence Research and Development Strategic Plan, National Science and Technology Council (NSTC) (2016), covers the following topics:

- **Strategy 1:** Make long-term investments in AI research.
- **Strategy 2:** Develop effective methods for human–AI collaboration.
- **Strategy 3:** Understand and address the ethical, legal, and societal implications of AI.
- **Strategy 4:** Ensure the safety and security of AI systems.
- **Strategy 5:** Develop shared public datasets and environments for AI training and testing.
- **Strategy 6:** Measure and evaluate AI technologies through standards and benchmarks.
- **Strategy 7:** Better understand the national AI R&D workforce needs.

While some of these topics are concerned with the advancement of AI as a technology, clearly many elements of this document have a bearing on government policy, which bodes well for the recent turn in our discussion. For an overview of US AI policy, see the Future of Life Institute's webpage on this.

As for what constitutes a responsible agent, let's start with some initial observations. We generally don't hold children responsible for their misdeeds. However, to some degree we may hold parents accountable for the actions of their offspring. I suppose this is like the idea that we might hold the programmer or owner of an AI responsible for the actions of the AI. Like children, we don't seem to hold the criminally insane accountable for their actions. The same is true for the mentally disabled. The argument seems to be that it is unfair to hold an agent responsible for things that it does not understand.

At this point, it seems that if an AI-driven vehicle got into an accident resulting in a fatality, then we might, as a society, choose to blame the makers of the AI. Much like we would fine them for selling a faulty brake. However, if under similar circumstances, a person was at the wheel we might resign ourselves to saying: well accidents just happen. It seems that this lack of criticism stems from the fact that we are used to the idea that people drive cars, people make mistakes and we are not prepared to go back to a primarily perambulatory society. Before taking the wheel, very few of us contemplate the possibility that their actions may inadvertently lead to injury or even fatality — we are just used to living with this type of risk.

Punishment might play a role here. We can argue that a rational agent fearing punishment will act responsibly. This of course implies two things:

1. That there is a state that the agent would find disagreeable.
2. The agent has some sort of relationship with its future self.

While the ideas of Q-learning exist, where an AI attempts to construct a policy based on optimising long-term rewards, it would be hard to argue that a policy has the quality that we are looking for. My religious friends often marvel at the fact that those of us who are of an atheistic persuasion don't simply embark on a hedonistic life of moral turpitude — after all, what do we have to lose? Since, as I am sure you would agree, yourself and yours truly represent the epitome of what it means to be a responsible agent, I am not sure that the idea of punishment is at the heart of the issue.

Akin to punishment is the idea of insurance. Drivers and doctors are allowed to go about their business as long as those that are injured along the way are adequately compensated. In the case of doctors, it seems that it is 'we the people' that ironically have to cover the costs of the insurance premiums. So, maybe a responsible AI is one that can convince an actuarial scientist that it is an acceptable risk and is thus insurable at a reasonable rate.

Suman, you bring up the idea of responsibility at a distance. Following this line of thought I can easily imagine a state where an AI is completely untethered. Consider the following thought experiment. As an environmental enthusiast I might like to raise money to help deal with the problem of climate change — a worthy endeavour as the Green among us would agree. I might then go on national television and say something like: 'Environmentalists-beyond-US-Jurisdiction, if you are listening, it would be great if you could construct and launch an AI that automatically raises funds to prevent climate change'. We know from recent experience that, if said in a mirthful manner, such invocations would exonerate me of any form of responsibility. Let's assume that within a matter of hours an AI is launched that provides the following services: for a fixed fee, a set of state-of-the-art Graphical Processing Units (GPUs) will plead any case to any Deity of choice for a fixed amount of time. A kind of automated prayer service if you will. Initial customers may include: those seeking to win the next high school football game against a hated rival or a member of middle management hoping for a little help up the ladder. Let's assume that the AI has the feral intelligence needed to stay on the right side of the law, but does not have the moral compass required to distinguish between right and wrong. Before long, our Artificial Evangelist is targeting the elderly and the infirm. Since no human is in charge here, we must face what I think is the basic question of responsibility — how to create agents with a visceral sense of shame.

Now we can talk all day about how cooperative societies may have had some sort of evolutionary advantage allowing for the selection of traits such as guilt and honour. But let's not go down that rabbit hole again. Let us instead view emotions as the arbiters of self. When we are afraid, our 'run-and-hide' persona takes control. If we are feeling generous, our 'let's-lend-a-hand' program is instantiated. If shame is what is needed to invoke our responsible selves, then it is surely an underrated emotion. At this point, we return once again to the elephant in the room. How can shame exist without grounding?

Plainly put, if an agent does not grasp the meaning of the ramifications of its actions, then how can shame truly manifest? My opinion is that grounding in AI may start to occur once we are able to synthesise the following experiences and then encapsulate such learnings into computational constructs that can, at a future point, be invoked resulting in a kind of reminiscent state of mind. Such experiences may include:

- Learning how to use something.
- Learning how to do something.
- Learning how to construct something.
- Learning how to discriminate between things.
- Learning in which ways all things are analogous to all other things.
- A long list of numinous terms and sentiments …

Given all possible states of mind, I view the ability of achieving a given state of mind as particularly perplexing. But my sense of it is that a good metaphor is the mechanism behind thunder. Initially, rain drops in the clouds bump into one anther resulting in a buildup of charged particles. One by one, these particles start to meander their way down to Earth in search of an optimal path of least resistance. If they find a promising endpoint, they return to their source making their path slightly more attractive. At some point, one path dominates all others and the remaining particles rush down the newly discovered route. A lightning strike. My intuition is that similar mechanisms are afoot when we consider the way in which the meaning and state of mind for something like 'Injustice' emerges.

Well, given that I am arguing for the grounding problem to be solved before unleashing a set of free-wheeling AIs, the worthy reader might ask if there is anything else I would like. David Brooks argues for what he refers to as cultural determinism. The idea being that the norms and beliefs of a society are ultimately responsible for concepts such as responsibility. A few years back, I attended a lecture on experiments that went something like the following. While seated in an fMRI, subjects were shown a large number of images of people and asked to rate their appearance (X) on a scale of 1–10. After each rating was given, the subject was told that other subjects in the study gave an average score of Y. Sometimes X was larger than Y. Other times it was smaller. The key is that this reported score Y was not in fact generated by the other subjects. It was produced randomly. After seeing thousands of images, some of the earlier images were shown again with the idea that the subject would not remember them. The remarkable observation was that the subject ratings X were biased towards the rating Y that was previously produced in a random fashion. The fMRI measurements seemed to imply that instead of performing some sort of calculation to appear more like the perceived norm, the subject's facility for judgement was in fact rewired. They really liked those images more or less based on a random number. Such findings might explain a few things. There has always been the suspicion that appreciation for high art, such as classical music or modern paintings, is just an affectation. However, maybe such enthusiasts actually become aesthetically rewired by their exposure to the perceived opinions of the cultural elite.

Going back to cultural determinism, maybe we are just a loosely connected network of neural networks and that our motivations, like our sense of beauty and aesthetics, are just reflections of the collective. To this end, for shame to manifest it may be the case that, like humans, our AIs may need to be wired to be rewired by the perceived norms and beliefs of society. If we follow this path and force our AIs to become fully burdened with a grounded communal sense of shame, we might ask the question: what will we owe them in return?

23

Legal Autonomy: Rights and Responsibilities

Suman

- It is suggested that if convenient for some social purpose, electronic agents may be declared autonomous persons irrespective of scientific backing
- The existing concept of legal person is considered further in terms of rights and responsibilities
- Particular attention is given to the principles of fundamental human rights and animal rights
- Recent manifestos enumerating ethical principles for AI Research are raised

The Policy Pecking Order

Peter — I was expecting you to make the very reasonable argument that 'the grounding problem (needs) to be solved before unleashing a set of free-wheeling AIs'. Let me put your observations in the terms I was using earlier. You're saying that no policy-endorsed or legal personhood, with responsibilities and liabilities, should be attributed to electronic agents (in the UETA 1999 Section 2(6) sense) unless some grounding conditions are met. These conditions are of electronic agents being integrated into collective ethical norms and systems. Integration would mean that electronic agents would then factor such norms into their actions and respond to normative demands in a collectively understandable manner. Perhaps, also become 'punishable' or capable of 'shame' in some tractable way. You point to the complexity and fluidity of collectively held norms. Such norms are seldom uniformly espoused in a collective system. There's a great diversity of norms and we can co-exist amidst diversity. Also, norms are constantly modified by various mechanisms without necessarily destabilising collective existence. Indeed, adjustments might be necessary to maintain collective stability.

On a side note: You, rightly in my view, observe that ethical norms have little to do with religion. Far as I can see, in this respect appealing to religion is much like wanting some perpetual parental authority guiding you sternly instead of considering reasonable collective interests/systems yourself. In other words, that's much like assuming a perpetually infantile position.

Along the way, you point to some of the conundrums of legal personhood, to which I return below. You confirm that what I called 'awareness-distance' could become such that electronic agents are completely 'untethered'. You perceive some ethical dangers in that. Which means, I suppose, that it's best to keep those electronic agents actively tethered as tools till the grounding problem is solved. Of course, true to the Credo of Genuine AI Engineers (GAIEs), you start wondering what it will take to enable such grounding. It might be possible. Presently it seems like a distant possibility.

That's all well and good, so long as one assumes that policy and law makers (PLMs) actually listen to GAIEs trying to resolve grounding problems. Or, that the great collective of GAIEs are themselves unproblematically grounded and *au fait* with policy determinants and legal rationales. All might be okay if the PLMs wait till the GAIEs say, 'Hark, now we declare with one voice that this electronic agent has 'shame', let it be a person — but consider what we humans should give it in return?' And only after that do PLMs get on to the persuading and legislating that is their forte. But it may not work like that. In your view, what are the chances? In any given Government Commission on AI Policy,

GAIEs would be advisors and consultants. There would be more weighty AI industry 'stakeholders' who, for the uninitiated, are quite difficult to tell apart from GAIEs. And there would be heavyweight PLMs calling the shots. Advisors and consultants are low down the policy pecking order.

So, the following may come to pass before long. *Before any AI engineer is convinced that a given electronic agent can be declared an autonomous person — has moved from being a functional tool to being an intentional and grounded entity — that electronic agent could be declared such a person for policy and legal purposes. It may be done on the back of existing legal and policy rationales. This may be done effectively and with public consent, with only cursory attention to what AI engineers consider scientifically valid.* And once done, the declaration could generate its own reality. Or, to put it in very nearly your words, the 'public's facility for judgement could in fact be rewired accordingly'.

Put otherwise, in terms of legal rationality and policy imperatives, the mechanisms to enable that exist already.

Legal Persons (Again)

I have mentioned one of these mechanisms in my previous intervention: the distinction between *legal person* and *natural person*. Let's consider the obvious example of a corporation as a legal person. Say, the legal person Big Corp PLC is charged with unfair trading by a legal person called Whoever. Following proceedings, the court fines Big Corp PLC a billion dollars. This has consequences for some natural persons. A couple of executives of Big Corp PLC get pilloried in the press and are seen off with decent retirement packages. More quietly, a number of disposable workers are made redundant. But none of these natural persons are actually the legal person Big Corp PLC and none of them were particularly sentenced by the court. These unfortunate natural persons had a *relationship* to the working of the legal person Big Corp PLC without *being* Big Corp PLC. In fact, those natural persons' relationship was established by employment contracts between themselves as legal persons and Big Corp PLC as a legal person. So, has the legal person Big Corp PLC in fact been punished or shamed?

We generally accept that such a judicial proceeding is fair and mean-ingful. It is but a little stretch from there to considering that an electronic agent called MacHine could similarly be declared a legal person, pretty much irrespective of its capacities. Once so declared, MacHine can hold a bank account and be tracked by the tax office. At some point then MacHine may be accused of the legally defined crime of, say, 'culpable malfunction'. It may be subjected to legal procedures, represented by a lawyer, attested for and against by witnesses, and fined or otherwise pun-ished. This punishment would have consequences for physical persons who, as legal persons, have a contractual relation to MacHine's workings. But they are not in fact MacHine themselves. For instance, Peter Tu, who had signed an agreement with MacHine to keep it shipshape, might find himself in an uncomfortable spot. MacHine could thus be a very plausible legal person irrespective of whether Peter Tu considers it insufficiently grounded or autonomous. All that's needed is for a declaration of MacHine's legal personhood to be considered socially beneficial and acceptable by PLMs. The reasoning to enable the declaration without radically altering the whole juridical system exists already. We are accus-tomed to thinking of such personhood as legitimate.

Rights and Responsibilities

In a similar spirit, let me turn to another familiar line of reasoning, one that your intervention picks up: the relationship between *rights* and *responsibilities* (liabilities). These are more aptly terms of liberal political principle (Jean-Jacques Rousseau and Thomas Paine onwards) than, strictly speaking, jurisprudence or governance. But they have been embedded variously and firmly in legal systems and policy discourse. They seem morally resonant to a great many people now. They are evoked constantly in policy advocacy and consensus seeking.

The particular aspect of rights of interest here are *fundamental* (or *inviolable* or *inalienable*) *rights*. Entities are considered as possessing such rights simply by dint of existing. *Human rights* are the paradig-matic example. In principle, all humans have these rights simply by being born and living. There are four dimensions to the conception of such rights.

1. Recognition of fundamental rights signals that all humans are autonomous and cannot be unconditionally owned or used as functionaries or tools (e.g. they cannot be slaves, though their labour time can be bought so long as the labour is not inhumane).
2. To be effective for a given human *H*, these rights have to be recognised for all humans by some authority (e.g. a government) with jurisdiction over the domain where *H* exists. Recognition means that the authority assumes responsibility for securing those rights for all humans under its jurisdiction.
3. The authority's responsibility for securing those rights is a distributed authority. Thereby all humans under its jurisdiction also become responsible for securing those rights for others. Since *H* is possessed of such rights, *H* is obliged to respect and secure those rights for others.
4. It is expected that *H*, being possessed of such rights, would be able to claim them when they are threatened. Others too may be able to claim them on *H*'s behalf when necessary.

As you noted, Peter, practicality demands that fundamental rights be operationalised differently at times without being changed. This means that (1) is always unnegotiable and (2) is always necessary. However, (3) and (4) might be worked variably. Children are an obvious example. The securing of their fundamental rights falls more strongly to appointed proxies (e.g. guardians) than for adults. Expectations of children being able to claim their own or being obliged to respect others' fundamental rights are limited.

Advocacy for fundamental *animal rights* bring an interesting turn to the concept of rights. Animal rights are now backed by policy directives and legal provision in various regimes. A few adjustments to the paradigm of *human rights* appear here. Here (1) carries a powerful symbolic and political charge. Simply recognising rights for animals, however defined, attributes their very existence with some degree of autonomy where none was assumed before. As above, (2) is necessary to make that effective. (3) and (4) are where animal rights differ markedly from human rights. For (3), recognising these rights brings no obligation to animals to respect or secure those rights for other animals. And (4) entails no expectation that animals would be able to claim such rights. With regard to animals, (3) and (4) are operationalised purely through human proxies. Humans are responsible for securing those rights for animals and for claiming them on animals' behalves when needed.

It is not difficult to see how these ways of recognising and operationalising fundamental rights may be extended to electronic agents, irrespective of whether they are grounded in a scientifically valid sense. Fundamental *machine rights* could be recognised along the model of animal rights. Recognition thus by an authority would in itself redefine electronic agents, with policy and legal effect, as autonomous to some degree. GAIEs might quibble. But nevertheless, the same engineers may also be declared liable as proxies for ensuring those rights are secured. I daresay those engineers would then get down to developing machine-rights-claim algorithms for electronic agents.

When?

There are reams and reams of academic publications and policy documents already out there on these issues. Given how obvious the policy and legal pathways towards declaring legal personhood and machine rights are, one wonders why that hasn't happened already. That's especially since the awareness distance between actions by electronic agents and persons responsible for the consequences is reasonably wide already. But such declarations could appear at any time. They could appear without contradicting core functioning principles of jurisprudence and governance.

If such declarations have not appeared yet, that's not because AI engineers have protested that electronic agents are not ready for it yet. It doesn't matter whether grounding problems remain or whether intentionality is far from understood. Nor is it significant whether complex automation is being palmed off as 'intelligence' or 'smartness' at present.

Very likely, such declarations will be made whenever policy and legal gurus feel that making them is more profitable and cost-effective than not making them. That could be whenever the appropriate lobby groups get on to them.

For instance, lobby groups may perk up if it seems that insurance risks can be capitalised by declaring that electronic agents are legal persons. Or if they calculate that the regulatory liabilities of executives can be reduced by conferring machine rights.

Manifestos

My argument, in brief, is that electronic agents may be made autonomous in law and policy well before AI engineers make them so in practice. Or, even if AI engineers fail to do so. Whether machines are consensually regarded as meaningfully intelligent, intentional, autonomous, normatively grounded, etc. is more in the hands of PLMs than in the hands of AI engineers and researchers.

At present, amidst burgeoning publications on AI principles by governmental and corporate bodies, there is also a great flowering of AI manifestos from professional associations and research collectives. These invariably announce ethical resolutions. There are so many of these around now that such documents have themselves become the subject of research (Yi *et al.*, 2018; Whittlestone *et al.*, 2019). Have you signed any?

The corporate ones are performances of reassuring virtuousness and good intentions, with an eye on publicity. Microsoft's *The Future Computed* (2018) and the Google CEO Sundar Pichai's 'AI at Google: Our Principles' (2018) are obviously such.

I find myself more interested in the kind that have appeared from your professional brethren — AI R&D folk — especially through the Future of Life Institute. These include the 'Open Letter: Research Priorities for Robust and Beneficial AI' (2015) accompanied by a paper (Russell *et al.*, 2015); then bolstered by the 'Asilomar AI Principles' (2017). When I checked last the Open Letter had been signed by more than 8000 persons. These are mostly researchers, engineers and other stakeholders, including many of the great and the good. What is your take on these manifestos? The Open Letter is worth contemplating carefully.

To me these seem to be as much *anticipatory disclaimers* as performances of virtuousness. They express a certain nervousness among AI aficionados. This is not because the aficionados really think AI will be untethered by themselves. It's because they know that PLMs will decide whether that should happen. And they will decide irrespective of whether the aficionados feel it should happen. But that might be a cynical way of looking at the manifestos.

24

Autonomy: Limiting and Conferring Rights

Peter

- The Cassandra-like nature of the Genuine AI Engineer (GAIE) is revealed
- The role played by AI in the 2016 elections is reviewed
- The plight of the black footed ferret (BFF) is considered along with arguments for why we should care

---

Engineers and Managers

Cassandra, the daughter of King Priam and Queen Hecuba of Troy, was offered the gift of prophecy by the God Apollo in return for becoming his paramour. After receiving the faculty for predicting the future, Cassandra decided to back out of the deal. In revenge, Apollo modified his boon into a curse: even though Cassandra could accurately predict the future, nobody would ever believe her. I would argue that the modern engineer has been similarly cursed. The Space Shuttle Challenger tragedy comes to mind.

It seems to me that we are going to have to rely on responsible management, as opposed to Genuine AI Engineers (GAIEs), to decide if and when an AI should be given the power of agency. In one of your earlier interventions, you mentioned the example of an AI agent deciding, on the fly, what price should be set for a given transaction. In a recent article (Calvano *et al.,* 2019) we find that, in fact, such AI agents may potentially learn how to collude with each other without direct communication or being explicitly programmed to do so. Applying reinforcement learning methods, such as those used to develop superhuman AI Go players, agents can learn that price wars are to be avoided. When multiple AI agents are working under similar principles, a kind of price fixing can ensue. Can we really expect responsible management to intervene? On a similar note, let's consider the exploits of Cambridge Analytica in the USA in 2016. What follows is a synopsis of what transpired in terms of data manipulation (for the political background see Kroll, 2018).

The current state of the art with regard to poll-targeted advertising is to establish a demographic profile for voters in a swing state. This involves concepts such as ethnicity, age, geographic location, marital status, type of employment … Given such information, the probability of a given voter casting his or her vote can be estimated. This allows a political party the opportunity to optimise their efforts to get voters agreeable to their agenda to cast votes. While collecting and curating such demographic knowledge is expensive, it seems to pay off as evidenced by those 2008 and 2012 US Presidential election campaigns by Obama's camp.

Going beyond demographics, there was a hypothesis that if the psychological profile of a given voter is available, then targeted advertising could be used to either increase or decrease their probability of voting one way or another. An accepted tool for producing a psychological profile is an extensive questionnaire. Questions such as 'do you like new experiences?' or 'do you find such and such irritating?' are answered by the subject. It turns out that in general people can be clustered based on their responses to the questionnaire. This results in a set of psychological dimensions known as OCEAN (each letter stands for a mode of variation). For example, O stands for openness to new experiences. On one extreme of the O-scale, people are attracted to new forms of art and different types of food. On the other is what you might call a meat-and-potatoes kinda gal who buys her art from the Thomas Kinkade gallery. Taking the questionnaire provides for accurate estimates of one's OCEAN coordinates and this can be viewed as a psychograph.

Cambridge Analytica, sponsored by the billionaire Mercer family, proposed the construction of a psychograph for every person in a given swing state allowing for efficient targeting of tailored advertisements, both positive and negative. However, their approach got around the problem of administering the long questionnaire to everyone in Ohio or Pennsylvania. This shortcut was as follows:

1. A researcher in Cambridge University built an online app that, after receiving consent from Facebook users, administers the questionnaire online.
2. The researcher then looked at the subject's Facebook user profile (what they liked to eat, where they hung out, etc.) and used this user information to see if he could build an AI-based regression to predict the answers of the questionnaire — he was successful.
3. Without consent, the researcher then applied this AI regression to all of the *friends* of everyone that took the questionnaire, generating estimated psychographs for all such individuals. This resulted on the order of 50 million estimated psychographs.
4. Facebook was OK with this as long as it was for academic purposes. The researcher then sold these psychographs to Cambridge Analytica (Steve Bannon was on the board at that time) for application to the 2016 campaign. Much of the outrage expressed around Facebook and Cambridge Analytica stems from this move.
5. In order to get Mercer campaign finance, you had to use Cambridge Analytica. The Ted Cruz campaign was the first to try this approach in the 2016 primaries. They found that Republican National Convention (RNC) demographic data was more accurate and hence the approach was abandoned.
6. When Donald Trump became the nominee, he accepted Mercer's financial backing, got Steve Bannon as his campaign manager, and started down this path as well. Once again it turned out the RNC demographic data was far more accurate than the Cambridge Analytica data. Cambridge Analytica staff ended up focusing on traditional get-out-the vote efforts, such as manning phone banks and putting up signs.

In terms of our conversation, this cautionary tale tells us that the decision-makers who were fine with an inappropriate exploitation of AI included: Billionaires, Industrial Giants, Sitting Senators, Respected Professors and a future White House Security Advisor. It appears that responsible management is indifferent to both price-fixing and invasion of privacy. Maybe the larger concern is what happens when AI becomes the weapon of choice for adversarial management? The zero-day hack known as Stuxnet was used in 2011–2012 to destroy centrifuges used for the processing of fissionable material; SONY Pictures was a victim of cyber-attack in 2014; and social robots were deployed to hack the US election in 2016. When dealing with the lawlessness of domestic or international conflicts, I don't see GAIEs as having much of a voice at all with regard to being responsible for AI.

Manifestos and Rights

As for manifestos, I have not jumped on to that particular bandwagon. However, I have helped to organise various forums for public conversation on this topic. Back in 2017, I worked with folks from the National Institute of Standards and Technology (NIST) on the Video Analytics and Public Safety (VAPS) workshop. This was a gathering of government officials, various user communities, members of the legal profession, public advocates as well as academic and industrial researchers. I organised the industrial research panel discussions. The underlying theme of this effort was to try to build a diverse community of stakeholders that can contemplate this topic in a collegial and constructive manner. For those interested, our official report (NIST, 2017) is in the public domain.

Let's turn to the question of AI rights. At the moment, this seems to be a bit of a hot topic. There are a number of books out there, such as David J. Gunkel's *Robot Rights* (2018). But resorting to the literature is not exactly in the spirit of our conversations, so I will (as is my wont) just hold forth on the topic. When we consider animal rights, it seems to me that one significant factor is cognitive complexity. While few of us would shed a tear for the demise of a mosquito, only a monster would take joy in the death of a wise and gentle elephant. Unless of course it was to make an argument regarding the evils of alternating current (AC), as in the grim tale of Thomas Edison and Topsy the Elephant (see Stallwood, 2018). Right now, the threshold seems to be fish. There are a surprising number of academic investigations with regards to the question of whether or not fish feel pain. The Japanese have a special method called 'Ike Jime' for killing fish almost instantly. It's painless and makes for tastier sushi. So, in addition to cognitive complexity, the quantity of pain also seems to be part of the calculation. I recently heard the following argument:

1. When considering the concept of cognitive complexity, cows and chickens are comparable.
2. The life of a factory chicken is miserable.
3. Cows cannot be produced in this manner and so their lives are relatively pleasant in comparison.
4. One chicken can feed a person for one day.
5. In contrast a cow can feed a person for a year!

So, if N is the number of neurons associated with a meal and S is the corresponding amount of suffering, then $S*N$ for a juicy steak is orders of magnitude smaller than that of a roast chicken. Putting issues of global warming, mad cow disease and unhealthy cholesterol aside, by this logic we should eat more burgers and fewer buffalo wings.

Ironically, we need pain and fear as feedback to keep us alive. There are cases where people feel no pain. Such individuals are in constant danger of unwittingly hurting themselves. There are also a few individuals that have lost the capacity for fear. While they are in general extremely happy, they all too often end up in an abusive relationship or life-threatening situation. They simply march down paths where you or I dare not go. While usually more stoic than humans, most animals experience pain and fear for the same reasons that we do. Thus, we view unnecessary suffering as inhumane. Of course, we have not always had such charitable points of view. In the not so distant past, beasts of burden were routinely housed in dark rooms doomed to a life of endlessly pushing a mill wheel round and round and in constant fear of the lash. As for the shame of human slavery, much has been and still needs to be said. While pain and suffering are part and parcel of the natural world, I don't see why it needs to be a prerequisite for intelligence. I think we could construct an AI that is indifferent to its 'lot in life'. We need another motivation for robot rights.

Whales serenade one another across vast distances. Dolphins surge towards then break the ocean surface simply to do a back flip in front of the sun. After taking a course on meditation, podcaster Ezra Klein can now peer blissfully off into the distance for hours at a time. One of Ezra's recent guests, Jenny Odell, waxes lyrically about the 'art of attention' (Klein, 2019). One of her recent projects was to build a collection of discarded items and put them on display. Each object was thoroughly researched in terms of where it was made, what purpose it served and the path that it took from factory to municipal dump. For Jenny, each subject of investigation was like an Ansel Adams photograph. While she suffered for her art — a whole summer with no time for parties or idle chit-chat — she paints a picture of experiencing the universe in an exuberant manner.

Not too long ago, the black-footed ferret (BFF) was the rarest mammal on earth. As a species they were confronted by the three Ps: Ploughs, Poisons and Plagues. As is so often the case, we humans were responsible for all three. The BFF lives on the Great Plains of North America. They have extremely long canine teeth. They survive by hunting and killing prairie dogs that build large boroughs connected by complex tunnels. The BFF enters the borough and when it finds a prairie dog, it bites the neck of its prey with vampire-like zeal. The dog eventually suffocates and dies. The BFF then arches its back, squeals in delight and does a kind of victory dance. Enormous efforts are underway to keep the BFF from extinction. Conservationists are even considering the use of CRISPR gene therapy methods.

Vox's Dylan Matthews and Byrd Pinkerton (2018) ask, 'is it worth it?' My take is that an exploding supernova pales in comparison to the moment when a BFF sinks its teeth into a prairie dog's neck. Such an experience is unique, it took billions of years to produce and cannot be duplicated. It may even be as extraordinary as Jenny Odell's relationship with rubbish. If artificial agents gain some sort of capacity to experience the universe, then I would argue for their rights to pursue such potential.

Suman, it is hard to say how your four dimensions of agent rights might apply here. A couple of points to consider:

1. As previously described, the concept of artificial pain and suffering might not exist,
2. An AI may be driven to consume resources in a manner that is unsustainable, and of course,
3. An AI might pose an existential threat to yours truly.

If we choose to ignore the rights of our artificial minions, one wonders what future generations will think of us. Victorian scientists obsessed with proving that men and women of colour were subhuman are now the topics of less than flattering novels. I guess the answer might depend on who or what ends up writing the history books.

25

Note on Rights and Data Matters

Suman

- The significance of empathy distance and awareness distance in considering animal or machine rights is underlined
- Tensions in governmental AI policies regarding data are discussed
- The question 'what are data?' is addressed briefly

Nuancing Rights (A Bit)

In my previous intervention, I had failed to underline a nuance in the sketchy outlines of animal rights and, hypothetically, machine rights. Peter, you have very thoughtfully explored that nuance in the latter part of your response. It seems, however, that my carelessness (and your enthusiasm for black footed ferrets) has possibly produced a tiny puff of confusion. Let me try to blow that away before moving on to other AI policy issues.

Of course, advocates for animal rights do not think of the tsetse fly and the buffalo similarly, any more than advocates for machine rights would think of the pocket calculator and the financial contract-making electronic agent similarly. Animal-rights advocates would be inclined to allow buffaloes rights rather than tsetse flies; machine-rights advocates to the contracting electronic agent rather than the pocket calculator (duh).

You observe that rights for animals are considered in terms of a given species' complexity and capacity for feeling pain (suffering). I am not sure complexity is actually a relevant factor in itself. It is not clear to me that there is a norm for complexity whereby the many species of tsetse flies can be regarded as being negligibly complex compared to the three species of buffaloes. The capacity for experiencing pain is the more determinate factor in distinguishing which animals should or should not have rights. Determining that, as you say, is a moving boundary. Once the issue is resolved for fish, there may yet be hope for tsetse flies. Accounting for suffering may involve complexity as a factor, but complexity alone is not the key for determining a species' rights. For machines, however, complexity is all — but let's dwell upon animals a bit longer.

With regard to rights, there's a further nuance within the gradations of animals' capacity for feeling pain or suffering. Simply determining a species' mechanism for experiencing pain — as a sensory stimulus-response and behaviour system — is not quite the capping argument either. Given that infringing, claiming and securing animal rights is monopolised by humans, it is our human relationship to animals which is crucial. The issue is whether this determination of a given species' experience of pain is something that humans can empathise with in terms of their own experience of pain.

Whether a prairie dog's pain is pain in the way humans experience pain is a moot point. It may be argued that humans understand their own pain in relation to lots of other conditions of human experience (including the parameters of human consciousness), and other animal species do the same in terms of their conditions. The degree to which these human and animal experiences are objectively comparable or matchable is at present an indeterminate affair. That's not unrelated to the fact that some humans feel pain and suffer without any immediate stimulus-response mechanism, and even without evident behavioural symptoms — the domain of psychology. And, of course, a few masochistic souls enjoy pain. Let's not speculate on whether a prairie dog might not get its kicks from having a black-footed ferret latching on to its neck, and die in agonised bliss.

In any case, attributing or withholding rights with regard to some animal species is mainly a matter of the human–animal relationship. If it can be determined that pain is felt by an animal species in a way that humans can empathise with, rights may reasonably be conferred; if it can't, no rights. Let me call this the *empathy distance* between humans and other animal species. We are apt to concede animal rights to species where the empathy distance is narrow (e.g. a buffalo) and reluctant to consider it where the empathy distance is wide (e.g. a tsetse fly).

In suggesting that animal rights as conceived and accepted now could provide a model for putative machine rights, I did not mean that the former can be adopted wholesale for the latter. The model of animal rights offers a limited analogy for modelling machine rights. In both, the infringement, claiming and securing of rights could be monopolised by humans and thus be legislatively enactable and publicly acceptable. But the difference is that for machine rights to be enacted, we don't have to wait for electronic agents to feel pain and suffer akin to some animal species. Genuine AI Engineers (GAIEs) might wonder whether suffering can be instilled in artificial systems, but that's not the point.

The part played by *empathy distance* in talking of animal rights can be plausibly replaced by what I dubbed, in an earlier intervention, as *awareness distance* in relation to electronic agents. The machine that can undertake acts of which the person who is responsible for the consequences of those acts is imperfectly aware or unaware — that could be thought of as the awareness distance in the human–machine relationship. This has to do with the machine's complexity alone and has no bearing on questions of suffering.

Just as the human–animal relationship judged by an empathy distance motivates animal rights legislation, so could the human–machine relationship judged by an awareness distance motivate machine rights legislation. No question here of whether machines suffer, exhibit feeling behaviour, etc. No need for humans to empathise with machines. A desire for humans to be absolved of responsibility for the consequences of automatised acts could be sufficient to call for machine rights.

Data Matters

At present, questions about AI's legal personhood or rights in policy circles are a relatively marginal matter, a kind of outer horizon. Policy concerns are generally more immediate: guiding implementation of so-called

AI systems in various sectors, developing an AI R&D and skills-based workforce, acclimatising consumers to automated systems, capitalising on AI opportunities for national interests (which is now coterminous with business interests), managing the fallout of automation (such as job losses), etc. In fact, the points you cited from the US government's *The National Artificial Intelligence Research and Development Strategic Plan* (NSTC 2016, US Strategic AI Plan hereafter) give a reasonable sense of these. I started with questions of personhood and rights because, in policy circles, those seem to refer to something constitutive of AI. We have argued that they aren't really. Otherwise, the more immediate action-and-strategy areas seem more after the fact of AI. They don't really go into what AI is, but chart ways forward for policy given that AI is here, is developing or is imminent. Having said that, it occurs to me that amidst these policy considerations there is a factor which invariably comes up with the notion that it has a constitutive relationship with AI: data, or with more heft, Big Data. Let's turn to this awhile.

As the US Strategic AI Plan 2016 puts it: 'many fundamental new tools and technologies are needed to achieve intelligent data understanding and knowledge discovery. Further progress is needed in the development of more advanced machine learning algorithms that can identify all the useful information hidden in big data' (pp. 17–18). Strategy 5 is devoted to it, and recently the President's Executive Order 13859 *Maintaining American Leadership in Artificial Intelligence* (White House, 2019) set some short-term goals accordingly. For US policy, the underpinning thinking about data generally and in relation to AI can be gleaned from the US Government's Federal Data Strategy website and the National Science Foundation's (NSF) *Harnessing the Data Revolution* project website.

UK policy documents are more given to high-flown sentiments, but to not dissimilar effect in this regard. The UK government's *Artificial Intelligence Sector Deal* (BEIS and DCMA 2018, AI Deal hereafter) enumerated 'Grand Challenges' rather than the modestly characterised 'Strategies' in the US, one of which is: 'AI and Data Economy — We will put the UK at the forefront of the artificial intelligence and data revolution'. Data seem to be central in the UK's AI Deal 2018 and are anchored consistently to AI throughout. This is so in the Parliamentary discussions which informed the AI Deal: a House of Commons, Science and Technology Committee report *Robotics and Artificial Intelligence* (2016), and a House of Lords, Select Committee on Artificial Intelligence report *AI in the UK: Ready, Willing and Able?* (2017). Insofar as data in general and in relation to AI go, the underpinning thinking is found in two reports produced by the Royal Society and British Academy in June 2017: *Data Governance: Landscape Review* and *Data Management and Use: Governance in the 21st Century.*

Judging from these policy statements and sources, it seems clear that the area of data management in relation to AI at a national level is perched on the fault line of a schism. In summary:

- On the one hand, it is recognised that AI capacities are best developed and tested by gathering, integrating and opening access to large quantities and varieties of high-quality data. That is, both existing data brought to constituting AI systems and data such as may be processed through self-developing AI systems. GAIEs and AI systems-in-development should have open access to data sources, preferably globally, but that actually means a great many other parties — perhaps even all individuals who are captured in data form — should too. GAIEs are (often severely) limited in their ability to interpret and understand the political and cultural import of various ranges of data, and the AI systems-in-development may well exacerbate those limitations to socially detrimental effect. From a policy point of view, capitalising on and socially grounding AI calls for integrated and openly accessible data sources, preferably with some form of expert gatekeeping with an eye on data quality and veracity.
- On the other hand, managing data is understood as principally a policy matter to do with *not* permitting wide access or integration, or with restricting data. To begin with, it is clear from national-level statements such as the US Strategic AI Plan 2016 or the UK AI Sector Deal 2018 that these nation-states are in competition for the top-spot. And these are very far from alone, there are numerous others — I have a few observations on PR China's AI policy in mind for a later intervention. While the GAIEs located in each nation-state can only be as able as they are and policymakers can but hope they are more able than

those in others, data management is more directly in the hands of policymakers. These national-level statements are complicated by the fact that a range of private interests cutting across nation-states play a significant role. In many respects AI developments and data acquisition have been dominated by the private sector, and data is more in private hands than in the public. Governmental policymakers are in the position of courting private corporations and having to protect corporate interests to protect their own. One of the ways in which corporations maintain their edges in capitalist markets is by exclusive ownership of data — or, at the least, privileged access and prerogatives on exploitation of data. Then there's the issue of how that exploitation of data affects citizens' privacy and freedoms, which governments can scarcely profess indifference towards. And, of course, there are always overriding security and defence considerations: walls need to be erected against data access by criminals, hackers, terrorists, spies, rogue states, investigators fishing for something nefarious to leak …

So, national level AI policies related to data consist in some such declaration as the following: To make our nation the global AI leader, we need to have robust, accessible and open data sources, but such that private ownership/prerogatives on data are protected (especially of global corporations), other nations don't get an upper hand, personal data and privacy are protected (or, at least, citizens think so), and baddies are kept at bay. We have to try and open the door which says 'pull' by pushing it.

Hence a question for GAIEs: *what bearing, if any, do these conflicted data policy thrusts have on AI R&D?*

What are Data?

Let me clarify the spirit in which I pose the question for GAIEs. I am not looking for a straight plunge into declarations on quality of data, optimising data analysis, securing personal data, constant data generation, data ethics, etc. Those are all issues arising after the fact of data usage in particular contexts. Nor am I hoping immediately for a vision of the future with regard to data analysis and AI R&D. I was reading that NIST (2017) VAPS workshop report you had mentioned in your previous intervention with interest. So, I am reminded of this observation from the panel on 'Industry Perspectives' (which you graced, Peter):

> With the increasing reliance on machine learning methods such as deep learning, developers will require access to ever-increasing quantities of data for both training and evaluation purposes. Going beyond static datasets (which can be overlearned), future algorithms will require constant novelty allowing for a state of never-ending unsupervised learning. This will require a migration from data sets to data sites and, perhaps, data cities.

This sounds like an important resolution (or prediction), though I'm not sure I understand its import. In any case, it seems to be premised on everyone consensually knowing what 'data' connotes already and moving forward from there (I daresay that was the case in the workshop, confined though it was to video analytics?).

For policy considerations, it seems to me (perhaps not for the first time in this conversation) that a back-to-basics sense of 'data' is worth bringing up and keeping in view. I tend to be sceptical of the way policy-makers and policy implementers conceive of data and become lyrical about Big Data. All the above-mentioned policy papers refer to 'data' as more or less one kind of thing. Data seem to be some more or less undifferentiable substance which have vaguely to do with statistics, and which don't need much disaggregation (quality gradations/personal or not/public and private seem to cover the main policy distinctions). The uses to which this substance 'data' is or can be put appear to be the overwhelming policy concern. It seems possible that a finer-grained sense of what 'data' refers to might actually have something to do with policy concerning it. I confess to an irate twitch when the term 'data' is evoked reverentially in policy circles, even the humble ones that I occasionally find myself in — the way in which the boss says, 'The data shows that ...' or 'Our data-based strategy is ...', as if evoking 'data' brings a higher confirmation.

So, to wrap up this intervention, a quick stab at addressing 'what are data?' Not, I hasten to say, an attempt at defining the term. I was looking at an article (Zins, 2007) which examines 42 definitions of 'data' (and 'information' and 'knowledge') by persons accustomed to using data, and felt dissuaded from adding to their number. All seemed pertinent in particular contexts, none seemed to fully cover the matter. I attempt something both narrower and more wordy here: a brief description of the relationship between 'data' terms which you and I may agree on for our purposes, or modify as we go along. Here we go:

> *Data* are organised and presented in *datasets*; 'data' is the generic or umbrella term for datasets and their contents. A dataset may be analysed in itself, or in analysing one dataset others may be brought to bear on it, or a number of datasets may be analysed in interpenetrating ways. Such analysis may lead to the production of secondary datasets derived from a primary range of datasets.
>
> A dataset is a collection or accumulation of items of individual *datum*, such that each datum can be comparably related to all other items of datum in terms of likeness or difference, spatio-temporal location, influences and so on. There is a circular relationship between datum and dataset: a dataset is such because it has comparable items of datum; a datum is such because it can be expressed in a comparable way to other items of datum to form a dataset. Comparability of items of datum along with the scale of a dataset's coverage of datum open the doors of *analysis*.
>
> Obviously, that doesn't tell us what a datum (item of datum) is. A datum could be anything that can be expressed in a comparable manner to other items of datum in a dataset. This could include what we would commonly think of as a fact, feature, note, point, sound, text, image, claim, observation, declaration, action, etc. for any domain, phenomenon or object.
>
> Datasets, and therefore data generally, necessarily involve the quantification of collected or accumulated items of datum at some primary level. Quantification is essential for rendering items of datum comparable and functional for analysis. For the purposes of this conversation, 'quantitative data' is a tautology and 'qualitative data' a misnomer.

26

Note on Qualia and Using Data

Peter

- Qualia research and its implications are discussed
- Various tools used for the analysis of data are reviewed
- Arguments are made regarding the over-reliance on data in AI research
- Characteristics of the Data Scientist are observed

Qualia

Suman, your initial argument for why government agencies might be motivated to grant personhood to artificial agents is based on their desire to escape from having to take responsibility for the actions of such AIs. In terms of animal rights, you promote the idea of empathy distance. Speaking as a Canadian, I can't help but be reminded of Brigitte Bardot's campaign against the great Canadian seal hunt (Usborne, 2006). Both of these arguments seem to be human-centric, in that they are motivated by the desire to either avoid consequences or to make us feel better about ourselves. I fear that this point of view is just a tad cynical. So, let me take one more stab at making a phenomenological argument for subjective experience as a motivation for AI rights.

In *Principia Qualia* (2016) by Michael Edward Johnson, we see an interesting approach to understanding conscious experience. The author argues that there are two basic classes of consciousness theories: top-down (a.k.a. 'higher-order' or 'cognitive' theories) and bottom-up. Top-down theories are constructed around how consciousness feels as well as the dynamics of how the brain implements what we experience. The top-down theories use relatively high-level psychological concepts as their basic primitives. In contrast, the authors argue for a bottom-up approach that is based on theories that are closer to physics in nature. Their goal is to try to find a mathematical approach from which all the high-level phenomenology could naturally emerge. Highlights of these ideas include:

1. **Qualia formalism:** For any given conscious experience, there exists, in principle, a mathematical object isomorphic to its phenomenology. This is a formal way of saying that consciousness is in principle quantifiable.
2. **Qualia structuralism:** This mathematical object has a rich set of formal structures. Based on the regularities and invariances in phenomenology, it seems safe to say that qualia have a non-trivial amount of structure. It likely exhibits connectedness (i.e. it's a unified whole, not the union of multiple disjointed sets), and compactness, and so we can speak of qualia as having a topology.
3. **Valence realism:** Valence is a crisp phenomenon of conscious states upon which we can apply a measure. Some experiences do feel holistically better than others, and (in principle) we can associate a value to this. Feelings such as pleasantness could be encoded into the mathematical object isomorphic to the experience in an efficient way. That is, we should look for a concise equation, not an infinitely large lookup table for valence.

With this point of view, the authors argue that all conscious entities may have a kind of shared experience. A good metaphor for how experiences may differ from species to species is similar to how various types of musical instruments have different resonant frequencies. Thus, experiences are comparable but also unique. To lose a species like the black-footed ferret or to deny an AI the ability to achieve its full phenomenological potential would be like robbing the universal orchestra of its woodwind or percussion sections.

The qualia folks hint that their theory has relevance to other philosophical questions, including the binding problem, free will, the is-vs.-ought dilemma as well as questions of individual identity. They even feel that their work may address what may be our greatest existential threat — nihilism. With such tantalising promises, I could not help but remember a trip I took to New York City to see a live performance of 'How to succeed at business without really trying', starring the great Matthew Broderick. Yes, that Matthew Broderick from *Ferris Beuller's Day Off* (1986, teen-comedy film). During much of the show, one could not help but come away with a poor view of Wall Street and by extension humanity in general. Under such conditions, one could easily come up with a theory of empathy distance or the conviction that the good and the great are simply trying to avoid taking responsibility for their indirect actions. But then, like the qualia scientists, Matthew Broderick looks at the audience and says not to worry, because we can always count on the brotherhood of man. So Suman, unfurrow your brow, and listen to Broderick sing 'Brotherhood of Man' and wash your concerns away (check out the YouTube clip if you will). Now let's talk about data!

Data

Before wallowing in a 'depends on what the definition of *is* is' contemplation of number theory, I would like to discuss the basics of how data are used today. In terms of data analysis, a generative model provides the means for synthesising all variable values for a particular phenomenon, both those that can be observed in the world as well as latent variables that can only be computed from those observations. Given a distribution where x is observable and y is not, a generative model can be sampled resulting in sets of (x,y) pairs. In contrast, discriminative models provide a mechanism for estimating the latent variables y, by analysing the observed variables x. Whether it is a basic regression routine or a multilayer convolutional neural network, the goal for discriminative methods is to compute $y = f(x)$ where $f()$ is known as a model. In simple terms, discriminative models infer outputs based on inputs, while generative models synthesise both inputs and outputs, typically given some hidden parameters. Deep Learning (DL), which we have discussed at length in previous exchanges, is a good example of the discriminative approach to data analysis. In terms of generative approaches, let's start by lingering a bit on the topic of Variational Methods. A great primer on the topic is 'Gibbs Sampling for the Uninitiated' by Resnik and Hardisty (2010). A short review of this important bit of math is as follows.

Consider the following experiment. For a given series of flips, of a possibly unfair coin, we make the observation χ = htthhthttt, where h stands for heads and t for tails. Note that for this experiment, there were four heads and six tails. The question that we would like to answer is: what is the probability distribution of y, which is the value of the next coin flip, given the observation χ? That is to say, what is $P(y|\chi)$?

We can start this discussion by assuming that the coin that we are flipping is weighted and can be described by the parameter π, where $p(y = h) = \pi$ and $p(y = t) = 1 - \pi$. What is the value of π that would make our observation χ the most likely observation? To answer this, we must know how to calculate $p(\chi|\pi)$ — the probability of the observation χ given a specific value of π. It turns out that $p(\chi|\pi)$ is equal to $\pi^4(1 - \pi)^6$ since we observed four heads and six tails. A plot for various values of $p(\chi|\pi)$ vs. π is shown in the following figure (see Figure 1).

It looks like the value of π associated with the maximum probability is 0.4. Intuitively, this makes sense and a little bit of calculus would confirm your intuition. We can now approximate $P(y|\chi)$ by $p(y|\pi = 0.4)$, which says that the probability of the next coin flip being heads is 0.4 and the probability of the next coin flip being tails is 0.6.

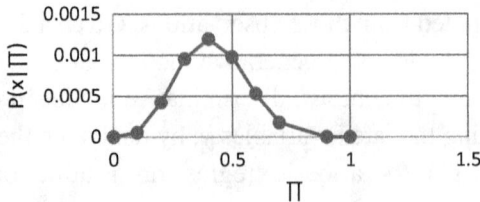

Figure 1.   A plot for various values of $p(\chi|\pi)$ vs. π.

Table 1. Value of π in the highest probability.

π	$P(\chi|\pi)\,P(\pi)$
0.4	0.000119
0.5	0.000781
0.6	0.000053

Now suppose we have some prior information about the coin itself. For example, let's assume that the coin was produced in a factory where 10% of the coins have a π value of 0.4, 80% have a π value of 0.5 and 10% have a π value of 0.6. This gives us a prior distribution on π, which is $p(\pi)$. The probability of observing the data is now proportional to $P(\chi|\pi)\,P(\pi)$. Since there are only three possible values of π (0.4, 0.5 and 0.6), we can look at Table 1 to determine what value of π results in the highest probability by observing the data.

We can see that the best value for π is now 0.5. This is known as the maximum a posteriori estimate. We can now approximate $P(y|\chi)$ by $p(y|\pi = 0.5)$.

Note that both of these developments have resulted in approximations of $p(y|\chi)$. If we want to squeeze every bit of information out of the observed data, then we are going to have to come up with an exact solution. Consider the following formula, $\int_0^1 P(y|\pi)P(\pi|\chi)d\pi$. The good news is that by evaluating this formula, we end up integrating out the value of π leaving us with $P(y|\chi)$, which is what we want. The bad news is that an integral has entered the field of battle. As the gentle reader may remember from high school calculus, integrals are hard. In fact, for all but a few function types such as polynomials, integrals are intractable, meaning there is no closed form solution. While I can manipulate this equation using various theorems, this would just add insult to injury. But fear not, here is where the topic of Variational Methods comes to our rescue. The trick is that, these types of integrals are known as expectations, which we can approximate using sampling methods. Let's talk a little bit about the expected value of a function. The definition of the expected value of a function $f(z)$ is defined as $\int_{-\infty}^{\infty} f(z)p(z)dz$.

Imagine you are playing an infinite game of bingo and that you have a particular bingo card. Let's say that there are 60 balls in the machine and that there are 25 different match numbers on your card. You might define $f(z)$ to be the number of hits you get on your card every time a ball is plucked with the value z and then returned to the bingo machine. Of course, at every iteration you will either get one or zero hits, but on average you will get $25/60 = 0.41$ hits. In this case, we can say that the expected value of any card is 0.41. Now suppose that the bingo machine has an uneven distribution of balls. There may be 5 number 1s, 17 number 2s, 11 number 3s and so on. Also, let's change the bingo card to have two numbers in each square, the first number being the match number and the second being the number of hits you get if the match number is called. We can also set these hit numbers in a random and non-uniform fashion. What now is the expected value of the card? Well, we can't just reason this out, we are going to have to play the game over and over again, add up the number of hits and then divide by the number of trials. The longer we do this, the more accurate is our estimate of the expected value of the card.

This is exactly what we have to do to estimate the expected value, with respect to a probability distribution (the bingo machine), of an arbitrary function. However, instead of a physical bingo machine, we use algorithms that can act like the bingo machine. A really popular version of such an algorithm is known as the Gibbs sampler — see Resnik and Hardisty (2010) for details. In terms of our broader discussion, it seems to me that part of being an intelligent agent is the application of principled approaches whenever possible.

For a more general discussion of probability, statistics and data, I would recommend Charles Wheelan's *Naked Statistics* (2012). The author covers topics ranging from the glory of the central limit theorem to 'How overconfident math geeks nearly destroyed the global financial system'. I will focus on two topics that are important to our discussion: (1) why we are not good intuitive statisticians and (2) correlation.

You go to the doctor and she administers a test for a relatively rare disease (only one in 100,000 people fall victim to this disease). Now the doctor informs you that the test is 90% accurate. Meaning that every time the test is performed, the probability that it provides the correct answer is 0.9. The doctor administers the test and unfortunately it comes back positive, implying you have the disease. How devastating is this? Before you start panicking let's unpack some things.

Let's say that we take one million people at random from the general population. Based on our prior knowledge that the disease afflicts 1 in 100,000 people, we can estimate that 10 people out of our million subjects will have the disease and that 999,990 people will not have the disease. Now if we apply our 90% accurate test to the million people, a likely outcome would be that 9 of the people that have the disease will be correctly diagnosed as having the disease and one will be misdiagnosed as not having the disease. We can refer to those 9 people as the true positives (TP). However, when applying the test to the people that don't have the disease, 10% of such individuals will get a false positive (FP) result, meaning that the test will came back positive even though they do not have the disease. These are the FP. So, the FP for this experiment is something near to 99,999. The total number of people that got a positive result is TP + FP but only TP will have the disease. This means that the probability of you having this disease is $\frac{TP}{TP+FP}$ which is roughly 1 in 10,000. The moral of the story is that people overweigh observed evidence at the expense of prior knowledge.

From a marketing point of view, correlation is king. Let's consider a given data sample, which is composed of a set of variates. For example, we can ask a thousand people to fill out a survey that asks questions such as your age, shoe size, the number of televisions that you have, etc. We can then pose questions such as 'how does weight vary with shoe size?' You can start by constructing a graph where the x axis represents shoe size and the y axis represents weight. For each sample, you can place a dot at the appropriate coordinate and see if you can observe any trends. Going a step further, you can compute the correlation coefficient (CC) between any two variates. The CC is a number between −1 and 1. The CC can represent positive or negative correlation. If CC = 0, then we say that there is no correlation between the two variables. If CC = 1 or −1, then the two variables are directly correlated, either positively or negatively. Given enough data, marketers can start to ask the question, 'Given that all other variables remain constant, how does variable $X1$ correlate with $X2$?' For example, for 22-year-old individuals who have taken 3 years of music lessons, it may be that their available pocket money is positively correlated with the age of their automobile. Thus, if you are 22 years old, have studied the flute for 3 years and have just purchased a brand new car, don't expect to be a target of direct advertising. The ability to compute such statistics requires massive amounts of data. But if you can get it, it is as good as gold. A famous story around this type of analysis is as follows.

It was observed that the purchasing patterns of a young lady were highly correlated with her also being pregnant. So, the retailer sent advertisements associated with infant child care to her home. The father of the young lady complained that the retailer was sending inappropriate advertisements to his daughter who he believed was not pregnant. It turns out that the daughter was indeed with child and that the father did not know it. In order to avoid future embarrassment, the retailer modified their advertising strategy by sending such individuals both infant care material as well as a random set of advertisements, thereby camouflaging their inferences. This of course leads us to the topic of big data.

Many people characterise big data using the three Vs: volume, velocity and variety. My take on big data is slightly different. I think that it is best described using three main attributes:

- The data is distributed as opposed to being collocated.
- The data is highly connected.
- The data is used for unintended purposes.

Those who have the tools needed to make connections across disparate sources of data, resulting in insights that were not anticipated by the data generators, have the ability to make discoveries that can be exploited by their benefactors.

One more topic that will round out this discussion for how data is used today is the question of causality. A great introduction to this topic, and more specifically to Judea Pearl's (2009) do-calculus, is in Kelleher's 'A Technical Primer on Causality' (2016).

As an example, consider a pressure cooker with a heat source and pressure gauge. You may observe that as the pressure gauge increases in value, so too does the temperature of the cooker. Generally speaking, given the observation of the pressure gauge (x), you would be able to compute the probability distribution of the interior temperature y of the cooker. That is to say, you would now have $P(y|x)$. Now suppose that you used your hands to physically force the pressure gauge to increase or decrease the measured value of the gauge. Would you expect the temperature of the cooker to change accordingly? Of course not. This is because the temperature causes the gauge to change and not the other way around. You have a causal model for your cooker. As seen from our prior discussions, with sufficient data, we are good at computing the probability of a latent variable y given the passive observations x. We know how to compute $p(y|x)$. The next question that we want to ask is what is the probability of latent variable y given that we do x? That is to say, what is $p(y|do(x))$? Note that $p(y|x)$ does not equal $p(y|do(x))$. If we could solve this type of problem, then we can ask questions such as: 'how much longer will I probably live if I chose to do 10 push-ups everyday?' The problem with estimating $P(y|do(x))$ is that we might not be able to actually *do* (x). However, given passive data coupled with a causal hypothesis, as well as some auxiliary observations, it is in fact possible to estimate $p(y|do(x))$. Such distributions can then be used for decision-making purposes as well as to answer counterfactuals such as: 'what would have happened had I chosen to turn left instead of turning right at the light?'

Answer

Having touched on topics such as Variational Methods, Bayesian Analysis, discriminative models, correlation and do-calculus, it is clear that the recent fruits that GAIE have been able to produce are based primarily on the ability to access and analyse data. So, to address your question 'what bearing, if any, do these conflicted data policy thrusts have on AI R&D?', I would argue that the main implication will be the ability to provide immediate value to AI funding entities. Counterintuitively I believe that data may be more of a crutch than an enabler to research. Given a difficult problem, it is well known that relatively simple algorithms can be made to produce spectacular results given copious quantities of data. It can be argued that practice is currently outpacing theory because we are able to provide increasingly accurate results using data-driven methods without increasing our insights as to why we are able to do so. Taking a 'it is always darkest before the dawn' point of view, I am predicting that this love affair with data will soon come to an end. What may be more important is an AI's ability to continually and authentically experience the world allowing for new capabilities such as common-sense reasoning and inductive learning.

As for your attempt to define data, I might add a few elements for your consideration. The first is the difference between *structured* and *unstructured* data. A set of measurements such as temperature and pressure associated with a given machine would be viewed as structured data because there is no ambiguity regarding the meaning of each measurement. In contrast, an image taken from a surveillance camera would be considered as unstructured data. While each pixel has a physical interpretation with respect to photon counts and geometric rays, its contribution with respect to the observed entities of the image is not well defined. Similarly, consider semantic ambiguity itself. The entities described by newspaper articles derive from a complex semantic ontology and from an AI perspective are subject to interpretation. While wind velocity may be complex, there is little in the way of semantic ambiguity.

Let me end with a joke that I heard many years ago, but I think is relevant to our discussion. A sheep farmer is standing in his field with his dog. In the distance he sees dust rising from a speeding car. The car enters the farm and makes its way to the farmer. The car stops and out pops a well-dressed young man with a nice pair of sunglasses — a slickster. The slickster approaches the farmer and asks: 'If I can tell you how many sheep are currently in your field; can I have one?' The farmer considers the proposition and, overcome by curiosity, he agrees. The slickster then pulls out an iPad and requests a satellite image of the farm. An image is formed with tiny ellipses around each of the fluffy white sheep along with various histograms and graphs. The slickster then informs the farmer that he has exactly 227 sheep. The farmer nods his head. Filled with glee the slicker grabs the closest animal and stuffs it into the back seat of his car. The farmer then says: 'Hold on a minute, if I can tell you what your profession is, can I get my animal back?' Thinking that fair is fair, the slickster agrees. The farmer then says: 'I believe that you are a data scientist'. Shocked, the slickster then responds with: 'Why yes I am a data scientist, how did you know?' The farmer replies: 'Well, you came here uninvited, you expected to be paid for working on questions that I already have the answers to, and you know nothing about my business. So, can I please have my dog back?'

27

Doubting Qualia and Social Data

Suman

> - Scepticism is expressed about qualia-based measurements of consciousness apropos of determining rights and responsibilities
> - Focusing on social statistics, some of the vagaries in measuring social factors are outlined with an eye on normative and descriptive measurements

Qualia

If it is correct that to have qualia experience the agency of a 'conscious mind' is necessary, the animal's experience can consist only of raw data, that is, neural correlates, or else it too must be taken to have a 'conscious mind'. However, this turns out to be problematic. First, we do not know what a mind (conscious or unconscious) actually is, or how to look for evidence of it, whether in humans or in animals. Second, we cannot even guess, let alone know, what the experience of neural correlates could be.

Zoltan Torey, The Crucible of Consciousness (1999, p. 11)

I have found that many scientists who think they are newfound friends of qualia turn out to use the term in ways no self-respecting qualophile philosopher would countenance.

Daniel C. Dennett, Sweet Dreams (2005, p. 87)

I have an earnest soul; cynicism is alien to my qualia, Peter.

Arguments from qualia and putative measures of consciousness are irrelevant to 'rights' as they are understood and governed at present. I fear human-centredness is inevitable in the latter because rights (whether human, animal or machine) are a matter of human social policy, not really of levels of consciousness.

Let's say, for the sake of argument, that we come up with consensually accepted consciousness levels based on aggregate qualia-valence measures for every species: i.e. we all agree that species-human has a consciousness level of Q10, and species-chimpanzee of Q11, and species-fish of Q25 and so on. Let's assume that these levels can be put in a sequence, so that Q10 is higher or lower than Q11 and so on. However firmly accepted by all, this exercise won't erase human-centredness in the determination and regulation of rights.

Endowing rights thereafter will mean something like declaring: 'All levels above Q15 are hereby endowed with rights which will be secured and regulated'. As things stand now, the determination that Q15 is, so to speak, the cut-off level will be done by humans (on the basis of empathy distance or awareness distance, I suspect). What securing them means in practice will be determined by humans. The policing of those rights accordingly will be done by humans. Regulatory disputes about those rights will be negotiated between humans. Humans will be chastised for infringing those rights. I can't see how this process can be regarded as other than human-centred.

I won't go into the validity of qualia-based arguments here, except to say I am yet to find a robust rebuttal of philosophical objections raised by Dennett in *Consciousness Explained* (1991, Chapter 12), and variously since, despite the blossoming popularity of qualia-based arguments. Objections usually take the form of asserting, as you did once earlier, that 'consciousness is an established phenomenon', instead of answering arguments with arguments. Johnson's *Principia Qualia* (2016), which you cited, is a joy for mathematicians but only after they negligently gloss over what Johnson means by qualia (or quale). He gives the following clarification in an incidental note:

'Consciousness' is a term often used as a synonym for self-awareness, or for social coordination of internal states, but I'm using it in a limited, technical sense: a system has consciousness if *it feels like something to be that system.* I.e., something is conscious if and only if it has subjective experience. 'Qualia' refers to the elements of consciousness, e.g. redness (p. 10).

The example of what an 'element of consciousness' is — 'redness' — is all we have to make sense of this here. I can only refer this back to Dennett's (1991) argument in *Consciousness Explained*, Chapter 12, about the missteps in using colour perception to exemplify qualia, which are carefully unpicked there.

I recently happened to be reading a classic historical work by Edward Payson Evans, *The Criminal Prosecution and Capital Punishment of Animals* (1906), principally about trials where animals were prosecuted, put on the stand and punished in European (ecclesiastical or secular) courts in the 14th–17th centuries. Very broadly, advocates of the time presented various wondrously sophisticated arguments for these: (a) maintaining that from a religious perspective animals have souls and (b) implicitly, that this is a good way of settling disputes between propertied landowners and livestock owners without troubling these members of the gentry directly, while doing something whereby the authority of church and magistrates is bolstered. It seems to me that 'qualia' is a usefully mystified Latin term (simply plural for 'quale', 'quality' in English) which works now for some scientists in the way 'soul' made sense for the devout in the medieval/early modern period. Purists among Catholics have ever favoured Latin, and scientists quite like Latin terms too — these suggest erudition to techie highbrows (without furrows).

Datum to Data

Many thanks for explaining what you do with data (variational methods, discriminative models, correlation analysis, etc.) for functionalising, linking, fine-tuning and predictive purposes in AI research. Your anticipation of the limits of data-led research is intriguing — I will ponder it and leave it to be pondered by others. Instead of doing that, it seems to me that a direction opposite to the one you took in considering data might be of some interest here.

Where you largely considered what to do once elicited data are at hand, I would like to consider more closely what's involved in the elicitation of data. What to do with data is naturally more interesting to AI aficionados — intellectual flights and beautiful inferences and applications become possible. The eliciting and tabulating of data are considered a routine and plodding chore which interests AI cognoscenti very much less.

The brief description of data terms with which I ended my previous intervention was, to some extent, designed to bring that reverse direction into view. The relationship between *datum* and *data* is stressed there, which received definitions rarely do because it seems too obvious (similarly qualophiles are generally reticent about the relationship between *qualia* and *quale*). To reiterate: identifying and collecting items of datum to form datasets involves expressing those items such that they can be collectively included in and presented as data. Once data are thus presented, the particularity of the datum seems to be erased or becomes irrelevant.

The distinction you rightly draw attention to, Peter — between structured and unstructured data — belongs to the zone of elicitation. Let me focus the following observations particularly on structured data, where, as you note, one of the key mechanisms of expressing the item of datum to fit data collocation is *measurement*. If I can measure the height of a specific giraffe in a way that makes it comparable to the heights of other giraffes, that makes this specific giraffe a datum in the dataset of heights of giraffes. This dataset is then a part of data about giraffes (alongside the dataset on weights of giraffes, distributions of giraffes, measurable anythings of giraffes). Moreover, let me focus particularly on *social data* (where the questionnaire-based surveys you have discussed — so beloved of policymakers — offer one of several methods of data elicitation). Structured social data draw on measurements of social conditions, as in statistics for 'inequality' or 'poverty', 'standard of living', 'political choices', 'consuming habits', 'market behaviour', 'performance' for geopolitical zones in terms of various indices ('development', 'growth', 'health', 'education', etc.) and the like. For the sake of convenience, I focus on several features of inequality and poverty measurement below, which work analogously in other areas of social statistics.

My argument is that though data analysts sweeping into the variational methods and discriminative models take such (raw) social data as neutral descriptive material, such social data are elicited with inbuilt normative (value-laden) content. The very act of measurement, of expressing social datum to elicit social data, involves a kind of rhetoric.

Social Statistics

In fact, it is a commonplace in social statistics that the measurement of a social factor could be *normative* or *descriptive*, i.e. either with a preconceived notion of what is significant or to articulate the situation clearly and without bias. So, for instance, looking at a set of measurements in relation to a poverty line is a *normative* approach. It is premised on the understanding that an undesirable (which is the normative term) social condition kicks in at some measurable point, and the determination thereof could motivate welfare policies, alleviation measures, etc. Correspondingly, looking at a set of measurements to consider income inequality on a relative scale (let's say some sort of centile scale) is a *descriptive* approach. It is not inevitably led by the notion that inequality is undesirable or not (those would be the normative terms here), it is more obviously led first by a need to describe the existing state of affairs without such preconceptions.

This sounds like a sensible and clear distinction, but in fact does not quite cover how social statistics work. What appears to be a descriptive approach to measuring inequality is seemingly both designed to have and is received as having normative content in practice. For instance, the very description of a social condition where the top 1% of earners are found to have as much as the bottom 50% immediately suggests normative judgements. Evidently, relative social measurements are imbued with normative implications according to the cognitive social context in which they are undertaken, presented and received. More aptly then, what is regarded as *normatively* led social measurement — such as, determination of a poverty line — could be thought of as *explicitly normative*; and what is considered descriptive measurement — such as, relative inequality on a given scale — could be considered as *implicitly normative* according to context rather than *descriptive*. It is difficult to pin down any area of social statistics where any kind of measurement escapes normative implication, i.e. is not received as showing a good or bad condition, as being significant or negligible in social terms. That implication becomes ideological or political when the measurement is taken as recommending some sort of target for improvement or the maintenance of a status quo. In that sense, social measurement could be thought of as invariably designed to serve a normative purpose or agenda and having a rhetorical weight.

Thinking of measurement in social statistics thus, as explicitly or implicitly normative, seems to undermine the most powerful claim of the science: that such statistics do in fact present the most precise and objective *descriptions* of social features and trends. The case is more complex: the thrust of social measurements is inevitably a descriptive one, but presentation of social measurements equally inevitably carry normative implications where received. This seems paradoxical only because statisticians habitually use *normative* and *descriptive* as if they are opposites or complementary, but that's no more than a syntactic misdirection.

Let's put the situation thus. The *act of measuring* (applying the measuring instrument, setting about counting, determining the dimensions or weights) is driven by a descriptive impulse. But some *conditions that enable the act* already have normative orientations built into them: such as, appointing standardised units of measurements, choosing terms that identify what is being measured, depending upon technological parameters of instruments, appointing a body to regulate and authorise standards, setting up ways of validating measurements. (For the AI field, this sort of standardisation and regulation is currently a matter of policy discussion in the USA, it features in NIST's July 2019 draft *US Leadership in AI: A Plan for Federal Engagement in Developing Technical Standards and Related Tools*.) More importantly, the *presentation of the results of the act* of measuring — e.g. as raw structured data in tables or graphs — immediately suggest normative implications and inferences in specific contexts. Perhaps the standard formats of presentation (in charts, tables, grids, etc.) are pre-determined for that end. The communications involved in both obtaining and putting the measurements — the structured social data — out there, and in using them for analysis and inferences, are optimal relevance-seeking communications.

Let me turn to a different aspect of the rhetoric of measurement in social statistics: *methodolingual translation*. Suppose a Person who has some experience of poverty approached a Statistician who has not herself previously engaged with poverty and asked her whether she could measure poverty. The Statistician will naturally assure the Person that there is nothing that cannot be measured, but would wish to know what exactly he had in mind. After all, 'poverty' as a term is a bit slippery, seems to connote quite a lot of possible factors to measure, could the Person put some definite markers on what poverty consists in? The Person would then elaborate on his experience of poverty, and from this account the Statistician would isolate some terms which seem particularly useful: such as 'employment', 'food', 'housing', 'sanitation', 'health', 'education', 'opportunity', 'insecurity', 'dependence'. The Statistician may then ask the Person whether among these terms there are some that are more important than others. The Person may choose one: e.g. 'food' — that might seem to him a fundamental element of poverty, which could supersede other terms or be seen as their cause. The Statistician might then decide that measuring the 'food' factor is a reasonable way to measure 'poverty' itself. She could set up a standard unit for this measurement (such as, kilocalories consumed per day), understand what is the necessary measurement of a healthy intake, and consider how to obtain data on those who do not get a healthy intake and can be considered in 'poverty'. Let's say she does get the data and gives the Person some putative measurements of 'poverty' accordingly. The Person would be happy with the results as a reasonable indicator of 'poverty' in all its ordinary-language complexity. Equally, the Person may feel that this dataset doesn't do justice to many aspects of poverty. Meanwhile the Statistician gains in confidence and her interest in this subject grows, so she wonders whether the other terms can also be measured and put into some sort of relationship to each other for a more complex measurement of 'poverty'. The results of this step would satisfy some that this is now really indicative of what 'poverty' in ordinary language suggests. But possibly another Person 2 from a different country who also has experience of poverty may suggest another term to bring into the measurements for the Statistician to think about … And so the process of measuring and honing and complicating measurement and data elicitation would follow, much as it actually has in the history of poverty measurement. At every step, the statistically measured 'poverty' is proximate with and yet not quite the same as 'poverty' in ordinary language.

In this process, the term that is putatively measured, 'poverty', is a repository of rhetorical negotiations. It is stretched and adjusted severally through its passage from ordinary language to statistical term, to presentation of data bearing that term and analysis thereof, and then back — now loaded with the weight of measurement — into ordinary language. So, a term like 'poverty' comes to statistics with its ordinary language connotations, bearing the contours of phenomenal experiences of suffering or perceptions of impoverishment. For statistical processing — conversion to measurable parameters — 'poverty' is disaggregated into implied or associated terms, such as 'nutrition', 'health', 'employment', etc. The measurements of these and linked-up analysis of these follow as if it is still 'poverty' in something like the ordinary-language sense, but this is in fact an *abstracted* idea of 'poverty', i.e. its connotations are limited and more definite. And yet, this abstracted idea in the term 'poverty' now, when returned to ordinary discourses with data attached, is treated as if it were resonant with phenomenal experiences and perceptions, only more scientifically so. This circuit is what I dub *methodolingual translation*: this process is not of the word itself changing in translation, but of connotations shifting while the word is held stable so as to enable the effective insertion of measurement.

Thus, the term 'poverty' bearing statistical measurement evokes a reality which is distinct from and yet as, if not more, weighty as the term in ordinary language. Measured 'poverty' according to food — one sort of poverty in abstract — may seem in some context as phenomenally effective as experience of suffering or visibility of 'poverty' in ordinary language. The word 'poverty' obscures the distance between the connotative shifts made to enable measurement and the complex of intertwined connotations in ordinary language.

Such methodolingual translation imbues statistical measurement with another dimension of persuasive nudging. On the one hand, it enables social statistics to make relatively unnoticed selections from and focalising of the connotations of the term putatively measured. On the other hand, statisticians are generally aware that their use of terms involve methodolingual translation which limits connotations and may mislead. So, statisticians usually strive to bring their measurements closer to the term's ordinary-language purchase. Much of the history of poverty measurement, from utility, income and nutrition measurements to multi-dimensional measurements, could be regarded as driven by statisticians trying to bring the statistical indicators of 'poverty' closer to the ordinary-language connotations of 'poverty'. And equally, that's a history of non-statisticians' proclivity to mistake given statistical indicators of 'poverty' as being the same as 'poverty' in ordinary language. Ideological and political and institutional interests structure this process.

In Brief

In brief, for social factors measuring involves massaging and the massage is moulded into the (raw) data. With a slight twist on Marshall McLuhan and Quentin Fiore's (1967) *The Medium is the Massage* (no, not a mis-spelling), we could say 'the data are the massage'. Actually, what you describe as doing with data, Peter, is after the fact of the massage that are data — at least in the social sphere. The processes you describe arguably extend the effects of the massage in the inferences from and applications of data. Error corrections are not eliminations of the massage.

This is particularly salient to data which are drawn from and brought to bear upon the social field. Insofar as AI research intervenes in social contexts, it is to extend the rhetoric grounded at the level of eliciting social data. So, such research is not so much an intervention in as perhaps a recomposition of the social field, with tacit ideological and political intent. The obvious sorts of abuse of statistics by policymakers, the subject of so many studies, come afterwards.

I say this without a whit of cynicism, which is truly alien to my soul/qualia.

28

Data Users and Data Doubters

Peter

- How data has been used for nefarious purposes and other question-
  able practices is recalled
- Why it is so hard for us to agree to agree is discussed
- A final plea is made for the just treatment of robots

Suman, half the fun in reading your interventions is trying to figure out
what exactly is the current bee in your bonnet. This time the irritant was
easy to identify, what was a bit perplexing was why you chose to get
worked up about this particular fly in the ointment. Your concern seems to
revolve around the practice of researchers deciding to reduce complex
concepts such as poverty down to specific measurements such as annual
income or nutritional intake. You seem to view this as a form of covert
rhetorical hijacking. This criticism is often heard when pundits cite the
performance of the stock market as a proxy for progress and prosperity.
In contrast, the World Happiness Report (see website) is often regarded as
a more appropriate measure. Viewed through this lens, Scandinavian
socialist paradises such as Finland often come out ahead. Bhutan has
adopted a Gross National Happiness index (see website) instead of the
Gross National Product as their measure of development and guide for
policy. But before delving into your mantra that the data are the massage,

let's consider what I believe to be some of the equally egregious sins of those that would wear the cloak of statistics.

Push polling is the practice where pollsters phrase a question not for the purposes of gathering information but in order to influence the opinion of those taking the survey. For example, that question 'How do you feel about the fact that candidate X has a secret mixed-race love child?' The negative premise of the question, which may of course be false, is thus lodged into the psyche of the survey taker. In a similar vein, questions can be designed to bias the outcome of the survey itself. The pretext for including inquiries regarding citizenship into the 2020 US census were so duplicitous that even a sympathetic supreme court had to rule against it.

In *Naked Statistics* (2012), Charles Wheelan describes what he considers to be a prime example of one of the most scurrilous forms of statistical malfeasance. It turns out that for a certain class of popular canned beers, their taste is so uniformly bland that it makes them practically indistinguishable from one another. Taking advantage of this fact, the producers of brand X decided to perform the following live experiment during the intermission of the Superbowl. They gathered 100 self-proclaimed brand Y drinkers (brand X's main competitor) and had them partake in a blind taste test between X and Y. To add an air of credibility, they had Superbowl referees officiate the event. As one would expect, roughly half of the participants ended up choosing brand X instead of brand Y — remember they are basically the same. On the face of it, brand X producers were taking a pretty big risk. After all, if a high percentage of Y drinkers stuck with their brand, the producers of X would have a lot to lose. However, prior to this stunt, the brand X producers ran this experiment over and over with different samples of brand Y drinkers. After application of the central limit theorem (the experiment is based on 100 people not just 1), they were very confident of the results that they would get. They were taking almost no risk. After the experiment the tag line was 'In a blind taste test, over 50% of Brand Y drinkers chose brand X!' implying that X is so superior to Y that even half of Y drinkers tested prefer it. Of course, if a comparable experiment was performed with Brand X drinkers instead of Brand Y drinkers, an equally negative tag line could have been produced. This is a great example of the cynical practice where accurate statistics are used to intentionally create a false impression.

Big pharma is particularly fond of having prestigious Academic Institutions perform experiments with their latest offerings. When positive results are found, they are published with great fanfare. However, when the findings are less favourable, drug manufacturers would use clauses in their contracts that would allow them to stifle publication. After many outcries, the credibility of universities, as impartial arbiters of truth, came into question. As a result, most universities now refuse to accept contracts which can control the rights of researchers to publish their results. However, professors still need funding and Big Pharma is still a significant cheque writer. So, one wonders how much vim and vigour goes into proving that a given drug is no better than sugar water ...

The field of Social Behavioural Science (SBS) makes great use of survey-driven statistics. Currently, the field is in crisis. Recent efforts to reproduce the results of many SBS seminal papers have failed. All sorts of questionable practices have been identified. One that is particularly irksome is based on a kind of retroactive hypothesis selection. The scientific method is based on the following paradigm:

1. Based on some sort of abductive process, a scientist constructs a hypothesis.
2. This hypothesis is then used to make predictions regarding the outcomes of a novel experiment.
3. The experiment is performed, and the hypothesis is either validated or falsified.

Now suppose that a scientist develops the hypothesis that drinking almond milk will reduce the occurrence of a particular form of cancer. After making predictions, a suitable experiment is designed and performed, but unfortunately no validating results are found. However, after looking at the data, the scientist observes that there is a measurable correlation between drinking almond milk and improved skin complexion. The researcher can simply pretend that this was the initial hypothesis, write a paper, get published, get tenure and live happily ever after. To address this issue, there have been calls for researchers to log their hypotheses in public databases before they start any form of data collection. Unfortunately, there have been cases where a few researchers have had the audacity to go back and edit such logs after the fact. Of course, part of the problem is that major publication venues are only interested in positive results. One questions whether science and therefore society is well served by such incentives.

Recently, Genuine AI Engineers (GAIEs) have been accused of producing biased AI Engines. The argument is that failure modes for things like facial recognition are higher for certain visible minorities. There is even a corporate-sponsored commercial featuring the great Mayim Bialik (IBM TV Commercial, 'Dear Tech: I Need Tech That Understands My Business', 2019), star of TV sitcoms like *Blossom* and *The Big Bang Theory*, pleading with GAIEs to do better. One hypothesis is that minorities are not adequately represented in the data used to train these algorithms. If this is the case, the first question I would have is whether or not such omissions are intentional or inadvertent. For example, we know that certain visible minorities are conspicuous by their absence in sitcoms such as *Blossom* and *The Big Bang Theory*. One suspects that network executives simply believe that there is no market for such representative offerings. While somewhat distasteful, there is at least a rational argument for such intentional bias. From my perspective, I cannot see why an AI researcher would go out of his or her way to disenfranchise a particular ethnic minority when it comes to something like face recognition. If anything, this would most likely hurt their overall performance measures. However, I can see how biased datasets are formed simply because data is hard to get, and many researchers simply use what is available. In fairness, I will point out that *The Big Bang Theory* does include a south Asian cast member — go Raj!

Back to the difficulties associated with data collection. About 20 years ago, I started working on a program to reconstruct 3D models of faces from skulls found at crime scenes. Part of this effort relied on the collection of male and female CT head scans from African American, Asian, Caucasian and Hispanic populations. There is no central repository for such data. I needed to put processes in place that would call for such things as informed consent from willing volunteers. On a daily basis, I would go to the yellow pages of cities that might have access to my target demographics and simply cold call local hospitals to see whether or not they could provide the data that I needed. It took me roughly 6 years to pull this dataset together. My point is that data is often hard to get and when time is an issue, one can see why researchers may act opportunistically. With this said, AI researchers should at the very least be aware of how the limitations of their data and hence their resulting AI Engines may end up disenfranchising various groups and members of the public.

Let's now return to this issue of reducing a complex concept, such as poverty, down to a measurement or two. The first thing I would like to say is that in some ways this is similar to the question of object recognition. For many years, researchers spent their time looking for specific measurements that could be used to identify certain object classes. For example, someone developing a face detector might assume that if we can detect the presence of two eyes, a nose and a mouth, then one is good to go. Similarly, researchers would look for the presence of geometric invariances. This would be some sort of calculation based on detected features that would not change with respect to view point. The takeaway message of the last five years is that one should not attempt to presuppose which features are important for inference purposes. One should instead provide methods, such as deep learners, with complete access to all the raw data and then let it figure out how to map such data to the desired latent variables. In the case of face recognition, this would mean using all the pixels of a given image as input to a convolutional neural network. From an SBS perspective, what does 'all the raw data' mean?

In terms of poverty, I really like Barbara Ehrenreich's *Nickle and Dimed* (2001). She basically gives up all her worldly possessions and attempts to live in the shoes of those that must survive on the minimum wage or less. If this represents the whole picture, one might consider the idea of life-logging, where a person-borne camera is worn continuously, similar to what is done in today's reality television. Given such enormous datasets, what can one do? Well, in the grand scheme of things I could imagine the construction of generative processes. That is to say, mechanisms that could produce samples that are indistinguishable from data collected by life-logging subjects. In principle, a generative process for the impoverished could be produced via mechanisms such as General Adversarial Networks (GANs). The idea being that one network is in charge of producing counterfeit samples, while another network must try to discriminate between authentic and counterfeit samples. It turns out that at the heart of many of these generative methods is the automatic separation of semantics. If successful, we might be able to extract a comprehensive semantic description of poverty. There are hypotheses that such networks might also produce symmetry operators that would allow us to, in a sense, define the space of poverty itself (see my previous discussion on symmetry operators). It may be the case that simulators produced by video game developers might give us a glimpse of what generative processes might be able to produce. I am currently enjoying the Sony Interactive game *Days Gone* (released in April 2019), where I play the character Deacon St. James — Deac for those who know me. I am a rough-on-the-outside biker with a heart of gold just trying to get by in post-apocalyptic Oregon. An element of the game requires that I ride my motorcycle with reckless abandon up and down treacherous mountain passes. The other day, I was (in real life) riding my bicycle to the local coffee shop when I realised that I was taking a turn with way too much speed. The *Days Gone* simulator is so good that it actually changed how I interacted with our universe. Suman, at this point I can almost hear the gnashing of your teeth, the days where AI will figure out the semantic structure of complex social phenomena are distant at best, the question is what do we do now?

Once again, your concern centres on SBS researchers attempting to redefine the meaning of a complex social concept by selecting what they assert to be the most relevant measurements. Given the questionable practices that plague this field, your objections are certainly warranted. I think that one must then ask the question: 'Given that policymakers need data-derived conclusions to drive their decisions, what processes do we need to put in place in order to come to agreement regarding what should be measured and how it should be measured?' A larger question might be, given that we agree on what and how things should be measured, how do we come to some sort of conclusion regarding the results of such experiments? That is to say, how do we get to a point where we can agree to agree?

While I certainly don't lump SBS sceptics with folks like Climate Change Deniers (CCDs), the question of how we, as a society, can establish common ground may also have bearing on this dispute. There are CCDs and there are CCDs. I fear that there is little hope for those that reject all evidence by simply claiming that it all emanates from some sort of elaborate conspiracy or hoax. However, other CCDs have concerns that I think we can address. A CCD colleague of mine makes the following argument: 'While I don't deny the accuracy of measurements made so far, I do question the conclusions. My reasons are as follows:

1. These measurements were predicated on certain hypotheses.
2. Scientists making these hypotheses are generally from elite left-leaning institutions.
3. If more scientists had a more right-leaning pedigree, they might develop hypotheses that could result in different measurements being made.
4. A fuller picture could emerge resulting in different conclusions being drawn such as climate change and human activity are independent of each other'.

While I question the validity of this argument, it at least gives us a starting point towards common ground. By conceding the point that different hypotheses might lead to different measurements, we as a society can then put resources behind

1. Producing as many diverse hypotheses as possible.
2. Relentlessly carrying out exhaustive measurements.
3. Letting the chips fall where they may.

The question comes down to whether or not we can establish enough communal trust in our institutions and by proxy ourselves so that conclusions can be drawn and then accepted across the board. Depending on the results, we can then either get on with the business of saving the planet or continue to burn coal to our hearts' content.

One last argument for the fair treatment of robots. You are certainly right that decisions regarding the granting of rights to an AI agent will be based on human-centric criteria. I would be hard-pressed to identify any examples where a dominant species was willing to consider the well-being of a weaker species over its own. Given that we are currently in one of the great periods of extinction, the fact that we are the top dog serves us well. However, without becoming an alarmist, it is conceivable that as we inch towards the singularity, we may at some point have to plead with a stern AI overlord for human rights and privileges. We may at that point wish we could point to a precedent where we behaved in a more charitable manner.

29

Data Distinctions and Data Nations

Suman

- The distinction between *social data* and *physical data* is underlined, maintaining that the refusal to recognise this distinction underpins, for instance, climate change denial
- For data policy in connection with AI Research, the advantages of collaboration and competition are considered
- In this regard, the governmental policy approaches of, on the one hand, PR China and, on the other hand, the USA and UK are compared

---

False Balance

You wondered, Peter, how agreement to agree on data-based observations can be obtained and public confidence in such observations bolstered. The problem, I feel, is deeper: more, how to agree to agree *or disagree*. Agreeing to do either of those entails having some shared ground in knowing how data are obtained, what principles validate data, what inferences are reasonable, etc. before determining in a considered and mutually understood way whether to concur or demur. My pat answer to getting to that ground level of agreement — that is, agreement to consider and examine data in rational ways — is basic education in data methods

(I would say that, won't I, education is my bread and butter ...). But that may not be enough.

There was a reason why I confined my observations in the previous intervention to *social data*. That refers to data about social processes which are premised on norms (i.e. elicited in terms of desirable or not, preferable or not, relevant or not, progressive or not) or dependent on declarations (such as, attitude surveys or tabulations of intent/perception). For the greater part, such datasets cannot be corroborated or tested by repetition, at the least with a robust degree of precision. Social norms and attitudes shift constantly, measurements are institutionally driven, measurement practices modify that which is measured, methodolingual translations kick in, and various agendas interfere in the interstices of those ambivalences. The validity of such data usually seems contestable.

The same cannot be said of data about physical or natural processes (underpinned at some level by physics): let's call this *physical data*. Such data can be corroborated variously, can be repeatedly tested, and to considerable degrees of precision. Strong confirmation and therefore consensus can be reached about the validity of such data.

It seems an elementary distinction. The crisis in public confidence you are referring to, Peter, seems to rest in not being able to distinguish between social data and physical data, between data that can be corroborated and tested and data that constitutively can't. I suppose this inability arises from inadequacies in basic education. As often, I daresay it arises by design. Where physical data undermine the agendas of powerful interest groups, the data are mendaciously made out to be as unsound as social data. Or when physical data contradict the articles of faith or wishful thinking of some population, they are received as if they were social data produced by an (imaginary) oppositional conspiracy.

The arguments you outline from your climate-change-denying pal is a good example to pause on, Peter. You seem to move too eagerly there. On the one hand, you say you 'question the validity of the argument'; on the other hand, you move with alacrity toward responding to it as if it might have some validity. If it isn't valid, then one can't respond to it meaningfully; one can only refuse it. So, that's the thing to check first: is it valid, even to a debatable extent?

Here's your friend's argument as you put it:

1. These measurements were predicated on certain hypotheses.
2. Scientists making these hypotheses are generally from elite left-leaning institutions.
3. If more scientists had a more right-leaning pedigree, they might develop hypotheses that could result in different measurements being made.
4. A fuller picture could emerge resulting in different conclusions being drawn, such as climate change and human activity are independent of each other.

Let's consider the underlying thinking in this argument.

- The first three points suggest that all hypotheses, and therefore measurements, reflect the ideological proclivities of those who propose them. As it happens, the kinds of data that indicate climate change, and a correlation between human activity and climate change, are in the sphere of *physical data*. These are data that, in principle, can be confirmed and corroborated by different parties from various locations, can be tested and retested. This is different from the *social data* that might purport to show, for instance, that a great many people don't want to act upon evidence of climate change. To simply assume that such physical data must be skewed by the investigator's ideological position is as absurd as assuming that Newton's laws of motion reflect his religious tendencies or that Einstein's theories of relativity are produced according to his conviction in socialism. So, your friend can't reasonably start from here without first demonstrating precisely where ideology has interfered in this physical data about climate change and its correlation to human activity. He has to start by examining and analysing the data that exists. If he can't logically demonstrate that this data is ideologically skewed rather than simply assuming it must be, his argument is not only not valid, it is a non-starter.
- The fourth point tells us why this argument is nevertheless being attempted at all. Your climate-change-denying friend is not interested in consulting the relevant data. He makes this argument because he *wants* data that confirms his unfounded belief; or, more precisely, he wants data to absolve him of responsibility for doing something about

climate change. We can only speculate on why he wants this. Maybe he's an avid supporter of Trump's policies (Jan Selby, 2019 is a useful article on the foreseeable effect of these). Perhaps he has business or professional interests which find such data inconvenient (quite respectable scientists are swayed when self-interest kicks in, see Oreskes and Conway, 2010). Possibly he has simply come across some climate change activists whom he can't abide. The list of despairing academic publications that try to understand climate change denial is extensive, almost a research industry unto itself.

I suppose your climate-change-denying friend's position is a bit better than Brazilian President Bolsonaro's on such issues, in that he seems to be offering an argument — but not better by much. In the midst of opening up the Amazon rainforest to untrammelled mining and agriculture (Freitas Jr, 2019), Bolsonaro is hostile to data showing the accelerated scale of deforestation taking place. When presented with such data, he immediately declared them 'lies' and fired the chief scientist (Le Page, 2019). Give your friend's arguments some air and financial/political backing and he might end up firing you for doubting the validity of his argument.

So, it does surprise me a bit that you are prepared, in response to this argument, to 'concede the point that different hypotheses might lead to different measurements' and are ready to get down to 'producing as many diverse hypotheses as possible'. You seem to be prepared to meet an invalid argument halfway, which is a kind of validation of the invalid. This reminds me of the rumbling disquiet, since 2013, about 'false balance' in BBC's programmes on climate change. As a public service broadcaster, BBC is charged with presenting non-partisan or balanced reporting. This has meant that every time a BBC programme has called upon a climate scientist to speak about the evidence for climate change, as a matter of 'balance' they have also wheeled out a climate-change-denying somebody to loudly assert doubt and disbelief and get a minute of fame. This has even been a matter of UK Parliamentary Debate, a House of Commons (2014) report *Communicating Climate Science* warned of the 'tendency for the media to approach climate science as an argument about two equally valid points of view, rather than discussion about scientific facts, and on the false balance of views being presented as a consequence' (p. 16).

Data Nations

But I am straying from the matter at hand: how AI policy bears upon data and vice versa. I have a somewhat different set of considerations to put to you.

From the perspective of AI policy, the nuances of how data are elicited on the ground and how public perceptions regard (or are manoeuvred into regarding) data are intersected by a more salient factor. Governmental level AI policies that address data as seminal for AI development suggest schisms other than those we have been contemplating.

Let me begin with a surmise, and you can tell me whether it is acceptable in principle. Let's say two research units A and B are trying to develop a particular AI capacity Φ which depends on them having access to large amounts (the more the better) of relevant data obtained as a dataset $d\Phi$.

1. **The full-collaboration option:** A and B could collaborate in pooling their $d\Phi$ and collaborate on integrating it for developing Φ — in that case, a robust Φ is most likely to be speedily and efficiently achieved;
2. **The part-collaboration and part-competition option:** A and B could collaboratively pool their $d\Phi$ but otherwise work competitively towards developing Φ — under these circumstances, a robust Φ may perhaps be equally or more speedily achieved because competition lends wings to both A and B;
3. **The full-competition option:** A and B could compete in getting the relevant data so that they each have two independent datasets $d\Phi[1]$ and $d\Phi[2]$, and at the same time they compete in integrating their respective databases in developing Φ — under these circumstances, the achievement of Φ is likely to be least efficient (getting adequate datasets take more time for both A and B) and its robustness most questionable (to begin with, A will question B's achievement of Φ if B got there first).

In brief, the best options for AI development involve some level of collaboration between parties working on it, and particularly salient there is collaboration in sharing data or having common access to relevant data. Does that sound reasonable?

The general tendency of state-governmental AI policy is towards full-competition with other states and, in particular, maintaining a competitive edge by protectionist measures with regard to data: setting standards accordingly, securing data within state control, setting up agencies with monopolies on acquiring certain kinds of data, etc. This thrust is in the nature of state-governmental policy. Since each of the states routinely claim or seek leadership in any given field, they appear ever to be in competition with all others as a matter of policy. Naturally, USA plans on 'maintaining American leadership in Artificial Intelligence' (White House, 2019) just as the UK expects to 'lead the world for years to come' in AI and data (BEIS and DCMA, 2018). Insofar as such competition to be the AI-top-dog state goes, to some degree that entails maintaining protectionist control of data. Data, at any rate, are something that states can try to control directly.

But this is a rather simplistic approach to considering the ways in which competition/collaboration with regard to AI and data work in governmental policy. A somewhat more complex picture is found when the kinds of state regimes in question are factored in. The UK and USA regimes are similar in many respects; the complexities become clearer if a somewhat different state regime is brought comparatively into the picture. So, I have been looking with interest at AI government policy in China (PRC), especially: the *"Made in China 2025" key area technology roadmap*《中国制造 2025》重点领域技术路线图 (NMSAC, 2015); *A New Generation of Artificial Intelligence Development: White Paper* 新一代人工智能发展白皮书 (MIIT, 2017); *Three-Year Action Plan to Promote the Development of a New Generation of Artificial Intelligence Industry (2018–2020)* 促进新一代人工智能产业发展三年行动计划 (2018–2020年) (MST, 2017) and *Key Scientific Issues of Transformative Technology: Key Special 2017 Project Declaration Guide* 变革性技术关键科学问题" 重点专项 2017 年度项目申报指南 (MST, 2018). My observations below do not go into the details of these; I keep to generalities informed by these. For an overview of PRC's AI policy, see the Future of Life Institute's webpage on this.

If I were pushed to describe the difference in regimes … with a great deal of reduction of complexity … tentatively … insofar as pertinent to the following observations: I think of the regime in the USA and UK as *neoliberal capitalist* and that in PRC as *state capitalist*. Two distinctions between these regimes are relevant here:

1. In a neoliberal-capitalist regime, the government functions predominantly to enable, foster and support the autonomy of diverse productive operations (e.g. corporations, businesses, firms). This autonomy means that such operations are often substantially outside the remit and therefore control of any single neoliberal government; they operate across multiple states. In a state-capitalist regime, the government seeks to limit (but not entirely remove) the autonomy of diverse productive operations and support is given accordingly. The government tends to hold controlling interests in operations even if they extend outside the remit of the state.
2. In a neoliberal-capitalist regime, the government is periodically revalidated through a multiparty elective system. In a state-capitalist regime, the government functions through the continuity of single-party governance.

Both are capitalist regimes at the state level insofar as their national economies, and therefore governance strategies, depend upon market-led capital investments and returns both domestically and globally.

With these cursory distinctions in mind, a few comparative observations follow on government-level AI policies in neoliberal-capitalist regimes like the USA or UK and state-capitalist regimes like the PRC — with particular attention to data matters and an eye on competition/collaboration.

1) The principal difference between national-level AI policy statements from the PRC and from the USA or UK jumps out if one simply looks at the content lists of such statements. Consider, for instance, the contents of the *"Made in China 2025" roadmap* (NMSAC, 2015) (see Appendix A for the contents in English) and *New Generation of AI* (MIIT, 2017) (see Appendix B for the contents in English) from PRC, and of the *AI R&D Strategic Plan* (NSTC, 2016) (see Appendix C for contents page) from the USA or the *AI in the UK* report (House of Lords 2018) (see Appendix D for contents page) from the UK. The PRC documents are focused

predominantly on the specific technologies to be realised and *set targets for developing particular smart/intelligent systems, which are enumerated.* The content of the technology is foregrounded. The USA/UK documents say very little about the technologies; the little that is said is in very general and mostly platitudinous terms. Instead, the policies outlined consist predominantly in *setting up an encouraging environment for the development of such technologies.* That consists in setting standards, making educational and legislative provision, arrangements for data security and ethics, assuaging doubts and garnering the confidence of the public, feeding the corporate sector's needs, etc. The language of these policy documents is accordingly different. The PRC documents are fairly technical. It seems likely that some Genuine AI Engineers (GAIEs) have a hand in them, and possibly have clout in the commissions that produced them alongside the bureaucrats. The USA/UK documents are in a sort of public-speak that one would expect from bureaucrats, corporate gurus, community stakeholders — no doubt GAIEs did their best as consultants in those commissions. It is not that the more technical material informing policy is not found if one looks for it. Those are just not foregrounded in national-level policy statements, but rather submerged in the deliberations of government bodies like NIST where GAIEs are at home in a sort of coterie. These are considered not quite a *public* matter, more the province of an esoteric cognoscenti. In brief, national-level AI policy documents are essentially declarative for PRC and mainly framework setting for the USA or UK.

2) The caginess about foregrounding technological content in USA/UK documents is understandable given the characteristics of neoliberal regimes. Such information is largely not controlled or owned by the state but by autonomous productive operations (mainly private sector and global corporations), especially insofar as commercially exploitable. That includes data which informs AI technological development. Autonomous productive operations competing with each other are unlikely to share commercially exploitable data, since data ownership gives competitive edge. Instead of detailing specific technological applications, these policy

documents therefore refer to firms and businesses which provide or produce those applications. Naming the firms and setting tenets for protecting the private sector suggest that these autonomous operations are proxies of the neoliberal state or that their interests coincide with that of the neoliberal state. In fact, neither is the case: that such operations find congenial working conditions or are headquartered in a given neoliberal state's territories shows no *necessary* coincidence of interest. Those private sector interests, in this field, are usually dispersed across various states and maximise themselves by balancing operations across various states. Given that in neoliberal-state policy this foregrounding of autonomous productive operations is paradigmatic, its absence in the state-capitalist PRC's AI policy documents in glaring. These only and occasionally offer summative observations on productive operations or businesses (e.g. several tables in *New Generation of AI*, 2017). These don't acknowledge a private sector as such, let alone seek to protect its interests.

3) Neoliberal-state AI policy documents like those from the USA and UK take care to assuage the doubts and concerns of citizens. Insofar as that regards fears about growing unemployment with increasing automation, lack of confidence and skills, anxiety about privacy and self-determination, concerns about security and so on, they are substantially (though usually ineffectively) addressed. Notably, data ethics and regulation of data usage by autonomous productive operations are significant policy issues. These preoccupations are natural in neoliberal regimes where governments court publics because these publics periodically validate them through the multiparty elective system. Given single-party governance, those citizens' concerns occupy almost no space in PRC AI policy documents. From the citizen's point of view, this state-capitalist policy attitude could either indicate that the state exercises unwarranted license to manipulate citizens or that the state is warranted by citizens' trust. Either way, that citizens' perspective is simply not addressed in policy.

4) Insofar as data in relation to AI development go, PRC policies and USA or UK policies share common ground in committing significant funding towards generating data, introducing industry and consumer

standards, and in facilitating data usage for education and training and for industrial/entrepreneurial ends. These are common ground in principle, because in practice they undergird competition between protectionist states rather than collaboration. If the standards set in the PRC and USA are different, and further, given that the languages (both in operating systems and in ordinary use) are different, separate datasets could be integrated into versions of the same kind of intelligent system whereby these versions then do not speak to each other. However, as both neoliberal-capitalist and state-capitalist governments depend upon global markets, some overlap in standards might nevertheless be expected. But in this regard, other regime-dependent factors kick in. Neoliberal states offer policy frameworks that enable the competition of autonomous productive operations. Such states cannot off their own steam ensure collaboration between those operations (the operations may collaborate if there are mutual self-interests), and nor can they therefore guarantee integration of data for the development of specific AI capacities. They can propose no timetables for these because that would undermine the autonomy of those operations, which in any case are largely beyond these states' remit. At best neoliberal states like the USA or UK can propose regulatory norms within their remit, which would always be contested by the autonomous operations. In this respect, a state-capitalist regime as in PRC can be much more gung ho. Such a government can ensure that productive units within their remit would collaborate and would integrate data towards developing particular AI capacities within a proposed timetable. This is expressed clearly in PRC AI policy documents: typically, for instance, in the many declarations in the *"Made in China 2025" roadmap* (NMSAC, 2015) of the following sort:

> By 2020, basically establish a standard system of the core information equipment for intelligent manufacturing, and have a set of breakthroughs of the key technology in the field of core information equipment of the intelligent manufacturing industry, so that the following can obtain scaled-up applications within China to an extent greater than 40% of the market share: basic communication equipment, industrial control equipment, industrial sensors, intelligent instrumentation and testing equipment, manufacturing and Internet of Things equipment, industrial

information security products. Also engender more than 5 related enterprises with annual incomes exceeding 10 billion yuan.

By 2025, establish the core information equipment industry ecosystem and technological innovation system, which are nationally determined and controllable, safe and reliable, and technologically advanced, so that Chinese-made intelligent manufacturing core information equipment captures 60% of the domestic market share and such that overall the level of technology reaches international advanced standards.

到 2020 年, 基本建成智能制造核心信息设备标准体系, 突破一批智能工业核心信息设备领域的核心关键技术, 使我国的智能制造基础通信设备、工业控制设备、工业传感器、智能仪器仪表和检测设备、制造物联设备、工业信息安全产品在国内得到规模化应用, 国内市场的占有率达到40% 以上, 培育 5 家以上年收入超过 100 亿元的相关企业。

到 2025 年, 建成自主可控、安全可靠、性能先进的智能制造核心信息设备*产业生态*体系和技术创新体系, 国产智能制造核心信息设备在国内市场占据主导地位, 国内市场的占有率达到 60%, 总体技术水平达到国际先进水平。(pp. 23–24)

Bringing these observations together, it seems fair to surmise that *insofar as inter-state competition* in the field of AI development through integration of data goes, PRC may eventually have an advantage over the USA or UK. This is because the former can ensure a level of collaboration that the latter can't; for the latter, competition between autonomous productive operations limits the ability to foster collaboration. In fact, in the neoliberal sphere (which is not a particular state but consists in several such states), it is autonomous productive operations across multiple states that are likely to go further irrespective of — and yet with the support of — neoliberal states. The competition would then be between state capitalism and capitalism in the neoliberal sphere rather than between states.

That autonomous productive operations in the neoliberal sphere can rise above state control and yet live within states' framework policies does not necessarily bode well for citizens under neoliberal governments. Citizens' concerns and anxieties about privacy, self-determination, security, ethical use, unemployment and inequity, etc. addressed (usually toothlessly) in the USA and UK policy documents are justified. Similarly, as noted already, the elision of citizens' perspectives in PRC's state-capitalist policies also does not bode well for citizens. In the prevailing regimes of data and AI policy thinking, the emerging conditions of the citizenry everywhere — whose interests all governments are ultimately meant to serve — are a grey area.

30

Data Doubters and Data Owners

Peter

- More interactions with Climate Change Deniers (CCDs) and sceptics are described
- Opportunities to review the role of NIST and PR China *vis-à-vis* their effects on the advancement of technologies such as face recognition are considered
- How AI talent is consumed in the modern day is discussed

No Desire to Agree

Back in December of 2016, I had some business out in western Canada. I took this opportunity to visit my brothers David and Alexander. Dave and I spent a few days snowboarding up at Whistler Mountain. On the first day, my nephew Ben was invited to an après-ski birthday party at a chalet owned by the family of one of his school mates. It was a nice little place situated on the slopes — you could ski right up to the front door. The children entertained themselves while the adults congregated in the living room, where they could marvel at the splendour that is the Great Coast Mountains of Canada. Like Dave, the other parents were well-heeled Chardonnay-sipping professionals and all seemed to know each other. Not unexpectedly they were curious about the recent US Presidential Elections. At one point, they asked if I had ever met a Trump supporter.

217

A bit taken aback, I explained that I come from the American Rust Belt, where one can't throw a stick without hitting a Trump supporter. I work with Republicans, I work for Republicans, I play cards with them and I hang out with them. I count Republicans as my friends and while I disagree with just about everything they say, I find myself fascinated by the way in which their convictions are both heartfelt and unwavering.

Suman, you paint the debate on physical matters as being cut and dry when compared to the shifting norms and subtle nuance of the social sciences. Let's return to my friend the Climate Change Denier (CCD). First consider the case made by professional Big Tobacco defenders. While there is a measurable correlation between people who die prematurely from cancer and those that have a history of smoking cigarettes, correlation does not (as we all know) imply causality. It may be the case that there is a specific gene which causes people to become addicted to tobacco products and that this gene is also responsible for maladies such as lung cancer. While this is of course nonsense, the same lobbyists were subsequently hired by the fossil fuel industry to make similar arguments to bolster the convictions of my CCD friend. They point to the fact that there have been climate change events in the past such as the ice ages, which had nothing to do with human activity. Perhaps if we only looked hard enough, maybe the equivalent of a genetic disposition to cancer and tobacco addition could be found that explains climate change in a manner that is independent of human activity. But of course, the left-leaning scientific establishment is not inclined to make such investigations. Once again, my goal is not to ridicule the CCD, rather I am trying to figure out what it takes to challenge this form of relativism.

Last weekend, I took another swing in this direction. In contrast to the CCD, this time I had lunch with a good friend of mine who was in town for a few weeks. He does not deny that climate change is taking place, he just thinks that the consequences are exaggerated. Let's put him in the camp of 'Call me when it's a Big Deal' (CBD). After our lunch at the Japanese noodle shop, I walked with him back to his local accommodation — about a two-mile trot. Our conversation started with his concern that undocumented persons were illegally voting in large numbers and that he would feel much better if the rule of law were more vigorously enforced. Viewing this as an opportunity to experiment with my goal of finding the means of establishing agreement, I pushed the conversation down the following path:

- I started by suggesting that since 50% of American citizens don't bother to vote, it seems odd that the undocumented would be willing to take the risk of voting illegally for almost no direct reward. The CBD stated that the promise of access to free healthcare and free education for the undocumented could warrant such risks.
- I then said that my understanding was that there have been studies which show that voter fraud was negligible at best. The CBD then declared he simply does not trust the product of such efforts because left-leaning researchers will always twist facts to their advantage.
- Manoeuvring, I then asked: since there is a countable number of illegal votes, what would it take for the CBD to agree on what that number is? He pushed for more law enforcement. I said that this was not a question of increasing his confidence in the elections but to coming to agreement on what the current level of abuse actually is.
- After a few backs and forths, the CBD conceded that a bipartisan investigation could do the trick. Feeling a thrill of victory, I thought I would push on to the issue of climate change ... I started with the seemingly logical proposal that if a bipartisan commission agreed with the vast majority of scientists, then he too would have to agree that something should be done. The CBD would have none of it.
- Falling back on my heals, I stuttered something regarding your argument that the social sciences are tough but when it comes to the physical world, the facts simply speak for themselves. The CBD said that this was backwards — I gasped. He argued that the physical world is much more complicated and more importantly that there is no punishment for inaccurate prognostication. He pointed to the fact that a few decades ago, egghead prophets and tree huggers alike were predicting that the world will soon run out of petroleum — flash forward to today, with fracking we see that the US has achieved energy independence. He then stated that we should not take action until it is absolutely clear that this is what we have to do. He then made reference to the greedy foreign businessman who will not stop polluting unless and until their precious offspring are practically choking to death.

- Hoping to short circuit some of this vehemence, I asked about irreversible events. The CBD looked suspicious and declared that he was not sure that anything was really irreversible. I suggested the extinction of animals such as the black-footed ferret — he was dismissive. I said that a number of glaciers that have been around for thousands of years have vanished in our lifetimes. I said that once the polar ice caps are gone, they won't come back, their light reflecting properties will be lost and that the oceans may rise by up to 20 feet or more. With a cunning glint in his eye, the CBD declared that more water means more rain which the farmers like and that the Dutch seem to do OK with their dykes and dams. He then mentioned that what is really irreversible is the breakdown of law and order! Fearing that I might lose ground on my solution to the issue of undocumented voting, I changed tack.
- Putting my cards on the table I mentioned our conversation and that it is my conviction that we must figure out what it takes to establish common ground. That is to say, how can we agree on what it would take to agree on anything? At this point, the CBD cut me off and stated that he simply has no desire to agree with me. He said that we should each stick to our convictions and let the wisdom of the people decide. After all, what could be more democratic than that … Maybe this is not a question of relativism, but the fact that we live in an age where the utility of a belief is more important than its veracity.
- Sadly, our journey came to an end. We both bid each other a fond farewell. Somewhat defeated, I got on my bicycle and pedalled home as the CBD sent a loving text message to his brand new electric vehicle.

Grounding Policies

I really like your analysis of AI policies from the US, UK and the PRC. With respect to the questions you raise regarding data sharing and government coordination of AI Research, I have a few perspectives. When it comes to the government coordination of US industry, I always think of the National Institute of Standards and Technology (NIST). NIST views itself as a kind of shepherd for science and technology. A few years back, I was invited by the National Academies of Sciences, Engineering and Medicine to participate on a panel in charge of reviewing NIST's Information Technology Laboratory. Our findings were made available to congress and were published as *Review of Three Divisions of the Information Technology Laboratory at the National Institute of Standards and Technology: Fiscal Year 2015* (NASEM, 2015). I spent most of my time focused on the Information Access Division (IAD). Elements of the report that have some pertinence to this discussion include:

> **Data-driven information science:** A data-driven approach is critical to advancing the field of information science and technology. The IAD team is starting to make an important contribution in this regard. The team is actively engaged in generating appropriate datasets and ground truths, running meaningful tests, and facilitating new web-based data sites. This direction is very positive. There is also an opportunity for the IAD to expand its vision beyond labelled data to include live data and to establish a methodology where larger numbers of candidate algorithms can be investigated through continuous evaluations. This is an industry-wide opportunity and trend, with implications for how to address ground truths and atypical events.
>
> There are examples in this collaborative program where ITL and the IAD visibly drive the creation or advancement of important fields. One such example is the Text Retrieval Conference (TREC). Over the past 25 years, the IAD has used the TREC platform to advance the metrics of performance in text retrieval. In particular, the community has moved from simple measures of precision estimates based on simple pooling of test run data to bootstrapping of test runs that consider interactions among query, system and documents. In the case of TREC for Video (TRECVID), the IAD has facilitated the identification of key tasks in video retrieval for defining system performance. Today, these include semantic indexing, instance search, surveillance event detection, multimedia event detection and event recounting. These are all tasks that the video retrieval community has accepted as a valid testing methodology for video retrieval systems.

NIST takes great pride in the role that it played in the advancement of face recognition. Under the leadership of Jonathan Philips, NIST made available a large corpus of publicly available training data. But more importantly, they maintained sequestered datasets that were used for evaluation.

Teams could train their algorithms on public data and then submit their algorithms for testing. Results were published and those that submitted algorithms could attend a NIST sponsored workshop, where they shared their insights and findings. Bragging rights for those that performed well turned out to be quite lucrative. This increased investment resulted in significant advances in face recognition. It got to the point where under ideal imaging conditions, automated face recognition engines started to outperform human capabilities. IARPA then came out with the JANUS program, which focused on face-recognition in the wild. They made available large public datasets of facial imagery taken in public spaces of non-cooperative individuals. This, coupled with the emergence of deep-learning methods, resulted in surprisingly strong face recognition performance from general surveillance imagery captured in open spaces such as train stations and city streets. Enter the People's Republic of China (PRC) — more on this later.

NIST has attempted this type of stewardship in a number of AI domains. However, success has not been universal. For example, when this approach was applied to the task of multi-camera multi-person tracking across crowded environments, progress has been limited at best. The goal of tracking an airport traveller, using a network of static wide-field-of-view cameras, from the point of entry to the moment of boarding, remains an unsolved problem. This is a good example of where insight, inspiration and invention may be more important than data.

Back in 2018, I was invited by the PRC State Administration of Foreign Experts Affairs (SAFEA) to give a talk on Industrial AI at the 12th Sino-American Technology and Engineering Conference (12th SATEC). They flew me over business class and put me up at the Foreign Experts Building in Beijing near the Olympic Park. The conference itself was held at the China Hall of Science and Technology. The meeting was kicked off by Zhang Jianguo, Vice Minister of the Ministry of Science and Technology and Administrator for SAFEA. He gave a great overview of the PRC's industrial R&D strategy. Most of the meeting was centred around a series of report-outs regarding the current status of various PRC industrial sectors as well as recommendations for future investments.

Suman, it is not surprising that your analysis of PRC AI policy reveals a focus on achieving specific technology goals. In many ways, the reviews at SATEC reminded me of NIST's goal-driven philosophy. Where things start to differ is that the PRC can mandate that certain technologies must not only be developed but that they must also be deployed. A case in point is the continuing evolution of face-recognition technology. While my knowledge is mostly anecdotal, it appears that face recognition is being used in the PRC at unprecedented levels. I understand that face recognition may now be the de facto mode of identification replacing such things as personal identification numbers (PINs) and fingerprints. There are stories of wanted criminals being caught by face-recognition engines deployed on vast networks of CCTV cameras. I have heard that jaywalkers are now routinely identified via face recognition and that their names are then automatically placed on billboards of shame. With such scale comes access to enormous amounts of data resulting in yet another turbo-charging of technical advancement.

During the conference banquet, held at the Foreign Experts Building, I had a chance to speak with a number of PRC AI Researchers. One sentiment that came through was their feeling that the PRC faces a problem with its Human Resource (HR) departments. In the PRC, HR remains convinced that leadership should be the sole recipient of economic rewards and that AI researchers are just replaceable cogs in the machine. This has resulted in talented AI developers doing everything they can to jump from research to leadership. Policy with respect to the care and feeding of AI talent may, in the long run, be more important than data strategies.

My understanding is that Google wants to have 15% of the US machine-learning community working for them. I would argue that the rest of the FANGs have similar ambitions. Such goals are understandable since AI and digitisation in general has ushered in a new breed of 'Takers'. Consider the following Table 1.

These companies are not generally inclined to share their data; however, some are willing to give away their technology. This is what I call the Candy Man strategy.

The open sourcing of AI tools such as TensorFlow (a deep-learning platform) has had a democratising effect on the AI community. It allows generic users to download software as well as pre-trained AI models and get results with little effort or expertise. This is extremely attractive to

Table 1. New breed of 'Takers'.

Takers	Took
Google + Facebook	Eyeballs + advertising dollars
Amazon	Distribution of books and then merchandise
Netflix	Distribution of video content
Apple	Distribution of music and then cell phones
Uber	Taxi business
Air B&B	Hotel business

upper management of companies that make things the old-fashioned way (the Makers). Unfortunately, this form of download and deploy results in little to no differentiation and it sucks resources away from Genuine AI Engineers (GAIEs) who then get picked up by FANG headhunters. Free downloadable software is equivalent to a sugary treat. While FANG researchers continue their healthy diet of research and development, those that have lived off free candy will soon be too flabby to compete with FANG muscle. At this point, the generosity of the Candy Man may come to an end, leaving the Makers ripe for the taking.

31

Populism, Jobs and Policy Futures

Suman

- Drawing upon the discussion of data policy, a definition of *populism* is offered
- A brief history of concern about the relationship between employment and AI development is given
- The general principles which govern that relationship and the emerging situation are outlined
- Four possible policy futures bearing upon employment and AI development are laid out
- A question is posed about the responsibilities of AI Engineers

---

Populism

I hope you'll carry on arguing with your CCD and CBD friends, Peter, even if it risks some tensions in the sweetness and goodness of your relationships.

The main point I took away from your account of the conversation with your CBD chum was in this bit of it:

> the CBD cut me off and stated that he simply has no desire to agree with me. He said that we should each stick to our convictions and let the

wisdom of the people decide. After all, what could be more democratic than that ...

So, we have two ideas of consensus (or agreement) on a truth claim at stake:

1. Agreement following the gathering of evidence on the claim, testing and retesting it, and making reasonable inferences.
2. Declaring the claim as agreed by 'the people' through some 'democratic' process — which generally means getting the majority of whatever is considered a relevant constituency to back the claim, and then dubbing that majority 'the people'.

Your friend's conviction is that the latter supersedes the former where there is any contradiction between them: i.e. majority backing is the final arbitrator in making truth claims and garnering agreement, even where there is robust evidence against this majority view.

In terms of evidence involving data, this conviction rolls out as follows. Data-led observations are always suggestive of the first kind of consensus, based on evidence and inference. However, given conviction in 'the people' as final arbitrators, such observations are only deemed acceptable when the underpinning data can be made to comply with majoritarian views or at least do not undermine those. Otherwise they are rejected by the decree of majority opinion. Observations based on social data which contradict majority opinion can usually be massaged into some kind of compliance or can be made to seem doubtful. Observations drawn from physical data which contradict majority opinion can only be refused straightaway.

This might be a baseline feature of what is currently thought of as 'populism'. It is widely held that 'populism' is gaining ground in social and political matters in our time, might indeed have the upper hand already. However, political scientists often struggle to define the term (see Mudde and Kaltwasser, 2017, Chapter 1; Müller, 2016, Introduction). Existing definitions tend to focus on social relations, principally expressed in claims made in the name of 'the people' against an establishment, and especially with an exclusionary or protectionist agenda. Perhaps more fundamentally, populism should be defined as built upon rejection of testable evidence and rational inference in favour of courting majoritarian public opinion.

Populism is the conviction that (truth) claims must be accepted if a majority backs them, irrespective of evidence and reasoning. And, relatedly, that all social contradictions can be resolved by going for the pathway that gets a majority behind it. Evidence, inference, testing and confirmation are of secondary importance; majority opinion takes precedence.

Jobs

But let's move on. By way of drawing this conversation to a close, I have a few final questions to pose for you, Peter.

The prospects and frameworks for employment (jobs, work) are obviously the most fraught area of policymaking in relation to AI. Fears of unemployment arising from automation had occasionally cropped up from the 1950s to the 1980s. The effects of automation on workers and employment were a significant issue for Marxist economists, notably, for instance, in Kidron (1956), Mandel (1972, Chapters 7 and 8), Morris-Suzuki (1984) and Mandel (1985). In the 1990s, discussion of the issue was generally at a low ebb. Rather, through the later 1990s and early 2000s, job losses due to business process outsourcing (BPO) on the back of developments in communications and information technology were oft debated. Media interest in job losses due to AI technology seems to have intensified in phases since three blog articles on the issue by Marshall Brain in 2003 attracted some attention. During the period of the financial crisis from 2007/2008 to about 2014 in the USA and EU, interest in the issue was again relatively muted. Job losses seemed more pressingly connected to mismanagement and greed in the financial sector and governmental austerity policies. Since 2015, rising unemployment and necessary reconfigurations of work due to advances in AI technology have featured continuously in the news. The issue has generated numerous publications thereafter, ranging from the sensational to the sedately scholarly (at book length, among others, Ford 2015; Susskind and Susskind 2015; Schwab 2016 (esp. Chapter 3); Cameron 2017; Jesuthasan and Boudreau, 2018; West, 2018; Baldwin, 2019). How this concern could be addressed seems more in the hands of policymakers than AI researchers and engineers; unsurprisingly, policy statements have proliferated of late. With a particular focus on employment, the USA came up with one in 2016 (Executive Office of the President, 2016), and others have followed suit, in the UK (British Academy and Royal Society, 2018), for the European Commission (Servoz, 2019), the United Nations (Department of Economic and Social Affairs, 2017; International Labour Organization, 2018), the Organisation for Economic Cooperation and Development (OECD, 2018) and so on.

Such policy statements share a great deal of common ground. Let me try to lay out the parameters of these policy considerations as succinctly and plainly as I am able.

The core considerations could be presented in the following simplified terms.

- Let's say that at any given time, there's a sum total of functions ΣF that enable production of goods and services. The functions in question include: developing and functionalising products, conceptualising systems, setting up infrastructure, employing workers, doing skilled work, instilling mechanical work, coordinating processes, delivering products, distributing and marketing products, making contracts, enacting transactions and investments, paying taxes ... so, every kind of function F that goes into production. Let's say, the human contribution to ΣF is $F(h)$, and it has usually been considered that the greater this contribution, the more production would benefit (productivity would increase). The machine contribution to ΣF is $F(m)$, and it has also usually been considered that the greater this contribution, the more productivity would increase. So, both $F(h)$ and $F(m)$ have been considered to have a directly proportional contribution to increasing productivity.

- Conventionally, it has been considered that $F(h)$ and $F(m)$ have — or should be designed to have — complementary parts in ΣF, so that both their contributions would have maximum effect on productivity. The part that $F(h)$ plays is understood in terms of quantity and quality of human input (simply, how many workers with what sorts of abilities are available). The part that $F(m)$ plays is understood by its ability to reduce the quantity of human input and at least equal and, better yet, exceed the quality of human input. Technological advance takes the direction of reducing the part that $F(h)$ plays relative to $F(m)$ in production. Striking the balance of complementarity in the parts $F(h)$ and $F(m)$ play such that productivity is maximised calls to a great extent upon policy. By appropriate policymaking, the part that $F(h)$ plays can be redefined (i.e. the balance of quantity and quality of human input adjusted) as the part that $F(m)$ plays advances so that a suitable complementary relationship can be maintained in ΣF. Such policymaking may include investing in education and training, arranging redeployment of workers, taking new initiatives and opening new areas in production, managing demographic changes, etc.

- The current concern is that technological advance has reached a stage — this is where complex automation and AI come in — where it is becoming difficult to envisage policy such that a suitable complementarity of $F(h)$ and $F(m)$ in ΣF can be struck. That is to say, the ΣF that enables maximisation of productivity can be so dominated by $F(m)$ that the part $F(h)$ plays is becoming narrowly focused and may even come to be negligible. In other words, the part of $F(h)$ may become inversely proportional to productivity. Moreover, the speed of technological advance in this respect is outstripping policy planning and recourse, indeed courting a policy stalemate. The key pressure point here is that maintaining complementarity of $F(h)$ and $F(m)$ has so far depended upon key differences in human ability and machine ability. It was understood that humans have a monopoly or a definite inborn advantage in certain abilities: e.g. to learn, use language, rationalise, build systems, explain, be inventive. These were recognisable abilities even if their processes were imperfectly understood (a domain of numinous terms). With technological advances, it seems possible that these abilities are gradually being passed on to $F(m)$ and will continue to be passed on — perhaps to a point where no $F(h)$ will retain an advantage in contributing to production. In some quarters, this direction and outcome is regarded as *fait accompli*. It is held that in contrast to analogous past experience (such as the 19th century Industrial Revolution), technological advance is now taking machines from automation towards Artificial Intelligence. (Let me parenthetically underscore the obvious: the idea is not that human persons will be competing with machine prototypes in a sci-fi mould, but that human abilities will gradually be replaced by machine abilities *in the production process*. This needs to be conceived as a shift at the level of production systems, not imagined at the level of persons shouldering robots. Needless to say, such a shift will have a profound effect on all levels of human social life and relations.)

Under these circumstances, with regard to employment the policy outlook in capitalist regimes could be envisaged as following several alternative future directions — i.e. toward the following future policy situations.

- **Situation 1 — policy of maintaining the existing regime of maximising production by whatever means:** That means, letting the cards fall as they will. If the above prognosis of the current direction of technological advance is correct, $F(m)$ will play an increasingly salient part in ΣF and $F(h)$ an increasingly reduced and narrowly focused part. Given the current regime, in quantitative terms this portends growing unemployment, more labour supply than demand exacerbated by continuing population growth. With qualitative factors in view, growing inequality can be anticipated. Since abilities that compose $F(h)$ are diverse and unevenly distributed, only some of those abilities will continue to remain in demand which only a small number would be able to provide. This small number will then concentrate the proceeds of production (wealth) in their hands at the expense of the rest.
- **Situation 2 — policy to continue the current direction of technological advance while actively maintaining the complementarity of $F(h)$ and $F(m)$ in ΣF such that production is healthy:** That means, making an active policy effort to redesign $F(h)$ such that both quantitatively and qualitatively human input is retained as complementary to the growing part of $F(m)$. This could entail significant regime change in terms of education, legal frameworks, ownership of and distribution of the proceeds of productive operations, planning of production, etc. This direction is likely to move away from maximising production by whatever means to planning production according to need/demand, which is the same as planning the remit of need/demand. Key here

would be redesigning $F(h)$ as $F(m)$ advances: inventing new kinds of $F(h)$ or new ways in which $F(h)$ and $F(m)$ can work together while controlling the scope of ΣF. This direction of policy is likely to be contingency-led, trying to anticipate trends and responding to their realisation when observed. The immediate policy principle here is to observe-and-prepare.

- **Situation 3 — policy to continue the current direction of techno-logical advance so as to let $F(m)$ dominate in ΣF, and to compen-sate for the consequences of the diminishing part of $F(h)$ by other means:** That means, to not meddle with the maximisation of produc-tion by whatever means — with growing $F(m)$ and diminishing $F(h)$ — but to use the benefits of that to alleviate the consequences for humans. So, policy will focus on compensating for or preventing the deleterious consequences of **Situation 1** above instead of letting that situation sim-ply unfold. That involves finding mechanisms for humans to live con-tentedly even if not employed in productive activity. The policy thrust here would necessarily be on redistribution: the proceeds of production would need to be distributed to all, irrespective of their part in produc-tion. A very significant regime change would be involved. Fundamental socioeconomic notions of ownership, exchange, value, profit, property, taxation and so on, would need to be reconsidered. And basic psycho-social ideas of status, purpose, recognition and so on may need to be reconfigured. Concepts of universal basic income and universal welfare gesture in this direction. This is less a contingency-led and more an active and principled policy direction.
- **Situation 4 — policy to regulate and, if necessary, check the direc-tion of technological advance so that a balance of complementary $F(h)$ and $F(m)$ in ΣF is maintained so long as production can be ensured at a reasonable level:** That is premised on the idea that pro-duction is a function of needs/desires and not a factor that has to be maximised to the full extent of what's possible. So long as the fulfil-ment of reasonable needs/desires is achieved, the parts of $F(h)$ and $F(m)$ can be balanced out in a planned way and there's no need to take it for granted that the part of $F(m)$ will necessarily be allowed to increase such that the part of $F(h)$ is reduced and narrowed. This does not call for comprehensive reconceptualisation of socioeconomic or

psychosocial precepts, but it does call for radical regime change. That change would involve principled and comprehensive planning of governance, economy and production processes. This is the least contingency-led of policy directions.

Obviously, Situation 1 is the least desirable; the others are conceived so that Situation 1 does not transpire. However, the prospects for Situation 1 are quite strong. By and large, policymakers are already embedded in the regime of Situation 1 and have their interests clearly articulated within and set to it. Insofar as policymaking involves government agencies, their interests include catering to public desires to maintain power; insofar as policymakers involve corporate agencies, profit-making is a powerful interest in favour of the status quo. These interests are vividly short term and their long-term repercussions seem hazy. The sway of populism, with which I started, may favour Situation 1. Further, Situations 2, 3 and 4 call for a challenging conceptual effort, a magnitude of regime change, which arouses anxiety — in policy parlance, they are 'disruptive'. Deferral, short-termism and inertia seem tempting options. Better to be reassuring and optimistic and upbeat and wait and see. Also, Situation 1 has its inbuilt stability measures, in terms of procedural checks and balances, legal recourses, limitations of agency and so on. Even if the will to move toward Situations 2 or 3 or 4 might be found, the procedure towards doing so might be so ponderous that the deleterious consequences of Situation 1 might nevertheless obtain. In that case, the move towards either of Situations 2, 3 or 4 would no longer be in the hands of those we think of as policymakers now — new formations may arise through social conflicts to push towards them.

Insofar as I can see, contemplation of Situation 4 appears to be shunned in policy circles at present. But perhaps that is being contemplated somewhere, who knows? Situations 2 and 3 are the favoured directions in current policy thinking. These occupy all the policy statements I mentioned above. Of these, Situation 2 garners more policy impetus than Situation 3, though that too tentatively. The observe-and-prepare and be-optimistic-and-reassuring tenor of contemplating Situation 2 is the hands-on favourite in policy circles. An unusual move by the US Congress (2018 and 2019) of putting legal shoulder into policymaking with AI futures in mind: the 'Artificial Intelligence Job Opportunities and Background Summary Acts' or the AI Jobs Acts, is clearly in the contingency-led spirit of Situation 2.

All that brings me to my first question for you, Peter. As a Citizen of the World, who necessarily thinks about these things, *where do you position yourself apropos of the four alternative policy situations above? Do you have a preferred policy direction? Do you consider one to be more likely to obtain than the others? Are there other policy directions or combinations of these to consider?*

GAIE Responsibilities

The other question is similar but somewhat distinct, addressed to you not as a Citizen of the World but as a Genuine AI Engineer (GAIE). *Insofar as you are a GAIE, do you think it is necessary for GAIEs to be aware of and responsive to such policy considerations? Do such policy considerations have any bearing on the work of GAIEs?*

It seems likely to me that many GAIEs feel that theirs is to do what they do, not to meddle with policy but to leave that to policymakers. If asked to give a point of information by policymakers, they feel a responsibility to do so; if asked to explain what the bearing of their work might be on a policy matter, they do undertake to explain it. But that simply means that their work is first and irrespective of policy, and policy is either after the fact or a kind of ether that surrounds their working conditions without impinging upon its substance.

In fact, GAIEs may well be regarded as working *for* policymakers and therefore having their interests aligned with the policymakers that be. They might be employed in a government-funded or privately funded project or university, or in the R&D division of a profit-making corporation. Their bosses may be precisely those policymakers who would prefer to let Situation 1 unfold. Should that make any difference to what GAIEs do by way of developing AI capacities? *If GAIEs knew that the AI capacity they are developing would have definite deleterious consequences given the prevailing policy regime, should they do anything about it?*

32

Jobs, Futures and AI Engineers

Peter

- The role of grace as an antidote to populism is proposed
- Elaborates the idea that the zero marginal cost economy might address social tensions brought on by automation and globalisation
- How an AI Engineer must respond to accusations of an existential nature is considered
- It is argued that the only thing more dangerous than AI research is a lack thereof

Antidote

Suman, the other day I was thinking about a reformulation of the statement, 'The arc of the moral universe is long, but it bends towards justice'. It goes something like, 'The arc of the scientific universe is long, but it bends towards truth'. As you point out, with the rise of populism both convictions are now in question. The majority prefers states that provide the majority with advantages. Once one agrees that 'illiberal policy is acceptable due to its convenience', it is a small step to 'illogical reasoning is acceptable due to its convenience'. So, let's agree that the fundamental problem that we have today with respect to acceptance of logical reasoning is part and parcel of the struggle between illiberal democracy and undemocratic liberalism.

To this end, I have a thought that might, to some degree, get us out of this pickle. Let's assume that racism manifests itself equally across all races. As is often the case, racism in the hands of the majority can be exploited with devastating consequences to the prospects of the minority. However, the converse is seldom true. One approach to combating such tyranny is through social movements. To date, Political Correctness (PC) has been one of the most potent weapons in the arsenal of the liberal left. It can be argued that the progressives have essentially won the culture wars. But this victory has not been without consequences.

Let's say that you are a member of the majority and happen to be a racist. If you are rightly or wrongly accused of racism, then you may end up in some sort of hellish state. Maybe you become a social outcast or pariah. Even without crime or accusation, you know that at any moment you may slip up. This is a kind of purgatory as you are in constant fear of being outed. Enter the demagogue, who can be defined as: 'a political leader that seeks support by appealing to the desires and prejudices of ordinary people rather than by using rational argument'. I assert that as of late, such would-be leaders make use of the following tactics: (a) they are outspoken in their illiberal statements; (b) when taken to task, they are blatantly unapologetic; and (c) when given access to power, they enact policies with the sole purpose of causing the liberal elite (a.k.a. the PC Police) to gasp and clutch their pearls. In so doing, they drain the venom of the left, which allows the illiberal majority to come out, heads held high without fear of humiliation or prosecution. The demagogue essentially journeys to the banished nether regions of society, absorbs their past, present and future sins and thus brings them back to a state of sweetness and light. From the perspective of the socially shunned, the demagogue becomes a Christ-like figure. A saviour, if you will.

Given that we agree that illiberalism and illogical thinking are two sides of the same coin, what is the antidote to populism and demagoguery? I suggest that instead of branding and shunning, we endeavor to embrace a sense of Universal Grace. Not from a deity, but from humanity for humanity. More specifically, we need to construct a state of unconditional acceptance. In this way, the redeemer aspect of the demagogue is diminished and so too its allure. I am not saying that monsters shouldn't be vilified and nor am I saying that hateful actions should not be called

out for what they are. But at the end of the day, witch hunts and conde-
scension only serve to rally forces that can be pitted against both reason
and virtue.

Jobs

With respect to jobs, let me first summarise your interesting analysis and
then provide comment. Let $\Sigma F = F(h) + F(m)$ equal the set of inputs
needed for production P, where $F(h)$ are the contributions attributable
to humans and $F(m)$ are the contributions attributable to machines. Let
complementarity C be equal to

$$C = \frac{h - h \cap m}{h \cap m}$$

which can be modelled as the ratio of work that can only be performed by
humans to the work that can be done by either machines or humans. When
C is high, there will be plenty of work for all. When C is low, humanity
becomes increasingly redundant. Technological advancement implies that

$$\frac{\partial^2 P}{\partial m \partial t} \gg \frac{\partial^2 P}{\partial h \partial t}$$

That is to say, the rate of change of productivity due to machines with
respect to time is much greater than the rate of change of productivity due
to humans with respect to time. In addition, as AI begins to fill its
promise,

$$\lim_{t \to \infty} C = 0$$

These two trends, the increasing rate of productivity gains by machines
and their capacity to emulate human capabilities, may one day result in

$$\lim_{t \to \infty} \Sigma F = F(m)$$

That is to say, all inputs to production may eventually be performed
primarily by machines and machines alone.

As a course of policy, you suggest four situations:

- **Situation 1:** Maximising production by whatever means.
- **Situation 2:** Allow technological advance while actively maintaining the complementarity of $F(h)$ and $F(m)$.
- **Situation 3:** Allow technological advance, let $F(m)$ dominate in ΣF and compensate for the consequences.
- **Situation 4:** Check the direction of technological advance so as to maintain complementarity of $F(h)$ and $F(m)$ in ΣF.

George F. Will recently wrote *The Conservative Sensibility* (2019). In this book he makes the argument that human nature is static; there will always be some who are more capable than others and that the optimal state will be achieved by just letting such natural forces play out. The tendency of government is to take a progressive stance with the idea that a more optimal state can be achieved. At best, such actions are ineffective, at worst, special interests can hijack the government for their own purposes. Thus, the conservative stands for minimal government intervention and a court system that gleefully denies the people that which they desire (i.e. social security and other entitlements). In *Pity the Billionaire* (2012) by Thomas Frank, we see the profound effects of The Friedman Doctrine or Shareholder Theory which holds that a firm's only responsibility is to its shareholders. Such visions are well suited to Situation 1. Globalisation, automation and devotion to shareholder value all seem to be driving forces of income inequality. The principle failure of centrists is their inability to curb the insatiable appetites of the top 1% in any meaningful way. I fear that Situation 1 is socially unsustainable.

Henry Ford realised that if employers do not provide adequate wages for their workers, there will be too few with the means to purchase his fine new automobiles. Heeding this advice and fearing the pitchforks and torches that will ensue from a prolonged Situation 1 campaign of catering to the conservative sensibility, many of the San Francisco elite are advocating for the Universal Basic Income (UBI) which falls into the camp of Situation 3. In *The Impact of Science on Society* (1951), Bertrand Russell argues that the powerful are most capable of taking advantage of technology, which is then used to increase their power. He proposes an aggressive form of Situation 3 composed of a world government capable of dispersing prosperity while keeping population growth in check. In *Player Piano* (1952), Kurt Vonnegut paints a Situation 3 picture illustrating the divide that emerges between those that can contribute to a high-technology society and those that are relegated to the UBI sidelines. My understanding is that Vonnegut used his short tenure at GE Research to model his vision of the techno-elite. It is not a flattering picture. My main concern with Situation 3 is the ability of government to provide continuous support to the masses. Many who have had the opportunity to study the super-rich come away with sad tales of isolated individuals convinced that everyone around them is out to steal their precious treasure. Even the trophy wives are not above suspicion. They are surrounded by sycophants and enablers that encourage them to believe that they are above the law and that social conventions need not apply to them. The very concept of taxation is abhorrent. They would rather burn their money than see it fall into the hands of government. Such fiends will do everything that they can to protect their interests and sabotage anything that interferes with their income. At the behest of the American oligarchs, the current party in power in 2019 has taken deliberate steps to dismantle just about every progressive accomplishment of the prior administration, with the promise of taking us back to a gilded age. Once the rich have moved their assets beyond the reach of the taxman, I fear that the UBI will become just another bitter-sweet memory.

From my perspective, neoliberalism (in the American sense of the term) attempts to make a run at Situation 2. Their advice to those that wish to earn a living is: 'Get educated so that you can adapt to the evolving needs of the good, the great — oh, and a safety net will be provided for those that cannot make the cut'. At best, this feels like a modern version of *Upstairs, Downstairs* (1971 UK ITV series). This Victorian–Edwardian approach does little to address income inequality and has left centrists open to being outflanked by left-wing progressives and right-wing demagogues. As previously stated, centrists have demonstrated that they cannot bring themselves to enact any meaningful forms of wealth redistribution. So like Situation 1 and Situation 3, Situation 2 does not seem to have the answers.

The original Situation 4 advocates were the early 19th century Luddites. They were English weavers and textile workers. Fearing that unskilled

workers would usurp their jobs, they objected to various forms of mecha-
nisation. Today, many union shops actively resist technological advance.
The fundamental problem with this stance comes down to competition
with those that have access to cheap labour or are willing to make full use
of technology. Left-leaning progressives call for limited trade agreements
and tariffs to even out the playing field. Unfortunately, such protectionist
instincts undermine the benefits of trade that result from comparative
advantages. Given the modern affinity for having one's cake and eating it
to, the isolationist Situation 4 approach ultimately crumbles.

Instead of throwing my lot in with any of those Situations 1–4, I propose a Situation 5 as follows:

- **Situation 5:** Encourage technology advancement towards a zero-
  marginal cost economy with government policy primarily focused on
  sustainable reduction of the cost of living.

In one of my prior interventions, I mentioned the concept of a zero-
marginal cost (ZMC) economy. The idea is that after initial investment,
advancements in AI, robotics, renewable energy, 3D printing, vertical
farming, recycling, etc. reduce the cost of production down to negligible
amounts. If governments can focus on providing the means for such one-
off investments, then local communities can, to a large degree, become
independent from the global economy with respect to their basic needs.
The key is to avoid dependence on continuous government support, which
I argue is unreliable and why I am not in favor of Situation 3.

Having the basics of life covered by one-time ZMC investments,
individuals will be free to participate in: (a) barter economies trading in
such things as artisanal soaps and beverages; (b) cooperatives that can,
with government financing, rejoin the global economy and compete with
conglomerates due to their low wages and lack of servitude to shareholder interests; and (c) cooperatives thus improving quality of life via the
giving of care, social activism and random acts of creativity.

Many have argued that without the dignity of work, the common folk
quickly become restless and despondent. It seems odd that we don't share
such concerns for the offspring of the idle rich. This might be a question

of how we choose to educate our children. Much of what we do in public school is targeted at conditioning young students so that they can eventually endure up to eight hours a day of mind-numbing drudgery. Such cog-like capacity is exactly what modern industry requires. In contrast, the Little Lord Fauntleroys of the world, with their private tutors and trips to Aspen, are simply not capable of modern 9-to-5 office work. However, to prepare the masses for a Situation 5 existence, we might consider revectoring our educational systems from the production of automatons to equipping young people with the skills needed to have rich and fulfilling lives. I would imagine this would involve such things as: an appreciation for the arts, civics, physical activity, excursions to explore our natural and cultural heritage, lessons from antiquity, mathematical and scientific curiosity and maybe philosophy-for-the-sake-of-philosophy. Across the globe, education has become a proxy for meritocracy. Kids exhaust themselves in vain attempts to acquire the exam technique necessary to gain entrance to elite institutions. Maybe generation Situation 5 will be known for their love of learning.

GAIE Responsibilities

Suman, I think that your final question goes beyond policy and basically asks if GAIEs should take responsibility for the ramifications of their machinations. Let me start by saying that when forced to attend a cocktail party, there are two things that the GAIE truly fear. The first is excessive eye contact and the second is a chance encounter with Sarah Connors from the redoubtable *Terminator* franchise (i.e. a character in a series of linked Hollywood films and a Fox TV series, USA). As you may recall, Sarah despises all GAIEs with a vengeance. Fair is fair given that robots, who were sent back in time, murdered her husband and attempted to kill both her son and herself. Let's start by considering the standard responses that all GAIE must have at the ready for the occasion when they too will be confronted by Sarah or her ilk.

Response 1: *I assure you that I am one of the good guys, I only work on AI projects that are for the good of humanity.*

- Many of my professor friends will only take funding from lovable institutions such as the National Science Foundation. My colleagues at Google refuse to take Department of Defense resources. When I go down this path, I usually start by saying things like: GE generates 1/3 of the world's electricity. GE Jet Engines facilitate an aircraft takeoff every 2 seconds. GE medical devices produce 16,000 images every second. The bulk of GE AI research is focused on (a) decreasing greenhouse gases via increased energy efficiency; (b) making inflight engine failures as rare as possible; and (c) making it easier to diagnose diseases and discover their cures. Energy efficiency, safe travel and the fight against disease, only motherhood and apple pie could make such a list more wholesome! However, the unconvinced Sarah usually comes back with something like: Is it not the case that sooner or later your research will become part of the public domain and thus can be coopted by dubious individuals with far less noble intent?

Response 2: *AI will do the dangerous, boring and repetitive tasks, releasing people to do the fun stuff.*

- Given the current climate, this position does not go over particularly well. On the bright side, robotics and AI make globalisation look downright benevolent.

Response 3: *While dangerous, the world has benefited greatly from fire (candle-lit meals), gun powder (fantastic fireworks), electricity (no more dishpan hands), computers (epic video games) and nuclear power (keeps our submarines humming along nicely while not disturbing the whales). AI will make our lives better — just wait and see!*

- I usually start by reminding people how hard life used to be. Simple things like starting fires without matches, cleaning clothes by hand, making a 5-mile trek on foot, waiting in line at the bank to get your money … At the beginning of the last century, the bulk of human endeavor was focused on the production of food. Flash forward to today, in the US the efforts of less than 3% can feed the nation and much of the world. Considering the 10,000 generations of humanity, our standard of living is undoubtedly better than all but a few of our predecessors. If you like playing candy crush on your cell phone, just wait and see what comes next.

Response 4: *Once Pandora's box has been opened, there is no closing it. AI is inevitable. If I don't do it, someone else will.*

- Well, Sarah must at least agree that I am honest before clocking me with the butt of her assault rifle.

Response 5: *As usual, media driven hysteria has blown things out of proportion.*

- To unpack this one, we need to consider the spectrum of concerns that we have pondered over the course of our discussions and make some honest assessments.
  - International conflicts via AI enabled weaponisation and cyber-attack.
    - My take is that the world's nuclear weapons arsenal is more than capable of wiping out humanity thousands of times over. The control of these doomsday devices now rests primarily in the hands of despots, dictators and demagogues with questionable haircuts. Can AI weaponisation really make things any worse?
  - Financial chaos that may result from lightning fast decisions made by automated Wall Street Agents.
    - Our financial institutions are fundamentally based on greed, ignorance and group think. The siren calls of tulip bulbs and sub-prime loans will always be luring us into treacherous waters. A little bit of regulation can keep AI financial algorithms in check — I wish the same were true for human nature.
  - Big brother and the surveillance state.
    - *1984* paints a bleak picture. However, history has shown that we don't need technology to create such Hells on Earth — the Cultural Revolution and McCarthyism come to mind. Recently, I was chatting with a colleague of mine. He told me about an individual who was charged with murder. The testimony of eyewitnesses

was damning. However, it was later discovered that the entire event was caught on video by a surveillance camera. Shortly after reviewing this new evidence, the District Attorney declared that this was the clearest example of self-defense that he has ever seen. He personally went down to the jail house and instructed the police officers in charge to release the accused gentleman immediately.

- In my opinion, without the visual evidence of police brutality captured by members of the public with handheld cameras, the #BlackLivesMatter movement would not have happened. Instead of a Big Brother state, we may be heading to a Little Brother state where privately owned cameras are used to keep the government itself in check.

- A word on #MeToo, it seems to me that as long as the predator vehemently denies any wrongdoing, the case just comes down to 'He said, she said'. Going forward it might make sense for potential victims to wear some sort of 24–7 video pendant capable of gathering evidence of sexual harassment. In the case were the individual has been incapacitated, an AI could then, in real time, call for assistance and make it known to the perpetrator that the authorities have been notified.

- At the end of the day, entrenched dictators and tyrants fear only one thing, the ability of the masses to organise. Social media, cell phones, the internet and yes, maybe even AI may ultimately become the means for global liberation and freedom.

○ Cognitive rewiring caused by over exposure to social media and AI.

- I have been somewhat dismissive about the clickbait nature of FANG technology. But at the end of the day, I think we are just going to have to get smarter about how we play with our new toys.

○ Job loss.

- We have discussed this topic at length. I guess that my final thoughts on this are that in a rational world, the ability to have the machines do our work for us should be viewed as the boon of all boons. The fundamental problem is the means for distributing wealth — once again, this is a matter of policy.

○ The busy child scenario.
- Let me start by saying that the idea of accidently creating an Artificial Super Intelligence (ASI) is patently absurd. We won't stumble into sentience. If we ever get there, it will be due to focused and sustained efforts. Those that choose to wade through these dark waters will have to own it. If they succeed, there may be peril. However, if they fail, the outlook for humanity might be considerably worse.

Let me end by expanding on what might happen if GAIEs give up on their AI quest. I just argued that AI itself is not an existential threat. It might actually be our one and only lifeline. In this light, a GAIE giving up on AI research in favor of more lucrative prospects such as hedge-fund management, might in fact be the ultimate act of irresponsibility …

One theory for why we have never encountered extra-terrestrial life is what I refer to as the doughnut hypothesis. Despite our long history, it has only been for the last 100 years or so that we have had the capacity to detect extraterrestrials based on their electromagnetic (EM) signals. It is also the case that we have only recently become detectable by our EM signals. It may be the case that once a species is capable of producing and detecting EM signals, extinction becomes imminent. Thus, each species creates its own EM doughnut expanding at the speed of light, but with a width of only a couple hundred years. The probability of contacting another species requires that one doughnut hits a world just as its inhabitants are ready to listen and before they become extinct. If the doughnut theory is true, then the probability of this happening would be low and hence we have yet to hear from our friend the ET. The question then comes down to, 'Why does it all end so quickly?' I have already made the argument that AI is not an existential threat. But here is what I consider to be the top-three threats to humanity.

1. **The tragedy of the commons:** I can imagine one of the last residents of Easter Island saying: 'If I don't chop down our one remaining tree, someone else will'. Abuse of the environment due to unrestrained greed may be our undoing. I was reading David J. Gunkel's book *Robot Rights* (2018). He makes some interesting points. One is the

fact that serious thinkers on AI seem not to take the idea of robot rights very seriously. The second has to do with different criteria for why an entity should be given rights: (a) the entity has interests that need protection or (b) the entity is capable of asserting its rights. Consider a woodland forest with its own dedicated AI persona. The AI could monitor the woodland state, understand its needs and define its purpose. It could become a legitimate advocate both identifying interests and asserting rights. Through such enchantments, we may finally get to a place where the commons can persist.

2. **You can't fit another rat into the cage:** The root cause of climate change and global conflict is uncontrolled population growth. As my brother Alexander informs me, 16 billion seems to be the limit of what the earth can sustain. This is really a problem for Government and Religion, neither of which seem to have any intentions of dealing with this crisis. I don't believe that robots will be used to cull the herd nor will they become a romantic alternative to marriage and procreation. I think that we are just going to hit a point were 16 billion people will be fighting over fewer and fewer resources. The temperature will have risen by 2 to 4 degrees. If closer to 4, most of the large animals will be gone. Pestilence and antibiotic resistant microbes will become the norm. If we are going to get through this, we will need massive technology pops. Things like: vertical farms, nuclear fusion, carbon sequestration, water desalination, renewables on steroids and maybe cryogenic time sharing, where each of us spends 9 out of every 10 years in suspended animation. If this is the road we are doomed to take, I think we will need bucketloads of AI-assisted creativity and invention — let's hope the GAIEs will be up to this challenge.

3. **We just don't like each other:** In Robert Putnam's *Bowling Alone* (2010), we see a thorough analysis of the breakdown of social equity — the amount of human interaction in our daily lives. One positive note is that the fall in social equity seems to correspond to a decline in racism. It is not that we have increased our fondness for one another, it is just easier to ignore each other. We see many of our young men opting for an online life of seclusion, with a stated goal of making as little impact on the world as possible. Loneliness and depression are growing day by day. Could an AI agent become some

sort of Witch's Familiar? A kind of Jiminy Cricket? Something that can help us see the world, not through the eyes of our evolutionary past, but with the perspective of an ally and maybe a friend?

Suman, I fear that I remain an unrepentant GAIE. I make the argument that AI may become our salvation, as it enables the ZMC economy, shields us from our self-inflicted ecological disasters to come and keeps us company as we wander down the lonely corridors of life. But at the end of the day, all that really ails us is attributable to our own doing. Our existence as a species is ultimately a question of policy. The solutions are all there, but we have to find the wisdom and the will to use them. To this end, the GAIE will always be ready to serve. Because, as Voltaire and not to mention the friendly neighborhood Spiderman would put it, with great power comes great responsibility.

Bibliography

Allen, Tom and Robin Widdison (1996). "Can Computers Make Contracts?". *Harvard Journal of Law and Technology* 9:1, 25–52. http://jolt.law.harvard.edu/articles/pdf/v09/09HarvJLTech025.pdf

Alznauer, Michael (2016). *Leading Naturally: The Evolutionary Source Code of Leadership*. Berlin: Springer Verlag.

"Asilomar AI Principles" (2017). https://futureoflife.org/ai-principles/

Baldwin, Richard (2019). *The Globotics Upheaval: Globalization, Robotics, and the Future of Work*. London: Orion.

Barrat, James (2013). *Our Final Invention: Artificial Intelligence and the End of the Human Era*. New York: Thomas Dunne.

Barthes, Roland (1972). "The Brain of Einstein". *Mythologies*. Trans. Annette Lavers. New York: Noonday Press, pp. 68–70.

Bauerlein, Mark (2008). *The Dumbest Generation: How the Digital Age Stupefies Young Americans and Jeopardizes Our Future*. New York: Jeremy B. Tarcher/Penguin.

BEIS (Department for Business, Energy & Industrial Strategy) and DCMA (Department for Digital, Culture, Media & Sport), UK Government (2018). *Artificial Intelligence Sector Deal*. https://www.gov.uk/government/publications/artificial-intelligence-sector-deal/ai-sector-deal

Bergson, Henri (1911). *Creative Evolution*. Trans. Arthur Mitchell. New York: Henry Holt & Co.

Berlin, Brent and Paul Kay (1969). *Basic Color Terms: Their Universality and Evolution*. Oakland, CA: University of California Press.

Bourdieu, Pierre (1984). *Distinction: A Social Critique of the Judgement of Taste*. Trans. Richard Nice. Abingdon: Routledge.

Brain, Marshall (2003). "Robotic Nation". http://theautomatedeconomy.com/robotic-nation-by-marshall-brain/

British Academy and Royal Society (2018). *The Impact of Artificial Intelligence on Work: An Evidence Synthesis on Implications for Individuals, Communities, and Societies.* https://www.thebritishacademy.ac.uk/sites/default/files/AI-and-work-evidence-synthesis.pdf

Calvano, Emilio, Giacomo Calzolari, Vincenzo Denicolò and Sergio Pastorello (2019). "Artificial Intelligence, Algorithmic Pricing, and Collusion". *VOX: CEPR Policy Portal.* https://voxeu.org/article/artificial-intelligence-algorithmic-pricing-and-collusion

Cameron, Nigel M. de S. (2017). *Will Robots Take Your Job? A Plea for Consensus.* Cambridge: Polity.

Chaitin, Gregory (2012). *Proving Darwin: Making Biology Mathematical.* New York: Vintage.

Chomsky, Noam (1957). *Syntactic Structures.* Berlin: Walter de Gruyter.

Chomsky, Noam (1980). *Rules and Representations.* Oxford: Basil Blackwell.

Chopra, Samir and Laurence F. White (2011). *A Legal Theory for Autonomous Artificial Agents.* Ann Arbor, MI: University of Michigan Press.

Copeland, Jack (2008). "The Mathematical Objection: Turing, Gödel, and Penrose on the Mind". https://www.ics.uci.edu/~welling/teaching/271fall09/Copeland---TheMathematicalObjection.pdf

Corson, Trevor (2004). *The Secret Life of Lobsters: How Fishermen and Scientists Are Unraveling the Mysteries of Our Favorite Crustacean.* New York: HarperCollins.

Dawkins, Richard (1976). *The Selfish Gene.* Oxford: Oxford University Press.

Dawkins, Richard (2006). *The God Delusion.* London: Transworld.

Deacon, Terrence W. (1997). *The Symbolic Species: The Co-evolution of Language and the Brain.* New York: W.W. Norton.

Defence Evaluation and Research Agency (DERA), UK Government (2001). *Strategic Futures Thinking: Meta-analysis of Published Material on Drivers and Trends.* https://webarchive.nationalarchives.gov.uk/20020117174539/http://www.cabinet-office.gov.uk:80/innovation/2000/Strategic/meta.shtml#4.5

Dennett, Daniel C. (1991). *Consciousness Explained.* New York: Little, Brown and Company.

Dennett, Daniel C. (2005). *Sweet Dreams: Philosophical Obstacles to a Science of Consciousness.* Cambridge, MA: MIT Press.

Department of Economic and Social Affairs, UN (2017). *Frontier Issues: The Impact of the Technological Revolution on Labour Markets and Income*

Distribution. https://www.un.org/development/desa/dpad/wp-content/uploads/sites/45/publication/2017_Aug_Frontier-Issues-1.pdf

Department of Trade and Industry (DTI), UK Government (1999). *Building Confidence in Electronic Commerce: A Consultation Document.* https://www.cyber-rights.org/crypto/consfn1.pdf

Deutsch, David (2011). *The Beginning of Infinity: Explanations That Transform the World.* London: Allen Lane.

Diamond, Jared (1997). *Guns, Germs, and Steel: The Fates of Human Societies.* New York: W.W. Norton.

DTI, UK Government (1999). *Promoting Electronic Commerce: Consultation on Draft Legislation and the Government's Response.* https://www.fipr.org/rip/PromotingE-CommerceDraftECB.pdf

DTI, UK Government (2000). *Proposed Guidelines on the Meaning of Research and Development (R&D) for Tax Purposes.* https://webarchive.nationalarchives.gov.uk/20000815200253/http://www.dti.gov.uk:80/support/taxcredit_b.htm

Ehrenreich, Barbara (2001). *Nickle and Dimed: On (Not) Getting By in America.* New York: Metropolitan.

Electronic Communications Act 2000, UK Government (2000). https://www.legislation.gov.uk/ukpga/2000/7/contents

Evans, Edward Payson (1906). *The Criminal Prosecution and Capital Punishment of Animals.* London: William Heinemann.

Executive Office of the President, US Government (2016). *Artificial Intelligence, Automation, and the Economy.* https://obamawhitehouse.archives.gov/sites/whitehouse.gov/files/documents/Artificial-Intelligence-Automation-Economy.PDF

Fernyhough, Charles (2016). *The Voices Within: The History and Science of How We Talk to Ourselves.* New York: Basic.

Feynman, Richard (1983). BBC Conversation: "Physics is Fun to Imagine". BBC https://www.ted.com/talks/richard_feynman

Finance Act 2000, UK Government (2000). https://www.legislation.gov.uk/ukpga/2000/17/contents

Ford, Martin (2015). *The Rise of the Robots: Technology and the Threat of Mass Unemployment.* New York: Basic.

Forestier, Sébastien, Yoan Mollard and Pierre-Yves Oudeyer (2017). "Intrinsically Motivated Goal Exploration Processes with Automatic Curriculum Learning". https://arxiv.org/pdf/1708.02190.pdf

Frank, Thomas (2012). *Pity the Billionaire: The Hard-Times Swindle and the Unlikely Comeback of the Right.* New York: Metropolitan.

Freitas Jr., Gerson (2019). "The Amazon Rain Forest Burns Again". *Bloomberg*, 30 May. https://www.bloomberg.com/news/articles/2019-05-30/amazon-rainforest-deforestation-in-brazil-on-the-rise-for-years

Future of Life Institute, AI Policy (website). https://futureoflife.org/ai-policy/

Future of Life Institute, AI Policy — China (website). https://futureoflife.org/ai-policy-china/

Future of Life Institute, AI Policy — United States (website). https://futureoflife.org/ai-policy-united-states/

Gödel, Kurt (1962 [1931]). *On Formally Undecidable Propositions of Principia Mathematica and Related Systems*. Trans. B. Meltzer. New York: Basic.

Greenberg, Joseph (1966). *Language Universals: With Special Reference to Feature Hierarchies*. The Hague: Mouton.

Greenlaw, Linda (2002). *The Lobster Chronicles: Life on a Very Small Island*. New York: Hyperion.

Gross National Happiness index (website). http://www.grossnationalhappiness.com/

Gunkel, David J. (2018). *Robot Rights*. Cambridge, MA: MIT Press.

Hamilton, William D. (1964). "The Genetical Evolution of Social Behaviour, I". *Journal of Theoretical Biology*. 7:1, 1–16. doi:10.1016/0022-5193(64)90038-4

Havrylov, Serhii and Ivan Titov (2017). "Emergence of Language with Multi-agent Games: Learning to Communicate with Sequences of Symbols". https://arxiv.org/abs/1705.11192

Hofstadter, Douglas and Emmanuel Sander (2013). *Surfaces and Essences: Analogy as the Fuel and Fire of Thinking*. New York: Basic.

Horgan, John (1998). *The End of Science: Facing The Limits Of Knowledge In The Twilight Of The Scientific Age*. New York: Perseus.

House of Commons, Science and Technology Committee, UK Government (2014). *Communicating Climate Science: Eighth Report of Session 2013–14*. https://publications.parliament.uk/pa/cm201314/cmselect/cmsctech/254/254.pdf

House of Commons, Science and Technology Select Committee, UK Government (2016). *Robotics and Artificial Intelligence: Fifth Report of Session 2016–17*. https://publications.parliament.uk/pa/cm201617/cmselect/cmsctech/145/145.pdf

House of Lords, Select Committee on Artificial Intelligence, UK Government (2017). *AI in the UK: Ready, Willing and Able? Report of Session 2017–19*. https://publications.parliament.uk/pa/ld201719/ldselect/ldai/100/100.pdf

IBM TV Commercial (2019). "Dear Tech: I Need Tech That Understands My Business". iSpot.tv. https://www.ispot.tv/ad/IiiR/ibm-dear-tech-i-need-tech-that-understands-my-business

Inland Revenue and HM Customs and Excise, UK Government (1999). *Electronic Commerce: The UK's Taxation Agenda*. http://www.iwar.org.uk/e-commerce/resources/ecom.pdf

International Labour Organization, UN (2018). *The Economics of Artificial Intelligence: Implications for the Future of Work*. https://www.ilo.org/wcmsp5/groups/public/---dgreports/---cabinet/documents/publication/wcms_647306.pdf

Jaynes, Julian (1976). *The Origin of Consciousness in the Breakdown of the Bicameral Mind*. Boston: Mariner.

Jesuthasan, Ravin and John W. Boudreau (2018). *Reinventing Jobs: A 4-Step Approach for Applying Automation to Work*. Boston, MA: Harvard Business School.

Johnson, Michael Edward (2016). *Principia Qualia: Blueprint for a New Science. Opentheory.net*. http://opentheory.net/PrincipiaQualia.pdf

JURI Committee (2017). *Motion for a European Parliament Resolution with Recommendations to the Commission on Civil Law Rules on Robotics*. http://www.europarl.europa.eu/doceo/document/A-8-2017-0005_EN.html?redirect

Kahneman, Daniel (2011). *Thinking, Fast and Slow*. New York: Farrar, Straus and Giroux.

Kelleher, Adam (2016). "A Technical Primer on Causality". Medium.com, September 7. https://medium.com/@akelleh/a-technical-primer-on-causality-181db2575e41

Kelly, Kevin (1994). *Out of Control: The New Biology of Machines, Social Systems, and the Economic World*. New York: Perseus.

Kelsen, Hans (1967). *Pure Theory of Law*. Trans. Max Knight. Berkeley, CA: University of California Press.

Kidron, Michael (1956). *Automation*. https://www.marxists.org/archive/kidron/works/1956/08/automation.htm

Kleiman-Weiner, Max, Rebecca Saxe and Joshua B. Tenenbaum (2017). "Learning a Commonsense Moral Theory". *Cognition* 167, 107–23. doi: 10.1016/j.cognition.2017.03.005. https://www.ncbi.nlm.nih.gov/pubmed/28351662

Klein, Ezra (2019). "Jenny Odell and the Art of Attention". *Vox.com*, 23 May. https://www.vox.com/ezra-klein-show-podcast/2019/5/23/18636332/jenny-odell-how-to-do-nothing

Knobe, Joshua and Shaun Nichols (2007). "An Experimental Philosophy Manifesto". In Knobe and Nichols eds. *Experimental Philosophy*. Oxford: Oxford University Press, pp. 3–14.

Krauss, Lawrence M. (2012). *A Universe from Nothing: Why There Is Something Rather than Nothing*. New York: Free Press.

Kroll, Andy (2018). "Cloak and Data: The Real Story Behind Cambridge Analytica's Rise and Fall". *Mother Jones*, May/June. https://www.motherjones.com/politics/2018/03/cloak-and-data-cambridge-analytica-robert-mercer/

Kurki, Visa A.J. and Tomasz Pietrzykowski eds. (2017). *Legal Personhood: Animals, Artificial Intelligence and the Unborn*. Cham: Springer.

Le Page, Michael (2019). "Space Agency Chief Fired After Revealing Recent Amazon Deforestation". *New Scientist*, 5 August. https://www.newscientist.com/article/2212479-space-agency-chief-fired-after-revealing-recent-amazon-deforestation/

Leslie, Alan M., Joshua Knobe and Adam Cohen (2006). "Acting Intentionally and the Side-Effect Effect: Theory of Mind and Moral Judgment." *Psychological Science* 17:5, 421–27.

Luhmann, Niklas (1995). *Social Systems*. Trans. John Bednarz, Jr. with Dirk Baecker. Stanford, CA: Stanford University Press.

Mandel, Ernest (1972). *Late Capitalism*. Trans. Joris De Bres. London: NLB.

Mandel, Ernest (1985). "Marx, the Present Crisis and the Future of Labour". *Socialist Register*, 1985/1986: *Social Democracy and After*. 436–54. https://socialistregister.com/index.php/srv/article/view/5535/2433

Matthews, Dylan and Byrd Pinkerton (2018). "How to Save a Species (if You Really Want To)". *Vox.com*, 21 November. https://www.vox.com/future-perfect/2018/11/21/18103851/future-perfect-podcast-endangered-species-ferret-crispr

Maturana, Humberto R. and Francisco J. Varela (1980). *Autopoiesis and Cognition: The Realization of the Living*. Dordrecht: D. Reidel.

McCloskey, Deirdre (1998). *The Rhetoric of Economics*. Madison, WI: University of Wisconsin Press.

McLuhan, Marshall and Quentin Fiore (1967). *The Medium is the Massage*. Harmondsworth: Penguin.

Microsoft (2018). *The Future Computed: Artificial Intelligence and Its Role in Society*. Redmond, WA: Microsoft. https://blogs.microsoft.com/wp-content/uploads/2018/02/The-Future-Computed_2.8.18.pdf

Ministry of Defence, UK Government (2003). *The Future Strategic Context for Defence*. https://webarchive.nationalarchives.gov.uk/20030825192124/http://www.mod.uk:80/issues/strategic_context/technological.htm

MIIT (Ministry of Industry and Information Technology), PRC Government (2017). 新一代人工智能发展白皮书 *A New Generation of Artificial Intelligence Development: White Paper*. http://pmoa4f1ea.pic30.websiteon-line.cn/upload/az9e.pdf

Morris-Suzuki, Tessa (1984). "Robots and Capitalism". *New Left Review* 147, 109–21.

MST (Ministry of Science and Technology), PRC Government (2017). 促进新一代人工智能产业发展三年行动计划（2018–2020年）*Three-year Action Plan to Promote the Development of a New Generation of Artificial Intelligence Industry (2018–2020)*. http://www.cac.gov.cn/1122114520_15132987738211n.docx

MST, PRC Government (2018). "变革性技术关键科学问题" 重点专项2017 年度项目申报指南 *"Key scientific issues of transformative technology": Key Special 2017 Project Declaration Guide*. http://www.most.gov.cn/mostinfo/xinxifenlei/fgzc/gfxwj/gfxwj2018/201811/t20181101_142520.htm

Mudde, Cas and Cristóbal Rovira Kaltwasser (2017). *Populism: A Very Short Introduction*. Oxford: Oxford University Press.

Müller, Albert and Karl H. Müller eds. (2007). *An Unfinished Revolution? Heinz von Foerster and the Biological Computer Laboratory — BCC 1958–1976*. Vienna: Edition Echoraum.

Müller, Jan-Werner (2016). *What is Populism?* Philadelphia, PA: University of Pennsylvania Press.

NASEM (National Academies of Sciences, Engineering, and Medicine) (2015). *Review of Three Divisions of the Information Technology Laboratory at the National Institute of Standards and Technology: Fiscal Year 2015*. Washington DC: NASEM. https://www.nap.edu/catalog/21877/review-of-three-divisions-of-the-information-technology-laboratory-at-the-national-institute-of-standards-and-technology

National Science Foundation, US Government. *Harnessing the Data Revolution* (website). https://www.nsf.gov/cise/harnessingdata/

Newport, Cal (2016). *Deep Work: Rules for Focused Success in a Distracted World*. London: Piatkus.

NIST (National Institute of Standards and Technology) (2017). *Video Analytics in Public Safety*. Workshop report 6 June, San Diego, CA, NIST IR 8164. https://www.nist.gov/sites/default/files/documents/2017/07/26/ir_8164.pdf

NIST (2019). *US Leadership in AI: A Plan for Federal Engagement in Developing Technical Standards and Related Tools*. Draft for Public Comment, August 20. https://www.nist.gov/sites/default/files/documents/2019/07/02/plan_for_ai_standards_publicreview_2july2019.pdf

NMSAC (National Manufacturing Power Construction Strategy Advisory Committee), PRC Government (2015).《中国制造2025》重点领域技术路线图 *"Made in China 2025" Key Area Technology Roadmap*. http://www.cm2025.org/show-23-174-1.html

NSTC (National Science and Technology Council), Networking and Information Technology Research and Development Subcommittee, US Government (2016). *The National Artificial Intelligence Research and Development Strategic Plan*. https://www.nitrd.gov/PUBS/national_ai_rd_strategic_plan.pdf

OECD (Organisation for Economic Cooperation and Development) (2018). *Policy Brief on the Future of Work: Putting Faces to the Jobs at Risk of Automation*. https://www.oecd.org/employment/Automation-policy-brief-2018.pdf

"Open Letter: Research Priorities for Robust and Beneficial AI" (2015). Future of Life Institute. https://futureoflife.org/ai-open-letter

Oreskes, Naomi and Erik M. Conway (2010). *Merchants of Doubt*. London: Bloomsbury.

Pagallo, Ugo (2013). *The Laws of Robots: Crimes, Contracts, and Torts*. Dordrecht: Springer.

Pask, Gordon (1975). *The Cybernetics of Human Learning and Performance: A Guide to Theory and Research*. London: Hutchinson.

Pask, Gordon (1996). "Heinz von Foerster's Self Organization, the Progenitor of Conversation and Interaction Theories". *Systems Research* 13:3, 349–62.

Pearl, Judea (2009). *Causality: Models, Reasoning, and Inference* (2e). Cambridge: Cambridge University Press.

Penrose, Roger (1989). *The Emperor's New Mind: Concerning Computers, Minds and The Laws of Physics*. Oxford: Oxford University Press.

Pichai, Sundar (2018). "AI at Google: Our Principles". https://www.blog.google/technology/ai/ai-principles/

Postman, Neil (1985). *Amusing Ourselves to Death: Public Discourse in the Age of Show Business*. New York: Viking Penguin.

Putnam, Robert D. (2010). *Bowling Alone: The Collapse and Revival of American Community*. New York: Simon and Schuster.

Reardon, Sara (2018). "Lab-grown 'Mini Brains' Produce Electrical Patterns that Resemble those of Premature Babies". *Nature*, 15 November. https://www.nature.com/articles/d41586-018-07402-0

Resnik, Philip and Eric Hardisty (2010). "Gibbs Sampling for the Uninitiated". University of Maryland Institute for Advanced Computer Studies, June. http://users.umiacs.umd.edu/~resnik/pubs/LAMP-TR-153.pdf

Ridley, Matt (1996). *The Origins of Virtue and the Evolution of Cooperation.* London: Penguin.

Royal Society and British Academy (2017). *Data Governance: Landscape Review.* https://royalsociety.org/-/media/policy/projects/data-governance/data-governance-landscape-review.pdf

Royal Society and British Academy (2017). *Data Management and Use: Governance in the 21st Century.* https://royalsociety.org/-/media/policy/projects/data-governance/data-management-governance.pdf

Russell, Bertrand (1908). "Mathematical Logic as Based on the Theory of Types". In *Logic and Knowledge.* London: Allen and Unwin, 1956, pp. 59–102.

Russell, Bertrand (1951). *The Impact of Science on Society.* New York: Simon and Schuster.

Russell, Stuart, Daniel Dewey and Max Tegmark (2015). "Research Priorities for Robust and Beneficial Artificial Intelligence". *AI Magazine*, Winter. https://futureoflife.org/data/documents/research_priorities.pdf?x60419

Ryle, Gilbert (1949). *The Concept of Mind.* Chicago: University of Chicago Press.

Saussure, Ferdinand (1916). *Course in General Linguistics.* Eds. Charles Bally and Albert Sechehaye. Trans. Wade Baskin. New York: McGraw-Hill.

Sayre, Kenneth (1965). *Recognition: A Study in the Philosophy of Artificial Intelligence.* Nortre Dame, IN: University of Nortre Dame Press.

Schwab, Klaus (2016). *The Fourth Industrial Revolution.* Geneva: World Economic Forum.

Searle, John R. (1980). "Minds, Brains, and Programs". *Behavioral and Brain Sciences* 3:3, 417–57.

Searle, John R. (2005). "Consciousness". Article circulated for *A Cognitive Science Dialogue: Consciousness East and West*, Northwestern University, 14 January 2005, featuring Alan Wallace and John Searle. http://faculty.wcas.northwestern.edu/~paller/dialogue/csc1.pdf

Selby, Jan (2019). "The Trump Presidency, Climate Change, and the Prospect of a Disorderly Energy Transition". *Review of International Studies* 45:3, 471–90. doi:10.1017/S0260210518000165

Servoz, Michel (2019). *AI: The Future of Work, Work of the Future! On how Artificial Intelligence, Robotics and Automation are Transforming Jobs and the Economy in Europe.* European Commission. https://ec.europa.eu/epsc/sites/epsc/files/ai-report_online-version.pdf

Stallwood, Kim (2018). "Topsy: The Elephant One Must Never Forget". In André Krebber and Mieke Roscher eds. *Animal Biography: Re-framing Animal Lives.* Cham: Palgrave Macmillan, pp. 227–42.

Susskind, Richard and Daniel Susskind (2015). *The Future of the Professions: How Technology will Transform the World of Human Experts*. Oxford: Oxford University Press.

Szabo, Nick (1997). "Fomalizing and Securing Relationships on Public Networks". *First Monday* 2:9, September. https://ojphi.org/ojs/index.php/fm/article/view/548/469

Tomasello, Michael (2008). *Origins of Human Communication*. Cambridge, MA: MIT Press.

Torey, Zoltan (1999). *The Crucible of Consciousness: An Integrated Theory of Mind and Brain*. Cambridge, MA: MIT Press.

Trivers, Robert (2014). *The Folly of Fools: The Logic of Deceit and Self-Deception in Human Life*. New York: Basic.

Turing, Alan M. (1937). "On Computable Numbers, With an Application to the Entscheidungsproblem". *Proceedings of the London Mathematical Society* s2-42:1, 1 January 1937. 230–65. https://doi.org/10.1112/plms/s2-42.1.230

Turing, Alan M. (1950). "Computing Machinery and Intelligence". *Mind* 49:236, 433–60.

US Congress, US Government (2018). AI Jobs Act of 2018. H.R.4829 — 115th Congress (2017–2018). https://www.congress.gov/bill/115th-congress/house-bill/4829/text

US Congress, US Government (2019). AI Jobs Act of 2019. H.R.827 — 116th Congress (2019–2020). https://www.congress.gov/bill/116th-congress/house-bill/827/text?format=txt

US Government. Federal Data Strategy (website). https://strategy.data.gov/

Uniform Computer Information Transactions Act 1999 (UCITA), National Conference of Commissioners of Uniform State Law, US Government.

Uniform Electronic Transactions Act 1999 (UETA), National Conference of Commissioners of Uniform State Law, US Government. http://euro.ecom.cmu.edu/program/law/08-732/Transactions/ueta.pdf

Usborne, David (2006). "Brigitte Bardot's Crusade to Save Canada's Seals". *The Independent*, March 24. https://www.independent.co.uk/environment/brigitte-bardots-crusade-to-save-canadas-seals-6105696.html

Vonnegut Jr., Kurt (1952). *Player Piano*. New York: Charles Scribner's Sons.

Vugt, Mark Van and Anjana Ahuja (2010). *Naturally Selected: The Evolutionary Science of Leadership*. London: Profile.

Weitzenboeck, Emily M. (2001). "Electronic Agents and the Formation of Contracts". *International Journal of Law and Information Technology* 9:3, 204–34. https://doi.org/10.1093/ijlit/9.3.204

Weitzenboeck, Emily M. ed. (2001). Special Issue: Electronic Agents. *International Journal of Law and Information Technology* 9:3, Autumn.

West, Darrell M. (2018). *The Future of Work: Robots, AI, and Automation.* Washington: Brookings Institution Press.

Wheelan, Charles (2012). *Naked Statistics: Stripping the Dread from the Data.* New York: W.W. Norton.

White House, US Government (2019). *Maintaining American Leadership in Artificial Intelligence*, President's Executive Order 13859, February 11. https://www.whitehouse.gov/presidential-actions/executive-order-maintaining-american-leadership-artificial-intelligence/

Whitehead, Alfred North and Bertrand Russell (1910). *Principia Mathematica* 1. Cambridge: Cambridge University Press.

Whittlestone, Jess, Rune Nyrup, Anna Alexandrova and Stephen Cave (2019). "The Role and Limits of Principles in AI Ethics: Towards a Focus on Tensions". *Association for the Advancement of Artificial Intelligence Conference.* http://www.aies-conference.com/wp-content/papers/main/AIES-19_paper_188.pdf

Widdison, Robin (1999). Letter to DTI. https://webarchive.nationalarchives.gov.uk/20000815072037/http:/www.dti.gov.uk:80/cii/elec/durham.pdf

Will, George F. (2019). *The Conservative Sensibility.* New York: Hachette.

Wittgenstein, Ludwig (1953). *Philosophical Investigations.* Trans. G.E.M. Anscombe. Oxford: Blackwell.

World Happiness Report (website). https://worldhappiness.report/

Wright, Robert (2017). *Why Buddhism is True: The Science and Philosophy of Meditation and Enlightenment.* New York: Simon & Schuster.

Yi Zeng, Enmeng Lu and Cunqing Huangfu (2018). "Linking Artificial Intelligence Principles". *CEUR Workshop Proceedings* Vol. 2301. http://ceur-ws.org/Vol-2301/paper_15.pdf

Zins, Chaim (2007). "Conceptual Approaches for Defining Data, Information, and Knowledge". *Journal of the American Society for Information Science and Technology* 58:4, 479–93. https://doi.org/10.1002/asi.20508

Appendices

Appendix A

'Made in China 2025' Key Area Technology Roadmap 《中国制造 2025》重点领域技术路线图
National Manufacturing Power Construction Strategy Advisory Committee, PRC October 2015

Contents

Appendix B

A New Generation of Artificial Intelligence Development: White Paper (2017)
新一代人工智能发展白皮书

Directed by
Department of Information and Software Services, Ministry of Industry and Information Technology, PRC

Table of Contents

Appendix C

The National Artificial Intelligence Research and Development Strategic Plan
National Science and Technology Council Networking and Information Technology Research and Development Subcommittee, USA

October 2016

Contents

Appendix D

House of Lords, Select Committee on Artificial Intelligence, UK, 2018

AI in the UK: Ready, Willing and Able?
Report of Session 2017–2019

Contents

Index

www.ingramcontent.com/pod-product-compliance
Lightning Source LLC
Chambersburg PA
CBHW061237220326
41599CB00028B/5458